P9-CSG-429

Cooking Across America

Over 175 Traditional and Regional Recipes

2012
Cook with
Your Senses!
Chef Nicole

Sharing recipes makes
Lasting memories!
Best,
Mary Elizabeth

By Mary Elizabeth Roarke and Chef Nicole Roarke

Foreword by Chef Frank Tramontano

Hatherleigh Press is committed to preserving and protecting the natural resources of the Earth. Environmentally responsible and sustainable practices are embraced within the company's mission statement.

Hatherleigh Press is a member of the Publishers Earth Alliance, committed to preserving and protecting the natural resources of the planet while developing a sustainable business model for the book publishing industry.

This book was edited and designed in the village of Hobart, New York. Hobart is a community that has embraced books and publishing as a component of its livelihood. There are several unique bookstores in the village. For more information, please visit www.hobartbookvillage.com.

Library of Congress Cataloging-in-Publication Data is available.
ISBN: 978-1-57826-414-8

Country Comfort: Cooking Across America is available for bulk purchase, special promotions, and premiums. For information on reselling and special purchase opportunities, call 1-800-528-2550 and ask for the Special Sales Manager.

Cover design by Nick Macagnone
Interior design by Nick Macagnone
Cover photography by Ken Cromer (www.kencromerphotography.com)

Printed in the United States
10 9 8 7 6 5 4 3

DISCLAIMER
Any similarities to existing recipes are purely coincidental.

I dedicate this book to my mom and dad, for sharing their love of baking and cooking; to my daughter Nicole, for collaborating with me and sharing her culinary passion and expertise; and to my husband Dennis and our other children Elizabeth, Dennis, and Christian: thank you for your constant love and support! A special thanks to my dear friend Margit, who introduced me to her colleagues from the Institute for Integrative Nutrition. Their contribution provides many healthy vegetarian and gluten-free recipes to our readers.

—*Mary Elizabeth*

To my family whom I love unconditionally, thank you! A special thank you to my mom, whom I could not have done this without. The level of dedication, hard work, and love that she puts into all that she does is unsurpassable. Thank you Daddy for doing all of the cooking, Christian for playing the music, Dennis for being supportive, and my loving sister Elizabeth for everything; especially while we were busy working on the book! Thank you to the sub-culture of chefs, cooks, and food-crazed people, of which I am proud to be a part!

—*Chef Nicole*

We would especially like to thank our dedicated editor Anna Krusinski for her continued support and expertise throughout the process of writing this series.

—*Mary Elizabeth and Nicole*

Thank you to all the chefs, cooking class instructors, food bloggers, private chefs, caterers, and creative home cooks across America who shared their favorite recipes.

Thanks to the following individuals for supporting our efforts and sending out our recipe requests to their network of chefs:

Philip Gutensohn, The International Culinary Center of the French Culinary Institute, New York, New York

Giulianna Galiano, Culinary Institute of America (CIA), Hyde Park, New York

Career Services, Institute of Culinary Education (ICE), New York, New York

The Star Career Academy, Syosset, New York

Kara A. Kenney, E Squared Hospitality, New York, New York

Food and Beverage Association of America

Table of Contents

Foreword

As I page through the eclectic collage of flavors and food styles presented in *Country Comfort: Cooking Across America,* I am reminded of the years that I had spent in Europe honing my culinary career and my time spent back in the United States—a true melting pot of history, steeped in tradition. The gathering of recipes in this book has created a festival of flavor, introducing a fabulous collection of regional foods throughout our nation. Mary Elizabeth and Chef Nicole have brought together some of the culinary world's most influential recipes, each a representation of the diverse cuisines of America.

As a child of Italian and Cuban parents, I grew up in a home centered around ethnic food. We spent most of my youth in Montauk, New York, on the east end of Long Island, a seafood wonderland surrounded by the freshest of catch from the Atlantic Ocean. This made for an awakening of my young palate. I remember, as a child, purchasing calamari in a bait store, far before it was considered "haute cuisine." In this book, you will find many other recipes that arose from humble beginnings as peasant dishes, and have now been reinvented with a new look at dining, while still maintaining their roots from various cultures. It is this transformation of culinary style that gives each region of the United States a unique combination of flavors. It is so refreshing for me to be a part of this national awakening of innovative food styles and culinary culture.

I find *Country Comfort: Cooking Across America* to be a fabulous culinary tour, and I know that these recipes will offer you a culinary awakening, opening your senses to such a distinct variety of styles, techniques, and flavor combinations.

In these pages, you will have the pleasure of finding some culinary styles that you may never have explored. Mary Elizabeth and Chef Nicole have painstakingly sifted through so many recipes, making this collection of national talent an obvious labor of love. Although these recipes highlight the unique flavors of each region, nearly all of the ingredients for these recipes are readily available throughout the

United States, creating an exciting adventure that anyone can embark on. I am honored to have contributed some of my own recipes highlighting the flavors of the Northeast, including my parent's heritage, which I hope you will enjoy.

So, let yourself go, and try some new things as you explore the diverse culinary styles found throughout the United States.

Congratulations, Mary Elizabeth and Chef Nicole: my chef's toque is off to you both with much appreciation for your time and devotion to this quest toward better living, and your discovery of the grand diversity of food styles across America.

—*Executive Chef Frank Tramontano*
Ever So Saucy Foods, LLC

Note to the Reader

Are you someone who is so passionate about food that simply eating it is not enough of an experience? Do you find yourself often wondering where ingredients originated when trying new food? As culinary-inspired individuals, we love to explore new cuisine, and we find it fascinating to discover traditional ethnic dishes that continue to be replicated and recreated on menus all across the United States. For both of us, traveling for business and pleasure is a common occurrence. Whether attending a conference in Chesapeake Bay or vacationing in the Florida Keys, we always feel compelled to request the respective signature dishes of that region, such as Maryland Crab Cakes in the Northeast, Key Lime Pie in the Southeast, Succotash in the Midwest, Wild Alaskan Salmon in the Northwest, or Enchiladas in the Southwest.

For the past two decades, Mary Elizabeth's career has required her to travel throughout the United States. For most business travelers, this often means an exuberant amount of complimentary hotel breakfasts, fast food eateries, working lunches, and catered corporate functions. Yet for "foodie" Mary Elizabeth, she thinks of this as an avenue to experience the surrounding area, its inhabitants, and, most importantly, the cultural influences through its food. Whether it is a charming country farmstand or a critically-acclaimed restaurant, Mary Elizabeth relishes in any opportunity to fully immerse herself in the local cuisine.

This experience includes asking a few key questions—what foods are specific to your region, and what has inspired these signature dishes? Most locals recall recipes that have been passed on through generations before them, fondly recounting memories of preparing these family favorites with ingredients indigenous to their hometown. Eager and proud, they describe every mouth-watering taste, aromatic scent, sizzling sound, characterizing texture, and aesthetically pleasing sight of their cherished dish.

The desire to collect and share recipes is a tradition passed down through most families. One of Mary Elizabeth's earliest memories is of her grandfather calling her mom at home to pass on a recipe he recently had tried. Her father, who was also an avid cook, was often found combing through the food section of the *New York Times*. Mary Elizabeth began collecting recipes herself when she coordinated a recipe exchange at work. Her and her colleagues called it "Food for Thought." Wanting to take her hobby to the next level, she attended culinary school for Pastry and Baking Arts. Since then, she has co-authored four of the cookbooks in the *Country Comfort* series.

The expression "the apple doesn't fall far from the tree" comes to mind when thinking of Mary Elizabeth's daughter Nicole. In fact, Nicole's first word was "apple." Many would say it was a coincidence that apples became her favorite food, and that she was born in the "Big Apple" in November, when the fall harvest treats us to an abundance of apples. On the contrary, Nicole believes that, like her ancestors, she has always been inspired by food. As a child, she would use recipes from her mother's repertoire to create a variety of menus for her family to serve on special occasions. As a teenager, her passion for cooking took a professional turn as she began working in several restaurants on Long Island.

As Nicole grew, so did her enthusiasm to cook and eat her way to becoming a chef. While accompanying her mother on a business trip to San Diego, California, Nicole was impressed by the terrain, food, and cooking styles, which were so different from what she was accustomed to on Long Island. Shortly thereafter, she lived and cooked her way through the Southwest and Southeast of the United States, learning how to prepare the regions' traditional foods. Eventually, Nicole returned home to the Northeast to attend the French Culinary Institute.

Driven by Mary Elizabeth's professional travels and Nicole's diverse regional cooking experience, and fueled by their innate love for food, this mother-daughter team has collected authentic recipes from chefs, home cooks, caterers, cooking classes, and culinary schools, as well as family, friends, and colleagues across the country; and they are proud to present *Country Comfort: Cooking Across America*.

The recipes in this book are sure to enhance your experience of eating American cuisine, and will enable you to invite new and exciting flavors from across America right into your own home. If you have traveled across the country before, then get ready to re-visit each and every region's local ingredients and signature dishes. If you have not yet had the privilege to go on such an adventure, then tell your taste buds to start packing.

Bon Voyage and Bon Appetite!

—Mary Elizabeth and Chef Nicole

Introduction:
America the Beautiful, Land of the Food

I can recall the smell of something as simple as a cherry tomato growing in the backyard. The scent of yellow onions swe ating in butter
evokes memories of Sunday dinners of pasta and sauce. Our recipe
for marinara sauce, which originated from our ancestors in Sicily, was
passed onto our relatives who immigrated to New York, and then followed my family to our home on Long Island. As commonplace as
it may seem, the routine of preparing a family meal has the power to
imprint an everlasting effect on generations to come. What do you
remember most about where you grew up? Is it food? Is it cooking
with your family? Where did the recipes come from, and what influenced them?

America itself is as beautiful as its popular anthem boasts. From
the magnificent mountain ranges to the sun-soaked canyon walls,
from the lush gardens and groves to the oceans' shores, America's
natural surroundings provide heavenly scenery as well as bountiful
edible resources. Depending on which region you reside in, America
is composed of radically different landscapes and foods.

Long ago, there was no other option but to eat what was fresh and
accessible. Despite the current industry's ability to buy and sell food
from all over the world, many reputable chefs and conscientious
cooks are enlightened by the challenge to only prepare locally and
seasonally sustainable food.

The Native Americans paved the way for this "living off the land"
cooking style. The survival of the early European settlers' was primarily based on the cooking lessons provided by the knowledgeable Native Americans. Being from countries such as England, Ireland, Italy,
Portugal, Germany, and Poland, these early settlers were not accustomed to the natural resources of their new land, so it was crucial
that they learned from the Native Americans how to utilize the food
sources around them. Later, when settlers from Africa, the Caribbean,
Puerto Rico, Asia, and India followed, they, too, were faced with the

challenge of melding their own cuisines with what was available to them in the United States. This "melting pot" of culture has brought us an endless combination of cultural dishes, which we are proud to feature in this book.

The Northeast region is famous for having four distinct seasons—from sticky and humid summers to wickedly frigid winters—and each season strategically yields its agriculture. For example, the temperate environment of the spring and fall seasons is ideal for growing produce such as asparagus and cauliflower. On the other hand, the winter soil of the Northeast gives life to an abundance of hard-shell butternut squash while the summer months allow us to cultivate delicate sun-kissed berries. Many of the Northeastern recipes collected for this book demonstrate the benefits of preparing what is found in your own backyard, given the current season.

Not only is the weather characteristically irregular throughout the Northeast states, but so is the terrain. In the state of New York alone, there are mountain ranges and farmlands, as well as beaches and heavily industrialized cities. Because of this varying terrain, we find a wide variety of resources that have been utilized in the region's cuisine. Additionally, the access to waterways such as the Great Lakes, the Great South Bay, and the majestic Atlantic Ocean gives the Northeast a consistent supply of fresh fish and shellfish, which is reflected in many of the area's favorite dishes.

While the Northeast is known for its cultural influence, agricultural availability, and resourceful coastline, the Southeast is characterized by an undeniable kindness and generosity extended toward its guests. "Southern hospitality" is a fitting expression for a culture that still invites the whole family, neighborhood, and fellow parishioners to a good old-fashioned low country boil.

In a land made of marshes, bayous, rivers, swamps, and shores touching the Atlantic Ocean and the Gulf of Mexico, along with record-breaking high temperatures, heavy humidity, and rainfall, the Southeast has some of the richest soil and the most desirable climate for vegetation to flourish. In addition, the wetlands and the multiple bodies of water are home to a variety of species of shellfish as well as fresh and saltwater fish. As a result, classic Southeast dishes often highlight the local catch of the day.

Southeastern styles of cooking such as Creole, Cajun, soul food, barbecue, Caribbean, Cuban, and Latin American are all unique to the area, each highlighting the cultures responsible for their creation. Southerners have always taken extra measures to ensure that their customs and traditional fare are passed on in the most authentic manner possible. The pride to preserve their individual identity began when the French, Spanish, African, and Native Americans were forced to share common ground of the newly established South. In order to keep their cultural identities, they continued to cook the food of their heritage, which we still enjoy today.

The vast landscape of the Midwest provides endless land for cattle and cows to graze, which, in turn, provides locals with some of the best grass-fed beef and dairy in the country. Additionally, the neighboring lakes, rivers, and streams are home to many freshwater fish, such as catfish and salmon. Because of this availability, a noticeable amount of the recipes from this region pair their locally-grown crops like ramps, cherries, morel mushrooms, and corn with a variety of beef and seafood selections. Often referred to as the "bread basket," the Midwest is home to many grain farms overflowing with wheat, rye and oats.

As settlers from the North and Southeast regions traveled further west through the Great Plains in search of gold, many stayed in the Midwest and made it their home. After the Civil War, Eastern European settlers inhabited the region, as well, and shared their knowledge of dry farming techniques, hearth cooking, and preservation methods. Midwestern cuisine currently showcases preparations such as artisan baking, smoking, and stewing, which truly reflect the influence of those earlier settlers. These techniques are regarded in all of America's "foodie" communities as retro, and yet modernly trendy.

The Northwest region is made up of the Rocky Mountain and Pacific Northwest states. With its moist and volcanic conditions, this region supports a long season to harvest fruits and vegetables, which are then exported throughout America. Thanks to their bountiful harvests, many Northwest recipes highlight activities of cultivating apples, pears, and berries, and foraging wild mushrooms, as their ancestors had many years ago.

The Northwest was originally pioneered by cowboys, miners, and frontiersmen venturing west via the Oregon Trail. The path was merely two wagon-wheel tracks drawn through uninhabited territory. Their chance of survival was contingent on their ability to utilize the natural resources that surrounded them, such as wild berries, game, and lake trout. They were also faced with the challenge of having to prepare food on the rugged trail. Today, the area's cuisine demonstrates a balance of these old-world cooking styles and touches of modern ingredients and techniques.

The first settlers to arrive in the Pacific Northwest were primarily Spanish missionaries, as well as French, English, Canadian, and Russian immigrants motivated by the lucrative fur-trade. Eventually, the Northwest Native Americans taught the new settlers how to increase their profitability by fishing along the local coast. Alaska, in particular, is still the United States' leading source of king salmon and king crab, as well as a tremendous amount of other cold water fish and shellfish such as halibut, rock cod, scallops, and shrimp. Again, what was once a necessity to consume local produce, meat, and fish has now become a popular food trend known as the "farm to table movement," which is especially evident in today's Northwestern recipes.

The Southwest is complete with picturesque views of the best natural landscapes that the country has to offer. A huge part of the Southwest is comprised of mountains, deserts, and plateaus, which can prove most difficult for propagation, but the local inhabitants have made the most of their surroundings by capitalizing on crops that thrive there, such as various types of chiles. On the other hand, the southern California coast and its salt-filled soil and temperate climate presently lead the nation's agricultural industry.

The Southwest is also home to an abundance of indigenous fruits and vegetables available year-round, like avocados, chiles, corn, jicama, mangos, and other tropical produce. The coast of southern California and the islands of Hawaii are also hugely populated with most of the countries sought-after fresh fish and shellfish, which are predominant in Southwest dishes.

Before the Gold Rush brought European settlers westward, the Southwest region had been occupied by Native Americans and Mexicans. Once the Spanish arrived, the three cultures influenced the

Southwest, and continue to do so today through Spanish-American, Baja Californian, and Tex-Mex cuisines. New Mexico and Texas borders both Mexico and the Midwestern states, which lend to many of the cattle ranches and the region's distinct style of barbecue. The first people who lived in Hawaii were referred to as Polynesians, meaning "people of the many islands." Consequently, today's Hawaiian cuisine represents a blending of several cultures, including Chinese, Filipino, Japanese, Korean, and Portuguese.

American cuisine as a whole is the sum of all its parts, each representing a particular region of our country. Each region is home to many signature dishes, indigenous ingredients, and cultural influences, all of which tell the story of how American cuisine originated. As you explore the recipes in this book, we invite you to journey across the United States and experience the diverse flavors that each region has to offer.

Part I

NORTHEAST

The Northeast region is made up of two distinct areas: New England and the Middle Atlantic states. New England includes Maine, Vermont, New Hampshire, Massachusetts, Rhode Island, and Connecticut, most of which are touched by the Atlantic Ocean. The Middle Atlantic is comprised of New Jersey, Delaware, Washington, D.C., Maryland, Pennsylvania, and New York.

The Northeast's dramatic change in seasons heavily influences the availability and cost of local fruits and vegetables. The famous fall harvest contributes to both sweet and savory dishes, like Apple and Maple Mashed Sweet Potatoes (page 56) and Roasted Butternut Squash Salad with Maple Dijon Vinaigrette (page 24). Apples, above all other agricultural gems, are most commonly associated with Northeast crops, and apple picking is by far one of the most popular family outings in the Northeast. To the credit of the earliest New England and Mid-Atlantic state settlers, recipes such as Apple Crisp (page 66), Baked Stuffed Apples (page 65), and Apple Strudel (page 67) have been passed down from generation to generation.

Come springtime, the asparagus stalks begin to resemble tree trunks. Their annual harvest has inspired refreshing and simple dishes like Asparagus Soup with Seasoned Dill Yogurt (page 14).

Summers in the Northeast provide the best environment to grow sweet, juicy strawberries and blueberries. The locals are notorious for preparing breakfast favorites like Blueberry Cobbler Doughnuts (page 7) and Crêpes with Blueberry Marmalade (page 5), as well as desserts like Rhubarb-Strawberry Crumble (page 68).

New York and New Jersey gardens are home to herbs such as basil and dill, along with tomatoes of all varieties. The simple preparation of a vine-ripe Beefsteak Tomato and Mozzarella Platter (page 23) or a deliciously complex Tomato Chutney (page 61) both highlight the versatility of these local favorites.

Perhaps the largest contribution toward traditional Northeastern cuisine comes from its surrounding waters. The majority of the New England and Mid-Atlantic states are bathed by the Atlantic Ocean, as well as the many bays responsible for the extreme amount of fresh fish and shellfish. The mollusks of New England (oysters and quahogs) and the crustaceans of the Mid-Atlantic (lobsters and crabs) are infamous across America.

For us, growing up on Long Island near the Great South Bay meant that fresh seafood was always plentiful. One of our family's favorite late-August activities was going crabbing. Strolling along the dock, we would find sapphire-tinted crabs crawling on top of one another in white spackle buckets. Despite their earnest efforts, the crabs would slide down the walls, never reaching the top. Sometimes, we would set traps or tie a piece of chicken on a fishing line and lasso it over the dock, watching carefully until we would see the line pull, signifying that a crab was walking away with the bait. We would then call out, and a partner would swoop down with the crab net as we quickly brought in the catch. After we arrived home and boiled the crabs, our work began as we picked through the shells, exposing the succulent meat for making fresh Crabmeat Salad (page 26) or Award-Winning Maryland Crab Cakes (page 31).

Crêpes with Blueberry Marmalade

Eric Dupaix *(Gordon Ramsay Restaurant, New York, New York)*
Serves 4

> Blueberries are readily available in North America since Maine produces a quarter of all the low-bush blueberries.

Crêpes
1 cup all-purpose flour
3 eggs
½ cup milk
½ cup water
¼ teaspoon salt
2 tablespoons unsalted butter, melted

Chantilly Cream
1 cup heavy cream (see Baking Tips on whipped cream, page 326)
1 tablespoon sugar
1 drop pure vanilla extract

Blueberry Marmalade
½ cup water
½ cup sugar
2 (3- x ½-inch) strips fresh lemon zest (see Chef's Tips on citrus zest, page 311)
2 cups (10 ounces) fresh blueberries
1½ tablespoons fresh lemon juice

Crêpes

In a large mixing bowl, whisk together the flour and eggs. Gradually add in the milk and water, stirring to combine. Add the salt and butter; beat until smooth. Heat a lightly oiled Teflon®-coated crêpe pan or frying pan over medium-high heat. Pour or scoop the batter onto the pan, using approximately ¼ cup for each crêpe. Tilt the pan with a circular motion so the batter coats the surface evenly. Cook the crêpes for about 2 minutes until the bottom is light brown. Loosen with a spatula, turn, and cook the other side.

Chantilly Cream

In a mixing bowl, whip the heavy cream vigorously until stiff. Add sugar and vanilla.

Blueberry Marmalade

Boil the water with the sugar and zest in a 1-quart heavy saucepan, uncovered, for about 5 minutes. Discard the zest. Stir in the blueberries and simmer on medium heat for 5 to 7 minutes, stirring occasionally until the blueberries begin to burst and thicken. Remove from the heat and stir in lemon juice.

Spread the blueberry marmalade on the crêpe and fold the crêpe twice. Serve on a plate with Chantilly Cream. Another option is to replace the blueberries with Nutella® or orange marmalade.

Blueberry Cobbler Doughnuts

Executive Pastry Chef Julie Elkind *(BLT Steak, New York, New York)*
Yields 1 dozen large doughnuts

Dough
2⅛ cups whole milk
1½ ounces fresh yeast
4 eggs
7⅞ cups bread flour
1⅜ cups confectioners' sugar
3¼ teaspoons kosher salt
½ tablespoon ground nutmeg
Zest of 2 navel oranges (see Chef's Tips on citrus zest, page 311)
½ cup unsalted butter, room temperature
Vegetable or soy oil, as needed

Blueberry Filling
½ pound fresh blueberries (wild are the best)
⅓ cup granulated sugar
2 tablespoons light brown sugar
½ cup fresh orange juice
2 vanilla beans, seeded
1 tablespoon lemon juice
2 tablespoons cornstarch
2 tablespoons water (slurry for thickening purposes)

Cinnamon-Sugar mixture
1 cup sugar
⅓ cup light brown sugar
2½ tablespoons ground cinnamon

Dough

Warm your milk no hotter than 92°F (if too hot, it can kill your yeast, and will not allow the dough to rise). Place the yeast into warm milk and mix until combined. Place into a stand mixer with a dough hook, turn to medium speed, and add the eggs.

Combine all the dry ingredients and zest in a separate bowl and add this mixture to the milk mixture. Mix until it forms sticky dough. Lastly, add the butter to the mixture.

Leave the mixer on medium speed until the dough begins to pull away from the bowl (approximately 12 minutes).

Place the dough in a greased bowl and place in a refrigerator until it doubles in size (at least 6 hours).

Once the dough is proofed (doubled in size), remove from the bowl; do not knead the dough. Place on a well-floured, flat work surface and roll about 1/3-inch thick.

Cut the doughnut dough with a round ring cutter (or desired shape cookie cutter). Fry in 350°F vegetable or soy oil until dark golden brown on both sides.

Blueberry Filling

Place all the ingredients (except the cornstarch and water) in a medium sauce pot and bring to a boil for 5 minutes until it starts to thicken.

Combine the cornstarch and water in a small bowl to create a slurry (will look like whole milk).

Pour into the blueberry filling and whisk until the filling becomes thick (should heavily coat the back of a spoon). Place in a bowl and allow it to cool.

To fill the doughnuts, place a pastry tip or tube into a pastry bag or in the bottom corner of a large plastic freezer bag. Fill the bag with the filling and twist the opposite end of the bag closed. Then use the fitted tube to puncture a hole into the bottom of each doughnut and squeeze the bag until the doughnut is full with filling.

Cinnamon-Sugar Mixture

Mix all the ingredients in a bowl. Pour into a shallow pan large enough to hold the doughnut. Completely cover each doughnut in this mixture.

Cranberry-Orange Scones

Susan Warner *(Topsfield, Massachusetts)*
Serves 8

Cranberries, the state fruit of Massachusetts, are in season from autumn to mid-winter. Their growing season overlaps with oranges, making the natural pairing of these flavors a successful combination. This recipe features dried cranberries, which the entire country can enjoy year-round.

Story by Chef Nicole

2 cups all-purpose flour
1 tablespoon baking powder
½ teaspoon baking soda
¼ teaspoon salt
2 tablespoons sugar
1 tablespoon fresh orange zest (see Chef's Tips on citrus zest, page 311)
½ cup unsalted butter, cold
⅔ cup buttermilk
1 cup dried cranberries

Topping (optional)
4 teaspoons fresh orange juice
½ cup confectioners' sugar, sifted
Raw sugar, to taste

Mix the dry ingredients, orange zest, and butter in a food processor (or use a pastry fork), and combine until the butter is incorporated to a fine meal consistency.

Add buttermilk and cranberries, combine with a spoon, and knead with your hands into biscuit shapes (2½-inch circles, ½-inch thick).

Drop onto a cookie sheet or pizza stone. Bake at 425°F for 15 minutes or until light brown.

For a sweeter scone, sprinkle raw sugar on top prior to baking. Once cooled, mix the orange juice and the confectioners' sugar. Use a pastry brush to paint the mixture on.

Popovers

Lorraine Ott *(Boxford, Massachusetts)*
Yields 6 large popovers

> Every time we visit our dear friends in New England, we awake to the smell of fresh popovers and the crisp, woodsy air.
>
> *Story by Mary Elizabeth*

1 egg, room temperature

1 cup all-purpose flour

1 cup milk

1 tablespoon unsalted butter, melted

Pinch salt

Preheat an oven to 450°F. Spray a 6-cup popover pan with baking spray.

Place the empty pan on the middle rack of the preheated oven for a few minutes while preparing the batter.

In a large mixing bowl, beat the egg slightly and add the remaining ingredients. Beat until smooth (it is helpful to transfer the batter to a separate container or liquid measuring cup with a spout for easy pouring).

Without removing the pan from the oven, carefully pour the batter into popover cups until each is three-quarters of the way full, and quickly close the oven door. Bake for 15 minutes at 450°F, and then lower to 325°F. Continue baking for approximately 25 minutes until golden (do not open the oven door until done; otherwise, the popovers will deflate).

Grandma's Boston Brown Bread

Krysten Lindsay Hager *(Inspired by Boston, Massachusetts; resides in Bellbrook, Ohio)*
Serves 5

My grandma Lillian Bagrowski used to make Boston brown bread for every holiday and at my grandfather's (or any other family member's) request. She would serve it like you would a coffee cake, alongside breakfast and sometimes as a dessert. Grandma thought that it was best served with fresh butter, but my cousins loved slathering it with cream cheese. As a daughter of Polish immigrants, Polish cooking was her first love, but, through local church gatherings, she grew to appreciate and enjoy foods from other ethnic groups. Grandma remembered first having brown bread at church, where she met many Irish immigrants from Boston. She always taught us to be open to new experiences and how, sometimes, the door to exploring a new culture was through its food.

1½ cups water
1½ cups raisins (or dried cranberries)
1 cup sugar
1 tablespoon shortening
1 egg, room temperature
3½ tablespoons molasses
1 teaspoon pure vanilla extract
2½ cups all-purpose flour
2 teaspoons baking soda
½ teaspoon salt

Preheat an oven to 350°F. Combine the water and raisins in a small saucepan, and boil for 1 minute. Pour into a large mixing bowl and cool. Beat in the sugar, shortening, egg, molasses, and vanilla.

Sift together the flour, baking soda, and salt, and add it to the batter.

Mix thoroughly. Bake in five 11-ounce clean and dry soup cans, filling each can only half full; do not cover the cans. Place the cans onto a sheet pan and bake for 1 hour. Let the bread cool completely before removing it from the cans.

Rhode Island Jonny Cakes or Hoe Cakes

Chef Phillip Griffin and Malinda Coletta *(Professor Chef, North Providence, Rhode Island)*
Serves 6–8

> Rhode Islanders take their jonny cakes so seriously that they hold baking and eating contests every year. The original cakes were made from ground dry Indian corn (maize) kernels. The slaves working in the fields would prepare these and sear them on the flat side of a hoe, which was heated by the sun or over a fire.

2 cups boiling water
4 cups stone-ground white cornmeal
1 teaspoon kosher salt
1 tablespoon unsalted butter, at room temperature
½–1 cup molasses

Bring water to a boil in a saucepan on the stove; mix it into the cornmeal in a large bowl. Add salt, butter, and molasses; mix thoroughly. Dough should be quite stiff. (If necessary, add cold water 1 tablespoon at a time until the consistency is right. If you only use ½ cup of molasses, you will likely need to add some water.)

Spread the dough in a thin layer on the bottom of your griddle or frying pan, pressing down to spread out the dough and to make the cake as thin as possible. Set a griddle or frying pan on medium heat. Prick all over with a fork to aid in cooking the center of the cake.

When the cake begins steaming up through the holes, it is probably cooked on the underside, so loosen it from the pan, flip it onto a plate, and then slide it back into the pan to cook the other side.

Once finished cooking, these can be stacked on a plate. Serve immediately with butter or honey.

Asparagus Soup with Seasoned Dill Yogurt

Reshma Adwar *(New York, New York)*
Serves 4

> In springtime, asparagus are just coming into the markets. I happened to find a particularly tender bunch at my local farmers market, and decided to make a healthy and tasty soup. The asparagus picked at the peak of the season gave the soup a grassy, fresh finish, which was heightened by adding a dollop of the creamy, tangy seasoned dill yogurt. There is no cream in this, which trims calories, and the overall preparation of this is simple. Yet the results are exceptional.

1 teaspoon olive oil
2 leeks, white and light green parts only, chopped (or 1 medium white onion)
2 bay leaves
1 large carrot, chopped
2 celery stalks, chopped
1 garlic clove, smashed (see Chef's Tips on garlic, page 314)
1 pound asparagus, chopped (save a few of the tips for garnish)
2 cups low-sodium chicken stock
¼ cup plus 1 tablespoon chopped dill
1½ tablespoons fresh lemon juice
Zest of 1 lemon (see Chef's Tips on citrus zest, page 311)
3 tablespoons Greek yogurt
4 lemon wedges (optional)
Salt and freshly cracked black pepper, to taste

Heat olive oil in a medium pot. When hot, add leeks and bay leaves, and sauté until the leeks soften (about 5 minutes). Add carrot, celery, and garlic, and sauté until the leeks caramelize and brown (about 8 minutes; if the vegetables start to stick, add a little water). Add asparagus, and sauté until slightly tender (about 5 minutes). Then add chicken stock and bring to a boil. Add ¼ cup of dill, and remove the bay leaves. Remove from the heat, and blend the mixture with either an immersion blender or in batches using a traditional blender or food processor. Return the blended soup to the pot and bring to a simmer. Add the juice, zest, salt, and pepper to taste.

In the meantime, combine the yogurt with the 1 tablespoon of dill and salt to taste.

To serve, ladle the soup into serving bowls and add a dollop of the dill-yogurt mixture. Garnish with an asparagus tip and a sprig of dill, along with a lemon wedge on top for color.

Chef's Tip

Cut leeks before washing to expose the center of the stalk. Place them in a colander and rinse well (this removes all of the dirt and grit, which are hidden within the layers of the leek).

To prepare asparagus, hold the stalk by each end and bend together until the stalk snaps naturally (the asparagus will always break at the point where the asparagus is no longer tender and becomes extremely fibrous). Only use the end with the tip; discard the opposite end.

Roasted Butternut Squash Soup

Heather Pierce Giannone *(Fairfield, Connecticut)*

Serves 4

Connecticut is nicknamed the "Nutmeg State," although the spice is not indigenous to Connecticut. In the eighteenth and nineteenth centuries, it had been brought over by sailors returning from a voyage, and became a local favorite. Use freshly ground nutmeg in this recipe to make a big flavor difference.

Story by Chef Nicole

---

2 medium butternut squash
3 tablespoons olive oil, divided
1 large onion, diced
2–3 medium carrots, sliced into ¼-inch rounds
½ teaspoon cinnamon
¼ teaspoon ground ginger
Pinch nutmeg, freshly grated
4 cups chicken broth/stock or vegetable broth (see Index, page 343)
Fresh sage, toasted squash, or pumpkin seeds (see Chef's Tips on nuts and seeds, page 318)
Greek yogurt, for garnish
Sea salt and freshly cracked black pepper, to taste

Preheat an oven to 400°F. Slice the squash in half lengthwise. Drizzle 1 tablespoon of olive oil on a baking sheet, place the squash cut-side-down, and move them around to coat in the olive oil. Pierce the skins a few times with a fork. Roast the squash in the oven until tender (about 30–40 minutes). Take out the squash and let it cool.

Heat 2 tablespoons of olive oil in a large pot. Add onions, salt, and pepper, and sauté for 2–3 minutes. Add carrots, and sauté for another 2–3 minutes. Scoop out the seeds from the squash with a large spoon, and discard or reserve to toast as a garnish. Scoop out the roasted squash from the skin, and add to a pot. Add cinnamon, ginger, nutmeg, and broth, and bring to a boil. Lower heat to a simmer and cover for 20 minutes.

Remove from the heat and puree the soup with an immersion blender (if you do not have an immersion blender, remove the vegetables with a slotted spoon, puree in batches using a blender or food processor, and then add it back to the pot).

Season with salt and pepper to taste. Garnish with sage, toasted seeds, or a dollop of plain Greek yogurt, if desired.

Lemon-Dill Fish Chowder

Jon Drake *(Cape Cod, Massachusetts)*
Serves 4–5

Few dishes in my native New England are more iconic than creamy chowder. Growing up, the love that my grandmother put into her fish chowder made the best summer evenings more pleasant, and the coldest winter nights more tolerable. This is a rustic take on the Northeast classic that incorporates the brightness of lemon zest and fresh dill with a soft, buttery broth that would make anyone's grandmother smile.

2 medium yellow onions, diced
2 bay leaves
¼ cup unsalted butter
3 medium red potatoes, unpeeled, washed, and cut into ½-inch cubes
1½ pounds skinless haddock fillet, deboned
1 (½ oz.) can evaporated milk
1 cup half-and-half
1 tablespoon Worcestershire sauce
½ tablespoon soy sauce
½ teaspoon freshly cracked black pepper
¾ teaspoon ground coriander
½ cup fresh dill, finely chopped
Zest of 1½ lemons (see Chef's Tips on citrus zest, page 311)
1 teaspoon salt
Dill and freshly cracked black pepper, for garnish

Sauté the onions and bay leaves in butter until the onions become soft. Add potatoes, and stir together. Add enough water to just barely cover the potatoes, and then lay the haddock over the top. Cover and simmer gently for 10 minutes until the fish flakes apart. Break the fish into large pieces and mix in the remaining ingredients. Continue heating on low for 30 minutes, uncovered, until a thicker consistency is reached, stirring occasionally. Garnish with fresh dill and freshly ground black pepper. Serve with a piece of warm, crusty baguette.

Chef's Tip

By sautéing the bay leaves with the onions, you extract more flavor from the dry herb rather than if you had added them to the liquid later in the cooking process.

North Fork Cioppino

Chef Claudia Helinski *(Salamander's Bakery and General Store, Greenport, New York)*
Serves 8–10

> Chef Claudia loves to make this soup in October. Her store is found on the North Fork of Long Island, where most of the ingredients are sourced from the many farms, vineyards, and fishing docks located nearby.
>
> *Story by Mary Elizabeth*

1 cup extra-virgin olive oil
Pinch red pepper flakes
1 tablespoon garlic cloves, chopped (see Chef's Tips on garlic, page 314)
3 large Spanish onions, chopped
3 fennel bulbs, cored and thinly sliced
1 bunch scallions, sliced
½ bottle (350 ml.) local dry white wine
2 quarts tomatoes, super-ripe, peeled, seeded, and chopped, or canned plum tomatoes
Heaping teaspoon saffron
1 tablespoon turmeric
1 tablespoon fennel seed
2 pounds assortment of local littleneck clams, lobster, chopped, mussels, and/or scallops
2 quarts shellfish stock or good-quality fish fumet
2–3 pounds codfish fillets, deboned and cubed
Fresh parsley, for garnish
Sea or kosher salt and freshly cracked black pepper, to taste

Gently heat the olive oil in a deep, non-reactive pot large enough to hold all the ingredients. Add red pepper flakes and garlic, and cook to a light golden color. Add Spanish onions and fennel, cooking until translucent. Add scallions, white wine, tomatoes, saffron, turmeric, and fennel seed, cooking until the fresh fennel is tender (about 15 minutes). Add clams and lobster (if using) and shellfish stock (or fish fumet), and cook, removing the clams to a warm serving bowl as they open. Add cod and mussels, leaving any scallops to add to the stew at the very last minute after removing from the heat. Taste for seasoning and sprinkle with parsley. Serve with rustic bread and salad.

Lobster Gazpacho

Chef Audrey Patterson *(Blueberry Point Chefs, Perry, Maine)*
Serves 6

1 small cucumber, peeled and cubed
2 scallions, minced
6 fresh basil leaves
1 tablespoon Worcestershire sauce
¼ teaspoon salt
1 tablespoon freshly squeezed lemon juice
1 clove garlic, made into a paste (see Chef's Tips on garlic, page 314)
¾ pounds tomatoes, diced
1 dash cayenne pepper
2 tablespoons olive oil
½ medium onion, diced
1½ ounces vodka
⅓ bell pepper, diced
2 cups tomato juice
1 cup lobster, cooked and chopped (or a combination of lobster and crabmeat)
1 cup crème fraîche (available in the dairy section)

Set aside a small amount of cucumber, scallion, and basil for garnish, and then combine all the ingredients (except for the lobster and crème fraîche) in a blender, blending roughly.

In the bottom of a martini glass or champagne goblet, put ¼ cup of lobster meat. Top with ¼ cup of crème fraîche and ½ cup of gazpacho mixture. Garnish with cucumber, scallion, and basil.

Beefsteak Tomato, Red Onion, and Mozzarella Platter with Basil Drizzle

Serves 6–8

Dressing

½ cup good-quality mayonnaise

3 tablespoons white vinegar

2 tablespoons whole milk

1 teaspoon sugar

½ teaspoon salt

15 fresh basil leaves

2 tablespoons extra-virgin olive oil

Salad

2 large beefsteak tomatoes, thinly sliced

1 small red onion, thinly sliced

1–2 (16 oz.) logs fresh mozzarella, thinly sliced

Dressing

Place all the dressing ingredients, except the oil, in a food processor and blend. While blending, slowly pour in the oil. Once all the ingredients are incorporated, stop blending, pour into a separate container with a spout, and reserve.

Salad

Assemble the platter by alternately arranging tomatoes, red onions, and mozzarella. Immediately before serving, drizzle the sauce over the platter.

This dish is typically seen with balsamic vinegar drizzled on top. Mary Elizabeth serves it with a tangy dressing that her friend Chris shared with her.

Roasted Butternut Squash Salad with Maple Dijon Vinaigrette

Chef and Dr. Sonali Ruder *(New York, New York)*

Serves 4

Not only is this salad healthy and easy to make, it is also a great way to use up leftover butternut squash. Packed with fresh greens, maple-Dijon vinaigrette, and topped with sweet butternut squash, dried cranberries, toasted pecans, and a sprinkling of tangy goat cheese, this salad will make you feel like you are overindulging, even though you are not. I like to use a mixture of peppery baby arugula and mild baby spinach, but feel free to use your favorite salad greens.

½ medium butternut squash, peeled and cut into ¾-inch cubes (about 2½ cups)

1 teaspoon fresh thyme leaves, chopped (or ¼ teaspoon dried thyme)

6 teaspoons extra-virgin olive oil, divided

¼ cup chopped pecans (see Chef's Tips on nuts and seeds, page 318)

1 tablespoon cider vinegar

1 tablespoon maple syrup

½ teaspoon Dijon mustard

½ (2½ oz.) bag baby arugula, washed

½ (2½ oz.) bag baby spinach, washed

¼ cup dried cranberries

2 ounces reduced-fat goat cheese, crumbled

Kosher salt and freshly cracked black pepper, to taste

Preheat an oven to 425°F. Toss the butternut squash with the thyme, 1 teaspoon of olive oil, a pinch of salt, and 2 to 3 turns of pepper in a large mixing bowl. Spread it out in a single layer on a sheet pan. Roast in the oven for 20 minutes, and then flip the squash over and cook for another 10 minutes until fork-tender. Turn the oven down to 350°F. Spread the pecans on a baking sheet and toast in the oven until fragrant (6 to 8 minutes). Remove from the oven and cool.

In the meantime, prepare the vinaigrette. Vigorously whisk the vinegar, syrup, and mustard in one steady stream, slowly pouring in the remaining 5 teaspoons olive oil until emulsified (see emulsification in Chef's Tips, page 320). Season the vinaigrette with salt and pepper.

Immediately before serving, place the arugula and spinach in a salad bowl, and toss with the dressing. Arrange the roasted squash, pecans, cranberries, and goat cheese on top.

Crabmeat Salad

Serves 6

8 ounces lump crabmeat, cooked and shells removed
½ small cucumber, peeled
¾ cup mayonnaise
¼ cup finely chopped onions
1 hard-boiled egg, cooled and chopped
1 tablespoon fresh lemon juice
½ teaspoon fresh dill, chopped
Salt and freshly cracked black pepper, to taste

Place pieces of crabmeat in a large mixing bowl. Seed the cucumber by cutting it in half lengthwise, and scoop out the seeds with a teaspoon or a melon baller. Dice the cucumber and add to the crabmeat. In a separate bowl, mix the remaining ingredients until well incorporated. Season with salt and pepper. Combine this with the crabmeat mixture, toss, and chill until ready to serve. Place on a bed of lettuce alongside fresh croissants.

New England Lobster Rolls

Chef and Dr. Sonali Ruder *(Inspired by New England; resides in New York, New York)*
Serves 4

> One of my favorite classic lobster dishes is New England lobster rolls. There is something about the sweet, tender lobster meat in the warm, buttery roll that gets me every time. Now, I know that there is a lot of debate as to which is the best lobster roll recipe. Some purists simply put steamed lobster in a buttered, toasted bun with no mayonnaise or other accoutrements. I, however, prefer my lobster rolls with a light coating of lemony mayonnaise, some finely chopped celery for crunch, and Boston lettuce to keep the bun from getting soggy.

Lemon-Chive Mayonnaise
(See Chef's Tips on emulsification, page 320)
1 egg yolk, room temperature
1 teaspoon Dijon mustard
1½ teaspoons fresh lemon juice
⅛ teaspoon kosher salt
6 ounces canola or other neutral-flavored oil
2 ounces extra-virgin olive oil
1 teaspoon water, room temperature (optional)
2 teaspoons chopped chives

Lobster
2 cups cooked and diced lobster meat
¼ cup homemade lemon-chive mayonnaise or plain mayonnaise
3 tablespoons finely chopped celery
Kosher salt and freshly cracked black pepper, to taste

Rolls
4 top-split hot dog buns
3 tablespoons unsalted butter, melted
3 leaves Boston lettuce, sliced

Lemon-Chive Mayonnaise

Place the egg yolk, mustard, lemon juice, and salt in a large bowl, and whisk together.

Mix the canola and olive oils together in a measuring cup with a spout. While constantly whisking the egg mixture in the bowl, slowly pour in the oil in a steady stream until emulsified.

If the mixture gets too thick, add water to thin it out.

Taste the mayonnaise, and season it to taste with salt and more lemon juice, if desired. Stir in the chives. Store any extra mayonnaise in an airtight container in the refrigerator for no more than 3 days. *Yields 1 cup.*

Lobster

Mix the lobster, mayonnaise, and celery together in a bowl. Season the mixture with salt and pepper.

Rolls

Heat a large skillet over medium heat. Brush the inner and outer surfaces of the buns with butter. Open the buns and toast them in the skillet until golden brown on both sides. Arrange some lettuce on each bun and top with equal portions of the lobster mixture. Serve immediately.

Syracuse-Style Chicken Wings

Executive Chef Charles Voudouris *(Inspired by Syracuse, New York; resides in Anguilla, British West Indies)*
Serves 4 (10 wings each)

The appetizer of spicy chicken wings originated at the Anchor Bar in Buffalo, New York. The classic story stars a creative employee, her hungry son, and his fellow teammates. After a late game, they adjourned to the bar to celebrate and feast. After a long evening, the menu was sparse, and our star was forced to use the only ingredient left in the house. Up until this time, chicken wings were regarded as unusable parts of the chicken. However, after being seasoned, deep-fried, and tossed in a spicy butter sauce, this dish became famous across the United States. While working in Syracuse (another city in upstate New York), Executive Chef Charles created his own version, which he has shared here.

Story by Chef Nicole

Chicken

1 (1 oz.) packet ranch dressing mix
2 cups all-purpose flour
2 tablespoons garlic powder
2 tablespoons onion powder
5 pounds chicken wings, non-breaded wings and drums
1 gallon frying oil (see Chef's Tips on blended oil, page 309)

Sauce

2 cups Frank's® RedHot sauce
¼ cup distilled white vinegar
2 tablespoons red chile flakes
8 ounces unsalted butter, cold and cubed
1 bunch celery, washed and cut into sticks
Salt and freshly cracked black pepper, to taste

Chicken

Mix the dry ingredients together, add chicken wings, and dust over a screen. Place frying oil in a deep fryer or in a heavy, large, deep sauce pot on a stove top. Heat oil to 375°F. Working in batches, fry a few pieces of chicken at a time for 4 to 7 minutes each, depending on the size of the wings (they are cooked when they are golden brown with an internal temperature of 165°F, and the juices should run clear.) When fully cooked, carefully remove from the hot oil with a fryer basket, spider, or large slotted spoon. Place on a sheet pan and reserve.

Sauce

Bring the hot sauce, vinegar, and chile flakes to a simmer for 10 minutes. Take off the heat, and whisk in the cold butter cubes into the hot sauce. Toss the sauce with the chicken wings, or serve on the side as a dipping sauce. Garnish with celery and homemade bleu cheese dressing.

Bleu Cheese Dressing
Yields 2 ½ cups

¾ cup sour cream
½ teaspoon dry mustard
½ teaspoon freshly cracked black pepper
½ teaspoon salt
⅓ teaspoon garlic powder
1 teaspoon Worcestershire sauce
1⅓ cups mayonnaise
4 ounces bleu cheese, crumbled

In a mixing bowl, combine the first six ingredients and blend on low speed for 2 minutes. Add mayonnaise and blend on low, again. Increase the speed to medium, mixing for 2 minutes. Using a wooden spoon, stir in the bleu cheese. Best if refrigerated overnight before serving.

Award-Winning Maryland Crab Cakes

Chef Ben Tehranian *(Cook with Ben, Columbia, Maryland)*
Serves 4 (1 cake each)

Dressing
1 whole egg
½ cup mayonnaise
1 teaspoon Dijon mustard
1 teaspoon Worcestershire sauce
½ teaspoon Old Bay® seasoning
1 teaspoon fresh lemon juice
¼ teaspoon salt
½ teaspoon hot sauce

Crab Cakes
1 pound jumbo lump or lump crabmeat
2 slices white bread, crust removed, and diced
1 teaspoon fresh parsley, chopped
3 tablespoons vegetable oil, if frying

Mix the dressing ingredients in a bowl and set aside.

Carefully check the crabmeat for any shells, being careful not to break up the crabmeat. Gently fold in the crabmeat with the bread, parsley, and dressing, only mixing enough to combine the ingredients. Refrigerate for a few hours or overnight. Shape the crab mixture into four cakes. For frying, heat the vegetable oil in a non-stick frying pan, and sauté until golden brown on each side For baking, place in a preheated oven at 450°F for 15 minutes or until done. Garnish with tartar or cocktail sauce.

Crab Gratin

Angela Martinez *(Celebrity Kitchen, Wilmington, Delaware)*
Serves 4

1 pound jumbo lump crabmeat
1 tablespoon mayonnaise
¾ cup gruyere cheese, grated
1 tablespoon Old Bay® seafood seasoning
2 tablespoons fresh Italian flat-leaf parsley, minced
2 tablespoons heavy cream

Preheat an oven to 375°F. Carefully check the crabmeat for any shells. Gently combine all the ingredients with a spatula. Do not over-mix. Portion the crabmeat into four individual gratin containers. Place in the preheated oven, and bake until warm and bubbly throughout. Serve it at once with fresh herb-buttered croutons, thickly sliced, chilled cucumbers, or multigrain crackers.

Rhode Island Squid Rings with Pepperoncini and Garlic

Chef Phillip Griffin and Malinda Coletta *(Professor Chef, North Providence, Rhode Island)*
Serves 2

> The Northeast region is as famous for its fresh shellfish as it is for its cultural influence. Pepperoncinis, otherwise known as Tuscan peppers, are quite popular in Italian-American cuisine.

¾ cup all-purpose flour
1 teaspoon garlic powder
¼ teaspoon freshly cracked black pepper
1 pound squid rings and tentacles
Oil, for frying and sautéing (see Chef's Tips on blended oil, page 309)
3 garlic cloves, peeled and chopped
2–3 pepperoncini peppers, sliced
1 tablespoon fresh lemon juice

Mix the flour, garlic powder, and pepper in a plastic bag. Rinse the sliced squid, pat off the excess moisture, place in the bag, and shake.

Add about ½ inch of oil to a heavy skillet, and heat over medium-high heat until very hot.

Remove the squid from the bag and place in a fine-mesh strainer. Shake the squid in the strainer to remove the excess flour. Add some of the squid to the hot oil without crowding the pan. Cook in several batches until crisp and brown, turning once. Use a spider or slotted spoon to remove the squid from the oil. Drain the squid on a sheet pan lined with paper towels.

In a separate skillet, add 1 teaspoon of oil and three cloves of garlic, and sauté quickly. Add pepperoncini and lemon juice. Then add the squid; toss this mixture, heat through, then serve.

Blue Point Oysters Pernod

Executive Chef Frank Tramontano *(Ever So Saucy Foods, Yaphank, New York)*
Serves 6 (3 oysters each)

> "Blue Points" are the most abused of oyster appellations. After a century of exile, real Blue Points are, once again, growing in their ancestral home, Long Island's Great South Bay. The name has been undercut by boring and bland "New Jersey Blue Points," "Virginia Blue Points," and other pretenders. Oysters are grown in trays around the docks of the Great South Bay and deliver the full-salt assault that made Blue Points famous in the 1820s, along with fascinating pine and anise notes (hence, the Pernod in this recipe), which are most apparent in spring. Delivered straight to Manhattan restaurants, they are the genuine article.

3 strips thick-cut hickory-cured bacon
¼ cup extra-virgin olive oil
4 cloves garlic, chopped (see Chef's Tips on garlic, page 314)
6 shallots, chopped
¼ cup dry white vermouth
½ cup Pernod (or anise-flavored liqueur), divided
¼ cup fresh, flat-leaf parsley, chopped
½ cup fresh dill, chopped
2 dozen Blue Point oysters, shucked
3 lemons, cut into wedges
Kosher or sea salt and freshly cracked black pepper, to taste

Prepare all the ingredients so they are measured and ready to combine (see Chef's Tips on *mise en place,* page 309). Cut the bacon into 1-inch strips (about 8 to 10 strips). Bring 3 cups of water to a boil. Boil the bacon strips for 3 minutes, drain, and set aside to dry.

In a deep sauté pan, heat the extra-virgin olive oil over low heat. Add garlic, and sauté for 30 seconds, stirring until the garlic turns slightly pale to very light brown. Add shallots, sauté, and stir until soft (about 1 minute). Add vermouth, and reduce the liquid for about 5 minutes, stirring constantly. Add ¼ cup of Pernod, and the reduce liquid for about 3 minutes, stirring constantly. Add parsley and dill, and continue to sauté for about 3 minutes. Add salt and pepper to taste and the remaining Pernod. Remove from the heat and set aside. This can be prepared a day in advance. Do not refrigerate.

Arrange the chilled oysters on a foil-lined baking sheet. Add 1 tablespoon of mixture to each oyster. Top with bacon, and broil for about 2 minutes or until the bacon is crisp. Serve with lemon wedges.

Presentation Suggestions:

On an oven-safe dish, serve on a bed of warm rock salt or sea kelp garnished with lemon wedges, dill fronds, and parsley sprigs.

Rhode Island Stuffed Quahogs

Chef Phillip Griffin and Malinda Coletta *(Professor Chef, North Providence, Rhode Island)*
Serves 8

The quahog is a hard-shell clam that inhabits the mud flats along the Eastern coast. The word "quahog" is derived from the Native American word "poquauhock," meaning "horse fish." The Native Americans used quahog shells, which have a shiny, purple lining, to make beads that were used as a form of currency. The quahog's scientific name comes from a Latin word meaning "wages." Currently, Rhode Island has a huge population of these delicious mollusks, and, though they are no longer used for trade, they continue to call them by their historic nickname. Quahogs are typically served with a lemon wedge and Tabasco® sauce.

Story by Chef Nicole

10 quahogs
Approximately 2 cups white wine
⅔ pound chorizo, approximately 1½ sausages
1 red bell pepper, cut in half
1 green bell pepper, cut in half
2 small yellow onions, cut in half
1 stick (½ cup) unsalted butter
2 tubes butter-flavored crackers
1 tube saltine crackers
6 day-old torpedo/small hero rolls
1 teaspoon salt
1½ teaspoons freshly cracked black pepper
Hot sauce and lemon wedges, for garnish

Wash the quahogs. Add white wine to a pot, and insert a little steamer basket. Set the heat to high and wait for it to boil. Steam 10 quahogs until they have all opened (approximately 10 minutes should do the trick). Remove the quahogs, strain the remaining liquid, and reserve. Chop up the meat roughly by hand. Reserve the shells.

By hand or using a food processor, chop up the chorizo, peppers, and onions.

Melt the butter on low heat in a medium sauce pan. Add chorizo, peppers, and onions, and let it sweat until the onions are soft.

Crushing by hand or using a food processor, chop the butter-flavored crackers, saltines, and torpedo rolls. Mix the salt and pepper.

Combine all the ingredients in a large mixing bowl. To moisten the stuffing, add a bit of the reserved liquid from steaming the quahogs (you want the mixture to generally hold together, but not be mushy).

Take half a quahog shell, and mound about ½ cup into each shell. Place all of the shells, stuffing-side-up, onto a baking sheet. Place in a 350°F oven for about 45 minutes to an hour until you have a nice crust on the top. Serve with plenty of hot sauce and lemon wedges.

Rhode Island Clam Boil

Chef Phillip Griffin and Malinda Coletta *(Professor Chef, North Providence, Rhode Island)*
Serves 4–6

> This classic Northeastern preparation for seafood includes steamers, which are soft-shell clams found in New England waters. Fresh shellfish, some vegetables, a bottle of white wine, and some herbs make for a delicious one-dish meal that will impress your family and friends.

3 cups water
1 (750 ml.) bottle dry white wine
1 bay leaf (fresh, if possible)
3 tablespoons Old Bay® seasoning
10 sprigs fresh thyme
1 bunch celery, diced
4 carrots, sliced
3 medium onions, diced
3 pounds potatoes, diced
3 ears fresh sweet corn, sliced into thirds
2 lobsters, live
2 pounds each mussels, steamers, shrimp, and calamari, washed and rinsed
1 pound Alaskan crab legs (fresh or frozen and defrosted)
1 stick (½ cup) unsalted butter, melted

In a large pot, add water, wine, bay leaf, Old Bay® seasoning, thyme, celery, carrots, onions, and potatoes. Cook for 20 minutes on high. Add sweet corn, and cook for 5 minutes. Add the lobsters, and then add the remaining shellfish. Cook for 5 to 10 minutes until the lobsters are bright red, and the clams and mussels have opened up (discard any mollusks that have not opened during the cooking process).

Remove the shellfish and vegetables, and serve in a large bowl. Strain and reserve the broth (some people like to drink and/or dip the steamers into this broth). Dip the shellfish into melted butter.

Poached Blackfish in Coconut-Lime Broth

Reshma Adwar *(New York, New York)*
Serves 2

Every Saturday, my husband and I visit our local farmers market. My particular favorite to visit is the fishmonger. During the week, he goes fishing off of Long Island, and then comes back each Saturday with fresh, delicious catches. One week, we picked up some blackfish, which has a beautiful, firm, white-colored flesh and a mild, sweet flavor. Due to the freshness of the catch, I wanted to do something special, so I decided to make this Asian-style broth to poach the fish in. The sweetness from the coconut milk enhances the sweetness of this fish, and the lime, fresh spices, and herbs temper and balance the whole dish.

2 teaspoons coriander seeds

1 small Thai chile (optional)

1 piece ginger, 1½ inches long, minced

2 cloves garlic (see Chef's Tips on garlic paste, page 314)

1 teaspoon olive oil

1 shallot, minced

Zest of 1 lime (see Chef's Tips on citrus zest, page 311)

Juice of 1 lime

6 ounces coconut milk plus ½ cup water

1 cup fresh basil, chopped

1 teaspoon brown sugar

1 pound white-fleshed fish (such as blackfish, cod, or halibut)

Salt, to taste

In a small blender or mortar and pestle, mash together the coriander seeds, chile, ginger, and garlic until it forms a paste. Set aside.

Heat olive oil in a large, shallow saucepan. When warm, add shallots and cook for 1 to 2 minutes; then add the paste, and cook for about 3 to 4 minutes. Add the lime zest and juice, sautéing for a minute; then add the coconut milk and water, and bring up to a boil. Add basil leaves, brown sugar, and salt, and stir to combine. At this point, taste the broth and adjust any seasonings. To poach, lower the heat to between 165 and 180°F, add the fish, and bring back to a simmer. (If the fish is not completely submerged in the broth, baste it with the liquid, and turn once to ensure the fish gets cooked through.) When the fish is completely cooked, turn off the heat and let the fish rest a few minutes before serving. Serve with brown rice and steamed vegetables.

Dolce Gorgonzola-Battered Long Island Fluke Fillet

Executive Chef Frank Tramontano *(Ever So Saucy Foods, Yaphank, New York)*
Serves 5–6

Authentic Italian gorgonzola comes in two varieties—dolce (meaning sweet) and mountain (the sharper and firmer version). Dating back to ancient times, this member of the Stracchino family is one of the world's classic cheeses. Almost spreadable, gorgonzola dolce is supple and luxurious, with an unmistakable tangy creaminess. Its pale white interior is laced with streaks of blue, giving it a striking appearance to match its piquant flavor. This incredible combination of flavor will bring new life to your preparation of most white-meat fish fillets (such as fluke, sea bass, and flounder) by adding a supple sophistication and beguiling flavor.

2 sticks (1 cup) unsalted butter, divided
½ cup dry white vermouth, divided
½ pound gorgonzola cheese
2 eggs plus 1 yolk
1 cup buttermilk or heavy cream (sour cream may be substituted)
½ teaspoon ground white pepper
½ cup flat-leaf parsley, chopped, plus 3 sprigs
6 fresh fluke fillets, about ¼ pound each
2 cups panko (Japanese) breadcrumbs
1 cup Italian seasoned breadcrumbs
2 lemons, cut into wedges

Preheat an oven to 375°F. Prepare a 9- by 13-inch oven-safe baking dish by lining the bottom with 1 stick of the butter cut into small slices. Add half the vermouth.

Combine the gorgonzola cheese with 1 stick of the butter, and heat in the microwave for about 1 minute. Whisk together until smooth. Add the eggs and yolk, and whisk until smooth. Add the buttermilk, white pepper, and parsley, then whisk until smooth. Cut the fish fillets into serving-size pieces, and add to the batter mixture. Let stand for up to 1 hour in the refrigerator (see Chef's Tips on standard breading procedure, page 319).

Combine both breadcrumbs in a mixing bowl. Remove fish from the refrigerator, shake loose any excess batter, and coat with breadcrumb mixture. The fillets should be about the size of your hand. Roll the battered, breaded fillets and arrange in the buttered baking dish. With the remaining ¼ pound of butter, cut into small pats and top each rolled fillet. Sprinkle the top of the fish with the remaining vermouth, cover with foil, and bake in a 375°F oven for 40 minutes. Remove the foil, and bake for an additional 5 minutes or until light brown. Serve with lemon wedges and garnish with fresh parsley sprigs.

Sautéed Chicken with Caramelized Onion-Tomato Relish

Reshma Adwar *(New York, New York)*
Serves 4

> I stepped into my local farmers market one day, and all I could smell was basil. There were bunches of it stacked high, and it looked so fresh and lovely that I had to buy a bunch. I looked around for other ingredients to go with it and found some beautiful cherry tomatoes. I then picked up some onions and cooked up this fantastically fresh and flavorful dish full of healthy ingredients. The relish will have a fresh, sweet-tart flavor, which will pair beautifully with the chicken.

Chicken

1½ pounds skinless, boneless, thin-sliced chicken, preferably organic
1 tablespoon balsamic vinegar
½ teaspoon dried oregano
½ teaspoon dried basil
½ teaspoon salt
½ teaspoon freshly cracked black pepper
1 tablespoon olive oil

Relish

1 teaspoon olive oil
1 large yellow onion, sliced
¼ teaspoon sugar
¼ teaspoon salt
½ teaspoon pepper
2 cloves garlic, chopped
1 tablespoon balsamic vinegar
1 pint cherry tomatoes, halved
1½ cups basil, julienned
Crushed red pepper flakes, to taste (optional)

43

Chicken

Combine all the ingredients in a large bowl, and set in the refrigerator to marinate for a few minutes. Meanwhile, heat up a sauté pan and add oil. When the oil is hot, add the chicken in batches, cooking until browned. Flip over and brown the other side. Before removing the chicken from the pan, be sure to cook through on the inside (165°F). Set the cooked chicken aside and cover with foil.

Relish

Heat another sauté pan, and add oil. When the oil is hot, add the onions, and stir once to evenly distribute the oil. Allow the onions to cook, stirring occasionally, until they begin to brown and caramelize. You will get browned spots on the pan, so just scrape those in with the onions. Caramelization should take about 10 minutes; you want the onions to be very soft and browned. Add sugar, salt, pepper, and garlic, then continue to cook the onions for a few more minutes. Once they have caramelized, add the balsamic vinegar, and stir for a minute. Add tomatoes, and cook for about 7 to 8 more minutes until they are softened and slightly caramelized. Turn off the heat, and add crushed red pepper flakes (if desired) and basil. Stir together. Season with salt and pepper to taste. Pour a generous amount of relish over the chicken and serve.

Sausage-Spinach Calzones with Marinara Sauce

Giulianna Galiano *(East Brunswick, New Jersey)*
Serves 6

My grandma, Carol, gave me her spinach "pie" recipe. Whether eaten on the run, reheated in a dorm room microwave, or consumed right out of the frying pan, these pockets of goodness are irresistible. I usually come home with pies and end up yelling at my brother and father for eating nine of them by dinner. Growing up in an Italian household, I was bound to learn this recipe and record it for future use. Each ingredient is handled with love and care because of the effort put into preparation. The tomatoes, spinach, and sausage can all be purchased locally, especially during the summertime, when the Jersey Shore farmers markets are in full swing. You may ask, "Why are these called 'pies'?" Good question; I have no idea. My guess is my brother and I were too young to pronounce "calzone" when we started demanding these treats.

Dough
2½ cups all-purpose flour
¼ ounce package yeast
Sugar and warm water, for yeast
1 tablespoon salt
1 tablespoon olive oil
Water, as needed, to make dough tight

Filling
1 tablespoon unsalted butter
½ Spanish onion, julienned
3 cups chopped spinach (fresh or frozen and drained)
½ cup fontinella cheese, grated
½ cup asiago cheese, grated
4 sausage patties, cooked and crumbled
½ cup ricotta

Canola oil, for frying (see Chef's Tips on blended oil, page 309)
Kosher salt, to sprinkle on top of pies

Marinara Sauce

6 plum or roma tomatoes (see Chef's Tips on tomato concasse, page 321)
2 tablespoons olive oil (or enough to coat bottom of pan)
1 teaspoon crushed red pepper flakes
3 slices bacon, diced
1 bay leaf
2 cloves garlic, minced
2 tablespoons tomato paste
½ cup red wine (preferably a cabernet sauvignon or pinot noir)
Sprinkle of dried oregano, basil, thyme, and/or parsley
Salt and freshly cracked black pepper, to taste

Dough

To prepare the dough, measure the flour into a bowl. Bloom the yeast by placing it in a separate container with a sprinkle of sugar and a splash (approximately 1 tablespoon) of warm water (105°F). (When fresh yeast blooms or is activated, it may bubble. This takes approximately 5 minutes.) When ready, make a well or hole in the mound of flour, and slowly pour in the yeast mixture. Stir until the flour and yeast are incorporated. Add salt, olive oil, and some water to bind the dough together. Make sure that it is not too wet or sticky. If this occurs, add more flour until the dough is soft. Knead for 5 minutes until the dough forms a ball with a smooth surface. Place the dough in a large mixing bowl, cover with a clean towel, and allow to rest for 1 hour in a cool, dark place. Remove the dough from the bowl and place on a floured counter top. Knead for 5 more minutes, place back in the bowl, cover, and allow to rest for another hour. Knead for another 5 minutes, place back in the bowl, cover, and allow to rest for 30 minutes. Reserve until ready to fill.

Filling

Melt the butter in a pan and sauté the onions until caramelized (they should be sweet, brown, and soft). During this time, defrost the spinach (if frozen) and squeeze to remove any excess liquid, or chop by hand (if fresh). In a large bowl, mix the cheeses, spinach, sausage, caramelized onions, and ricotta. Season with salt and pepper to taste.

To assemble calzones, place the dough on a floured flat surface. Use a rolling pin to flatten the dough into an 8-inch circle. Spread approximately 3 heaping tablespoons of filling over half of the circle, leaving a ½-inch border. Fold the empty half of the dough over the filling and crimp the edges closed, like the edges of a pie crust. Add canola oil to a shallow, straight-sided skillet, and heat the oil until 325°F. Carefully lower each pie into the hot oil. Use a metal spatula or slotted spoon to flip the pies when the bottoms become light golden brown in color. When the other side is golden as well, transfer to paper towels on a rack, and immediately sprinkle with salt.

Marinara Sauce

To prepare the sauce, the plum tomatoes must be roasted to achieve a sweet flavor. Preheat an oven or toaster oven to 400°F. Score the ends and remove the stem of each tomato. Blanch in simmering salted water for approximately 1 minute (until the skin loosens). Use a slotted spoon to remove the tomatoes, and immediately shock them by fully submerging in an ice water bath until fully cooled. Remove from the ice water, peel, and discard the tomato skins. Place the whole tomatoes on a foiled, shallow sheet pan and oven-roast for 10 minutes. Rotate and flip tomatoes, roasting for an additional 5 minutes. Remove from the oven and set aside. Once cool, dice into small chunks and set aside.

Meanwhile, combine olive oil with crushed red pepper flakes in a saucepan over medium heat for 1 minute to infuse the flavor. Add bacon, and cook until crispy. Add bay leaf, garlic, and tomato paste, then stir until the garlic has softened and the paste becomes slightly darker in color (approximately 2 minutes). To deglaze the pan, pour in wine and simmer until reduced by half of its original volume. Add the roasted tomatoes, and crush with a wooden spoon. Season with the dried herbs, salt, and pepper. Simmer for 15 minutes. Enjoy this sweet and spicy marinara sauce with the fresh calzones. *Buon Mangiare!*

Balsamic Pork Chops with Apple

Tracy Holleran *(The Secret Ingredient Cooking School, Fairfield, Connecticut)*
Serves 4

> This one-pot meal only has a handful of ingredients, but it packs a flavorful punch. During autumn in the Northeast, apple orchards are brimming with families out for an afternoon of picking and sampling. Pairing apples with pork is a classic combination in New England, and by adding rosemary and a touch of balsamic vinegar to the mix, this simple dish turns into something spectacular.

4 boneless pork chops (about 1½ pounds)
1 tablespoon oil (see Chef's Tips on blended oil, page 309)
1 large or 2 small apples, peeled, cored, and sliced into wedges
2 tablespoons balsamic vinegar
2 tablespoons fresh rosemary leaves
1 tablespoon unsalted butter
Kosher salt and freshly cracked black pepper (see Chef's Tips on seasoning, page 320)

Preheat an oven to 375°F. Season the pork chops with salt and pepper on both sides.

Heat a large, oven-proof skillet (do not use a Teflon® coated pan) until hot. Add blended oil. Sear chops on both sides until golden brown. Add apples to the pan, and transfer into the preheated oven and cook for about 7 minutes or until the pork is gently cooked through and only a hint of pink remains.

Remove the pan from oven and return to the stove top. Remove the pork and place on a platter, tenting with foil to keep warm. Turn the heat to medium high, and add balsamic vinegar to the apples. Add rosemary, and cook for a few minutes until the apples are tender. Add butter, and stir until melted. Pour the apples and balsamic sauce over the pork and serve immediately.

Pork Belly Pot Pie with Carrots and Parsnips

Executive Chef Clifford Crooks *(BLT Steak, New York, New York)*

Serves 4–6

> This delectable dish is an example of how some of today's chefs are preparing classic comfort food such as pot pie using trendy ingredients like pork belly and root vegetables. I am especially impressed with Executive Chef Clifford's choice to confit the pork belly. To confit is a term that means to cook food in its own fat. This method results in the most tender and succulent piece of pork belly that you will ever consume.
> *Story by Chef Nicole*

¼ cup salt

1 cup sugar

½ teaspoon ground cinnamon

½ teaspoon ground ginger

½ teaspoon ground paprika

1½ pounds pork belly

2 pounds lard or duck fat, divided

½ pound carrots, peeled and sliced ¼-inch thick

½ pound parsnips, peeled and sliced ¼-inch thick

3 heads garlic, divided

4 springs thyme, divided

1 teaspoon black peppercorns

3 bay leaves

1 Spanish onion, thinly sliced

8 cloves garlic, thinly sliced

1 teaspoon butter

¼ teaspoon cumin

2 sheets puff pastry

1 egg, beaten

Crème fraîche, as needed

Mix the salt, sugar, cinnamon, ginger, and paprika in a bowl, and coat the pork belly liberally. Store in a refrigerator for 24 hours to cure.

Warm 1 pound of lard. Place the carrots and parsnips (in separate dishes) in two oven-proof dishes, and cover with the lard. Slice one head of garlic in half, and place one half with the carrots and the other half with the parsnips. Then add one sprig of thyme and a pinch of salt to each. Cover with foil and bake in an oven for 40 minutes at 275°F until just fork-tender. Allow the vegetables to cool in fat and remove, reserving the fat to confit the pork belly.

Pork

Remove the pork from the cure, rinse, and gently pat dry. Place the pork in an oven-proof dish with the remaining garlic heads (split), thyme, peppercorns, and remaining 1 pound of lard. Cover with foil and cook in the oven at 275°F for 4 hours. Let it cool before opening, and then remove the pork from the fat and rest it on a sheet pan. In a small pan over low to medium heat, sweat onions and the sliced garlic cloves with butter until translucent. Add cumin, and let cool while you shred the pork belly. Mix the pork belly and onion mixture together, and set aside.

Line a baking dish or pie pan with a layer of the puff pastry on the bottom. Blind bake the puff pastry by placing a sheet of parchment paper over the puff pastry, and fill with dry beans or baking beads. Bake at 350°F for 20 minutes to slightly set. To remove the beans or beads from the puff pastry, grab the edges of the parchment paper, and carefully lift and remove all of the contents. Layer half of the carrots and parsnips artfully in the bottom of the blind-baked puff pastry. Add the pork mixture on top, and then cover the pork with the remaining carrots and parsnips. Cover the top of the pie with the other sheet of puff pastry, and crimp the edges closed. Using a pastry brush, paint the top of the pie with an egg wash (a beaten egg brushed on right before baking will give your crust sheen). Cut a decorative hole or a few slits in the top of the pie (to release steam), place the baking dish on top of a sheet pan, and bake at 350°F for 45 minutes until golden brown. Cool the pie for 20 minutes before cutting. Serve with dollops of crème fraîche and enjoy.

Shepherd's Pie with Herbed Mascarpone Polenta

Tracy Holleran *(The Secret Ingredient Cooking School, Fairfield, Connecticut)*
Serves 4

The Northeast is heavily populated by Irish-Americans, where shepherd's pie is a favorite. It was originally created as a way to repurpose the Sunday supper's leftovers, and there are as many varieties of this dish as there are Irish families. In this version, the traditional mashed potato topping is swapped for creamy cheese-infused polenta, and the filling is embellished with spices, giving shepherd's pie a whole new identity.

Filling
1¼ pounds ground beef
¼ cup water
1 medium onion, diced
2 medium carrots, peeled and diced
2 tablespoons tomato paste
1 tablespoon all-purpose flour
¼ teaspoon freshly grated nutmeg (may substitute ground nutmeg)
½ teaspoon cinnamon
¾ cup peas (thawed, if frozen)

Topping
2 cups water
Pinch kosher salt
⅔ cup precooked yellow corn meal (instant polenta)
2 ounces mascarpone cheese (or cream cheese)
½ cup grated Parmesan cheese, divided
½ cup fresh parsley, chopped

Filling

Brown the ground meat in a large skillet over medium-high heat until no longer pink. Transfer to a colander to drain out the excess fat, and set aside. In the same pan, add water to deglaze the pan. Add onions and carrots, and cook for about 5 to 7 minutes until tender. Add tomato paste and flour, and cook for 1 to 2 minutes to remove the "rawness" of the flour. Return the meat to the pan, and add nutmeg, cinnamon, and peas. Stir to combine. Add ¾ cup of water. Simmer for about 10 minutes until the sauce thickens slightly. Transfer to a 9-inch pie plate and set aside.

Topping

Place water in sauce pot and bring to a boil. Add salt. While constantly whisking, add polenta, lower the heat, and cook until thickened (this should take around 5 minutes). Remove from the heat, and add mascarpone, ¼ cup of Parmesan cheese, and additional salt to taste. Stir until incorporated. Fold in chopped parsley. Spoon polenta over the filling and top with the remaining Parmesan cheese.

Bake at 375°F for about 20 minutes until the top is golden brown and the filling is heated through. Serve immediately.

Stinging Nettle Gnocchi, Maryland Crab, and Lemon

Executive Chef Amy Brandwein *(Casa Nonna, Washington, D.C.)*
Serves 1–2

> Gnocchi is a light and fluffy potato pasta or dumpling that is surprisingly easy to prepare. This particular dish offers another creative way to incorporate a Northeast regional favorite— the Maryland crab with locally grown nettles. This particular variety is called the stinging nettle, because of the hairs found on the tips of the edible leaves. The nettle leaves lose their sting when cooked or dried.
> *Story by Chef Nicole*

2 Idaho potatoes
1 pound nettles, leaves only (you may substitute spinach or Swiss chard)
½ cup all-purpose flour
1 teaspoon salt
1 egg
1 tablespoon olive oil
3 tablespoons pancetta, diced small
3 cloves garlic, thinly sliced
3 pinches hot pepper flakes
¼ pound Maryland jumbo lump crab, cleaned and shells removed
1 tablespoon unsalted butter
1 pinch lemon zest (see Chef's Tips on citrus zest, page 311)

Preheat an oven to 350°F. Pierce potatoes with the tines of a fork, and then bake for 40 minutes or until tender. While the potatoes are still hot, peel and mash them finely using a ricer, food mill, or potato masher. Set aside to cool.

Heat salted water to a boil in a saucepan. Add nettles, and blanch until bright green and fork-tender. Then shock them by placing them in a bowl of ice water. Once cooled, drain any excess water and finely chop.

Combine the potatoes, flour, salt, egg, and nettles. Knead until thoroughly mixed and the dough is holding together. Roll small amounts into 1-inch wide by 6-inch long "ropes". Cut the ropes into 1/2-inch pieces. Use a gnocchi roller or a fork to make an indentation on top of each piece, and then pinch between your fingers to plump them up.

Warm a sauté pan over medium heat and add olive oil. Render the fat from the pancetta by cooking the pancetta in a warm pan until crisp to extract its fat. Add garlic to the rendered pancetta fat and cook until lightly golden. Add hot pepper, crab, and butter. Cook the gnocchi for 2 to 3 minutes in boiling salted water until the gnocchi floats to the top. When ready, carefully remove the cooked gnocchi from the pot with a slotted spoon, and set aside in a lightly oiled bowl. Add a bit of cooking water to your crab mixture. Add the gnocchi and simmer for a minute to thicken. Add lemon zest, and toss thoroughly.

Baked Stuffed Potatoes with Smoked Bacon and Cheddar Cheese

Chef Ron Boucher *(Chez Boucher Cooking School, Hampton, New Hampshire)*
Serves 12

Chef Ron entered this dish into a fifty-state recipe contest hosted by the Idaho Potato Board. The first potato planted in the United States was in New Hampshire in 1743, so it seems very fitting that they won. Using all local New Hampshire products gives this dish its special personality.
Story by Mary Elizabeth

12 Russet potatoes, washed
⅛ cup vegetable oil
3 ounces unsalted butter, melted and divided
½ cup light cream
½ cup sour cream
6 slices smoked bacon, cooked, chopped, and fat discarded
2 scallions, chopped
½ cup grated New Hampshire cheddar cheese
4 tablespoons grated Parmesan cheese
Romano cheese, grated
Salt and white pepper, to taste

Preheat an oven to 400°F. Rub the potatoes with oil, salt, and pepper. Place on a sheet pan, and bake for 1 hour or until fork-tender. Remove from the oven and set aside. In a small saucepan, heat 2 ounces of butter with the light cream and sour cream over medium heat.

Cut a slice off the top of each potato. Using a soup spoon, scoop out the potato pulp, leaving a ¼-inch-thick border of potato in the shell. Process the pulp through a food mill or ricer, and place into a mixing bowl.

Pour the hot butter mixture over the potatoes and fold to incorporate. Fold in the bacon, scallions, and grated cheddar and Parmesan cheeses. Season with salt and white pepper to taste.

Place the mixture in a pastry bag and pipe into the reserved potato shell. Melt 1 ounce of butter. Using a pastry brush, paint the melted butter on the top of each potato, and sprinkle with romano cheese. Place back in the oven at 400°F for 15 minutes or until golden brown in color and heated throughout.

Apple and Maple Mashed Sweet Potatoes

Eve Lynn Kessner *(Brooklyn, New York)*

Serves 6–8

> Here is another stellar Thanksgiving (or any special day, for that matter) recipe. It is a recipe that my mom has "veganized" for us, and it tastes just as good, if not better, this way. It is perfect for any fall feast.

½ cup vegan butter or margarine, such as Earth Balance®
¾ cup maple sugar or maple syrup
3 Granny Smith apples, peeled, cored, and sliced
6 sweet potatoes, steamed, peeled, and cut into cubes (if preferred, use unpeeled)

Preheat an oven to 350°F. Grease an oven-proof dish large enough to hold all the ingredients.

In a sauté pan, melt the butter. Add the maple sugar (or syrup) and apples, and then mix.

Cover and cook 5 minutes until the apples are soft.

Add the sweet potatoes, and mix well. Place everything in a food processor and puree until smooth or to the desired consistency.

Transfer the sweet potato mixture into a prepared dish, and smooth out the top. Sprinkle the top with additional maple sugar, and place a few dots of butter on top. Bake for 20 minutes until light brown. Serve hot.

Spicy Spaghetti Squash

Jackie Damboragian *(New York, New York)*
Serves 4

> Personally, I love pasta because I love sauce, pesto, tomato, garlic, oil, etc. Any sauce that you put on pasta, you can mix with spaghetti squash. It is easy to make and is a simple, quick dish for those nights when you are craving pasta, but want something a little lighter and healthier.

1 spaghetti squash, cut in half
1 teaspoon plus 2 tablespoons extra-virgin olive oil
4 cloves garlic, minced
1 teaspoon red pepper flakes
Chives or basil, chopped
Salt and freshly cracked black pepper, to taste

Preheat the oven to 400°F. Take the squash halves, rub with 1 teaspoon of olive oil inside each half, and then season with salt and pepper. Place each half, skin-side-up, on a baking tray. Place in the oven for 45 minutes or until done (check it with a fork to make sure that the squash is very tender).

Remove from the oven and allow it to cool slightly (be careful, as the skin will be very hot). Wrap a dish cloth around the outside of the skin to hold it. Once you have the squash in hand, scoop out the seeds with a large spoon and discard. Use a fork to pull the strands of squash away from the skin. Place in a mixing bowl.

Place 2 tablespoons olive oil in a skillet, and then add the garlic and red pepper flakes. Heat on medium-high heat until the garlic is just starting to turn brown (about 1 minute).

Pour this mixture over the squash, add herbs, and mix well.

Boston Baked Beans

Susan Warner *(Topsfield, Massachusetts)*
Serves 6

> Like many family recipes, Susan says, "There really is no recipe written down, just one passed on by my mom and her mom before her."

1 (16½ oz.) can original-style baked beans
1 small onion, diced
¼ cup molasses
¼ cup brown sugar
½ teaspoon dry mustard
Dash water
1 tablespoon ketchup
3 strips bacon, diced

Mix everything in a large bowl and pour into a small baking dish. Bake at 350°F for 45 minutes or until bubbly.

Roasted Cauliflower and Walnut Pesto

Executive Chef Amy Eubanks *(BLT Fish, New York, New York)*
Serves 4

> One of the first signs of fall in the Union Square Farmers Market in New York City is the abundance of cauliflower—from basic white to Romanesco to Circus. I like to present this versatile vegetable with bold flavors like vinegars and spices. In this recipe, it is simply prepared as a side dish to complement any fall entrée.

Cauliflower

1 head cauliflower
2 tablespoons oil (see Chef's Tips on blended oil, page 309)
Salt and freshly cracked black pepper, to taste

Pesto

2 tablespoons walnuts, toasted and chopped (see Chef's Tips on nuts and seeds, page 318)
2 tablespoons chopped parsley
2 tablespoons chopped cilantro
¼ cup olive oil
1 tablespoon sherry vinegar
½ teaspoon paprika/pimento espelette (optional)
Salt and freshly cracked black pepper, to taste

Cauliflower

Trim the head of the cauliflower, discard the outer leaves and stems, and cut into florets. Slice each floret in half lengthwise. Bring a large pot of salted water to a boil over high heat. Add the cauliflower and blanch until fork-tender (about 3 minutes). Drain and shock by submerging in a large bowl of ice water to cool. Drain well and set aside.

Heat oil in a large frying pan over medium-high heat. Once the oil is hot, gently place the cauliflower florets in the oil (flat-side-down), lower the heat to medium, and sear until golden brown on one side. You may need to sear the cauliflower in batches. Season the cauliflower with salt and pepper to taste.

Pesto

In a medium mixing bowl, stir together walnuts, parsley, and cilantro. Add olive oil and sherry vinegar. Season the pesto with salt and pepper to taste, and set aside at room temperature.

Remove the seared cauliflower from the pan, and decoratively place them on a plate, seared side facing up. Drizzle the walnut pesto over the cauliflower and sprinkle with paprika, if desired. Serve immediately.

Tomato Chutney

Donna Mc Laughlin *(Inspired by New Jersey; lives in Lansdale, Pennsylvania)*
Serves 6–8

> This recipe was originally created by my neighbor Hazel Miller.
> It is a fabulous example of how to use the bountiful tomato
> crops available when summering on the Jersey shore. Store this
> chutney in your refrigerator so that, when guests drop by your
> beach house, you have an instant homemade appetizer. Serve on
> baguettes with a dollop of goat cheese.

3 pounds tomato concasse (see Chef's Tips on tomato concasse, page 321)
½ pound onions, chopped
½ pound apples, peeled and chopped
1 pint vinegar
¼–½ pound sugar
1 ounce pickling spice, tied in cheese cloth with butcher's twine
2 teaspoons salt

Place all the ingredients in a saucepan, and simmer until the majority
of the liquid is reduced and the chutney is thick and tender. Remove
the spice bundle. Serve warm or cool. Store in an airtight container in
the refrigerator for no more than 5 days.

Homemade Cranberry Sauce

Lorraine Ott *(Boxford, Massachusetts)*

Serves 8

Around 1815, the first cranberries were cultivated in Massachusetts and, today, it is their official state fruit. They were eaten raw or made into sauces, and baked into muffins, scones, and bread. Most Americans traditionally eat cranberry sauce on the Thanksgiving holiday, although in the state of Massachusetts, the bogs are exploding with these ruby red and mouth-puckering tart berries year-round. Lorraine's friend Susan has creatively combined the soft, sweet flavor of pear and the spicy punch of ginger to keep this version of the classic dish exciting and new.

Story by Chef Nicole

1 (12 oz.) bag whole cranberries
2 pears, peeled and chopped
Juice of half a lemon
1 cup sugar
⅔ cup water
¼ cup crystallized ginger, minced
¼ teaspoon cinnamon

Wash and sort through the cranberries, discarding any spoiled ones. Toss the pears with the lemon juice. Place the cranberries, pear mixture, and remaining ingredients in a pot, and bring to a boil.

Simmer until thick (about 2 hours).

Indian Pudding

Chef Phillip Griffin and Malinda Coletta (*Professor Chef, North Providence, Rhode Island*)
Serves 4

> This is a traditional New England dessert to serve during the holidays.

4 cups milk, divided
½ cup corn meal
⅓ cup brown sugar
⅓ cup white sugar
⅓ cup molasses
1 teaspoon salt
4 tablespoons unsalted butter
½ teaspoon each ground ginger, cinnamon, and fresh-grated nutmeg

Preheat an oven to 275°F. Heat 2 cups of milk in a saucepan until very hot. Slowly pour over corn meal, and stir constantly while cooking in a double boiler for 10 to 15 minutes until the corn meal is creamy. Add the remaining ingredients (except the additional 2 cups of milk). Spoon the mixture into a well buttered, 1½-quart casserole dish.

Bake the pudding in a water bath: Place a rectangular, shallow roasting pan in the oven. Then place the filled casserole dish in the center of the roasting pan. Carefully pour hot water into the roasting pan until the water almost reaches the level of the pudding inside the casserole dish.

Pour the remaining 2 cups of milk over the top of the pudding (it will look like it is way too much, but this is okay, as it will be absorbed). Bake for 2½ to 3 hours. The pudding will appear to be slightly firm when ready, though it will still jiggle in the center. Remove from the oven and carefully set on the counter top. Once cool enough, remove the casserole pan from the water bath. The pudding will become firm as it continues to cool.

To serve, warm in 275°F oven for 15–20 minutes, spoon into a dish, and serve with whipped cream or ice cream.

Honey Maple Roasted Pears

Angie Hamilton *(Guilford, Vermont)*

Serves 4–5

> This recipe was inspired by my grandparents Kathy and Peter Wilde, who lived in a farmhouse next door to my childhood home in Vermont. Between the house and the barn, there was a large pear tree that produced more pears than we could ever use. Every spring, my grandfather would lead the family in maple sugaring. Whether because of the plentiful fruit or because of her own desires, my grandmother was always baking. Growing up with an endless source of maple syrup has led to its frequent use in my kitchen.

4–5 pears, cored and quartered
1 cup local honey
½ cup Vermont maple syrup
2 cups pineapple juice
1 splash balsamic vinegar (see Chef's Tips on reduction, page 310)
1 teaspoon fresh ginger, grated
1 teaspoon cinnamon
¼ teaspoon nutmeg, freshly grated

Preheat an oven to 400°F. Place the pears, skin up, in a glass or ceramic baking dish. In a separate bowl, mix the liquids and spices together, and pour evenly over the pears. Cover and bake for 30 minutes. Uncover and bake for 10 more minutes. Carefully pour off the liquid into a small pot, and cook over medium-high heat for about 5 minutes or until the liquid is reduced by half and caramelized slightly. Serve the pears with a drizzle of the reduced liquid and vanilla ice cream, whipped cream, brie, goat cheese, or any other creamy mild cheese.

Baked Stuffed Apples with Walnuts and Raisins

Chef Andrea Beaman *(New York, New York)*
Serves 4

4 Empire or Cortland apples, cored
½ cup walnuts, chopped (see Chef's Tips on nuts and seeds, page 318)
2 tablespoons raisins
1 tablespoon honey
½ teaspoon cinnamon
Dash ground cloves
1 tablespoon brown sugar
2 tablespoons grass-fed butter or unsalted butter
½ cup apple juice

Preheat an oven to 350°F. Place the apples into a 9- by 9-inch baking dish. Combine the walnuts, raisins, honey, cinnamon, cloves, sugar, and butter in a bowl. Stuff the cored apples with the walnut mixture. Pour the apple juice into the pan. Bake the apples, uncovered, for 40 to 45 minutes.

The Best Apple Crisp

Ellen L. Madison *(Woody Hill Bed & Breakfast, Westerly, Rhode Island)*

Serves 6

Filling

10–12 Rhode Island greening apples, peeled, cored, and sliced
1 tablespoon cinnamon
¼ teaspoon salt
1½ tablespoons sugar
½ cup water

Topping

1 cup sugar
1 cup all-purpose flour
1 stick (½ cup) unsalted butter

Filling

Preheat an oven to 350°F. Fill a buttered 9- by 13-inch baking pan with the apples until quite full. In a separate bowl, combine the cinnamon, salt, and sugar. Sprinkle the mixture over the apples. If desired, add more cinnamon, and sprinkle over the apples until they are brown with the cinnamon. Pour water over the apples.

Topping

Mix together the sugar, flour, and butter with your fingers. Spread over the apples and bake for 45–50 minutes at 350°F. Serve with ice cream or fresh whipped cream, if desired (see Baking Tips on whipped cream, page 326).

Gluten-Free Apple Strudel

Amie Valpone *(New York, New York)*
Serves 8

> Amie treats us not only to her blogs, but to a recipe that she describes as, "One of the best gluten-free baked goods to come out of my tiny Manhattan apartment all season. You want this. Trust me; there's no such thing as just one bite."

1 tablespoon sugar

¼ cup fresh rosemary leaves, minced

8 large organic McIntosh apples, peeled and sliced

1½ cups gluten-free all-purpose flour

¼ cup sugar

1 teaspoon baking powder

⅓ teaspoon sea salt

2 teaspoons ground cinnamon plus more for topping

¼ teaspoon allspice

¼ teaspoon fresh, organic orange zest (see Chef's Tips on citrus zest, page 311)

2 tablespoons fresh organic orange juice

¼ teaspoon gluten-free almond extract

2 large eggs

Preheat an oven to 350°F. Spray a baking dish with baking spray. Sprinkle in the sugar and rosemary. Add sliced apples; spread evenly. In a large bowl, combine the flour, sugar, baking powder, sea salt, cinnamon, allspice, and orange zest. Add orange juice, almond extract, and eggs; mix well to combine and form a mealy texture. Transfer the mixture on top of the apples in the baking dish. Sprinkle with additional ground cinnamon. Bake for 40 minutes or until golden brown.

Rhubarb-Strawberry Crumble

Nicole Franzen *(Brooklyn, New York)*

Serves 6–8

> My boyfriend loves rhubarb. So, when June rolls around and I know it is in season, I stop by a local farmers market to pick some up, along with a heaping pint of the first strawberries of the season. This combination makes a perfect accompaniment.

Filling

4 cups rhubarb, cut off ends and chop into 1-inch pieces
2 cups strawberries, cut in half
¾ cup granulated sugar
¼ cup unbleached flour
Zest of 1 orange plus juice of ½ orange (see Chef's Tips on citrus zest, page 311)

Topping

1 cup rolled oats
½ cup plus 2 tablespoons firmly packed brown sugar
½ cup all-purpose flour
1 stick unsalted butter, softened

Preheat an oven to 350°F.

Filling

Place the rhubarb and strawberries in a bowl, and then add the sugar, flour, orange zest, and juice, tossing until the fruit is well coated. Set aside.

Topping

Put the oats, ½ cup of brown sugar, flour, and butter into a bowl. Mix thoroughly with your hands.

Place the strawberry rhubarb mixture in a 9- by 13-inch baking pan. Sprinkle the topping over it evenly. Sprinkle with the additional 2 tablespoons of brown sugar. Bake for 40–50 minutes. Serve with a scoop of vanilla ice cream or fresh whipped cream (see Baking Tips on whipped cream, page 326).

Wet Bottom Shoo-Fly Pie

Art Roman *(The Kitchen Workshop, Paoli, Pennsylvania)*
Yields 1 (9-inch) pie

Topping

2 cups all-purpose flour

⅔ cup packed light or dark brown sugar

½ cup solid vegetable shortening

Filling

½ teaspoon baking soda

⅓ cup boiling water

⅔ cup cold water

1 large egg, beaten

1 cup packed light or dark brown sugar

1 cup dark molasses

1 (9-inch) unbaked pie crust (see Index, page 339)

Topping

In a medium bowl, combine the flour and brown sugar. Cut the shortening into the flour and brown sugar using a pastry blender or two knives until crumbly.

Preheat an oven to 350°F.

Filling

Dissolve the baking soda in the boiling water, then add cold water.

In a small bowl, stir the beaten egg into the brown sugar, add the molasses to this mixture, and then add the baking soda-water mixture and mix.

Pour into a 9-inch unbaked pie crust and bake for 10 minutes. Reduce the oven to 325°F, sprinkle with the topping, and bake for 50 minutes longer or until done in the center. Allow to cool before slicing.

Rainbow Cake

Tiffanie Nickkia Bonneau *(New York, New York)*
Yields 1 Bundt cake

> My family is originally from Saint Croix in the Virgin Islands.
> As a child, I remember my grandmother making this beautiful,
> four-colored cake for everyone's birthday. She called it the
> "rainbow cake." It has a strong almond flavor and vibrant
> colors. Red is used for the radiance of Saint Croix, yellow for the
> shining sun, green for the lush hills, and blue for the crystal
> blue waters. Now, my family resides in a section of New York
> City called Harlem, along with many other Caribbean families
> who migrated to the Northeast.

3 cups cake flour
2 tablespoons baking powder
3 sticks (1½ cups) unsalted butter, room temperature
4 ounces cream cheese, room temperature
2 tablespoons shortening
2 cups sugar
1 (3 oz.) box instant French vanilla-flavored pudding mix
6 large eggs
3 tablespoons sour cream (or ½ pint heavy cream)
2 tablespoons pure almond extract
1 tablespoon pure vanilla extract
Red, yellow, green, and blue food coloring gel

Preheat an oven to 350°F. Sift the flour and baking powder into a
bowl, and set aside. With an electric mixer, cream the butter and cream
cheese in a large mixing bowl. Add shortening, sugar, instant pudding, eggs (one at a time), sour cream, and extracts. Continue creaming the ingredients together. Add the flour mixture gradually (½ cup
at a time). Evenly distribute the prepared batter into four bowls. Using
a toothpick, put a different color dot of each food coloring into each of
the bowls. Stir each until well blended. Spray bundt pan generously
with baking spray; evenly pour the bowls, side by side, around the
pan. Put in the oven for 45 minutes or until golden brown.

New York Cheesecake

Yields 1 (10-inch) cake

Crust

1¼ cups graham cracker crumbs
3 tablespoons sugar
Pinch salt
⅓ cup unsalted butter, melted

Filling

6 (8 oz.) packages cream cheese, softened
1 pint (16 oz.) sour cream
¾ cup sugar
1 teaspoon pure vanilla extract
6 large eggs, room temperature

Crust

Mix the crumbs, sugar, and salt in a bowl with a spoon. Add butter, and stir until the crumb mixture is moistened. Press an even layer on the bottom of a 10-inch spring-form pan. Chill in a refrigerator while preparing the filling.

Preheat an oven at 400°F.

Filling

On low speed, combine all the ingredients (except the eggs) in a standing mixer. Add eggs, one at a time, and blend for 30 minutes.

Lay a large piece of aluminum foil on your counter top. Remove the spring-form from the refrigerator and place in the center of the foil. Bring the edges of the foil up around the sides, but do not cover the top of the pan. Pour the cream cheese mixture into the center of the pan so it evenly spreads over the crust. Create a water bath by placing the pan into a large, rectangular baking/roasting pan. Carefully put this on the middle rack of the oven. Now, carefully pour hot water from a kettle or liquid measuring cup with a spout into the baking/

roasting pan, and allow the water to fill around the foiled pan until it reaches halfway up the sides. Bake at 400°F for 1 hour. Carefully remove the entire water bath from the oven. Once cool enough to handle, remove the cheesecake from the water bath, and let it thoroughly cool in the refrigerate for 24 hours. Serve with fresh whipped cream.

Homemade Whipped Cream

½ pint heavy cream

Pinch cream of tartar

1 teaspoon pure vanilla extract

¼ cup confectioners' sugar, sifted

Place the bowl and beaters in the freezer while you are assembling your ingredients. Beat the heavy cream and cream of tartar first until the peaks are formed or the heavy cream appears to double in volume; then add the vanilla and sugar. Continue to beat until blended.

Part II

SOUTHEAST

The Southeast region stretches along the East Coast through Virginia, North Carolina, South Carolina, Georgia, and Florida, and then west through the states of Alabama, Mississippi, Louisiana, Tennessee, and Kentucky.

While living in Saint Augustine, Florida, Nicole grew quite accustomed to the sights, sounds, and cuisine that are characteristic of the American South. Heavy humidity hangs in the air like the webs of Spanish moss from the trees. The sound of frogs and crickets permeate through the dense marshes scattered with crawfish. In the waters heading down the Atlantic Ocean around Florida's peninsula and up through the Gulf of Mexico, live multiple varieties of warm water shrimp. These reddish pink-shelled and plump, white meat-filled morsels are the main attraction in classic dishes like Shrimp and Grits (page 92). In fact, from any sweltering hot (and yet surprisingly comfortable) Southern kitchen, you will find that fish and shellfish are by far the most predominantly used ingredients.

Many Southeast residents are from Native American, Spanish, French, African, and Latin American descent, and each of these cultures have put their own twists on the cuisine. Cajun cooking (otherwise known as "country cooking") is based on many one-pot meals featuring local ingredients (known as "swamp-floor" ingredients) such as fish, wild game, and shellfish (see Cajun Delight, page 99). On the other hand, Creole food is known as "city food," and can be described as a sophisticated and refined cooking style marrying the flavors of the various ethnic groups found in New Orleans (see Shrimp Creole, page 98).

The Southern recipes in the following pages feature both sweet and savory ingredients. From Georgia's infamous peaches to the indigenous pecans of Alabama and Florida's nearly unlimited supply of citrus, these sweet indulgences are harvested and enjoyed throughout America. Although desserts like Bananas Foster (page 123), Key Lime Pie (page 130), and Kentucky Derby Pie (page 128) are replicated by chefs throughout the states, the Southeastern originals take the cake.

Peach-Raspberry Melba Muffins

Cindy Dickey *(Dickey Farms, Musella, Georgia)*
Yields 12 muffins

1 cup fresh Georgia peaches, washed and diced
½ teaspoon cinnamon
2 cups all-purpose flour
½ cup sugar
2½ teaspoons baking powder
½ teaspoon salt
½ cup walnuts, chopped (see Chef's Tips on nuts and seeds, page 318)
1 egg
1 cup milk
⅓ cup unsalted butter, melted
2 tablespoons brandy
1 (15¼ oz.) jar seedless raspberry jam

In a bowl, sprinkle the peaches with cinnamon and set aside. In a separate bowl, sift together the flour, sugar, baking powder, and salt; stir in the walnuts. In a separate bowl, whisk the egg, milk, butter, and brandy together, and stir into the peaches. Make a "well" or hole in the dry ingredients, and fill with the peach mixture. Mix lightly just until moistened. Fill twelve greased muffin cups halfway, place 1 teaspoon of raspberry jam in the center of each, and cover with the batter until two-thirds full.

Bake at 400°F for 20 to 25 minutes until golden brown.

Banana-Bourbon Scones with Walnuts

Lori Rice *(Lancaster, Kentucky)*
Yields 6–8 scones

Dough

1 tablespoon unsalted butter
1 overripe banana, mashed
2 tablespoons Kentucky bourbon
2 cups white whole-wheat flour
2 teaspoons baking powder
2 tablespoons raw sugar
½ teaspoon salt
¼ cup unsalted butter, cold and cubed
¼ cup walnuts, chopped (see Chef's Tips on nuts and seeds, page 318)
1–2 tablespoons milk or cream

Glaze (optional)

3 tablespoons confectioners' sugar
1 tablespoon maple syrup
2–3 teaspoons whole milk

Preheat the oven to 400°F. In a skillet over medium-high heat, melt the 1 tablespoon of butter. Add the banana, and combine with the butter. Carefully pour in the bourbon and cook on low heat, stirring often, for about 3 minutes. Set aside.

In a mixing bowl, combine the flour, baking powder, sugar, and salt. Add ¼ cup of butter, and blend with a pastry blender or fork until the dough is in pea-sized pieces.

Pour in the banana mixture and stir until incorporated. Add the walnuts. Slowly add the milk or cream a tablespoon at a time until a dough forms. It should be firm enough to roll out for cutting the scones.

Place the dough on a floured surface and use your hands (or a rolling pin) to press it out to about ¾-inch thickness. Use a biscuit cutter (or an empty washed and dried 16-ounce can) to cut out the scones. Place on an ungreased baking sheet.

Bake for about 15 minutes until the scone begins to brown and is firm in the center. Remove from the oven and place on a cooling rack.

Glaze

Mix the confectioners' sugar with the maple syrup in a small dish. Slowly add milk, 1 teaspoon at a time, until a thin, drizzling consistency is reached. Drizzle over the cooled scones and let set before serving.

Traditional Rice Calas

Elizabeth Pearce *(The Cocktail Tour, New Orleans, Louisiana)*
Serves 4

One of my favorite New Orleans foods to talk about during my walking tours is calas, a popular nineteenth-century rice fritter. Recently, it has been making a comeback in local restaurants. Eighteenth-century laws required that slaves be free from work on Sunday. Many slaves, however, took that time as an opportunity to work for themselves. Women made and sold candies and treats known as calas. The "Calas Woman" was a standard fixture on the streets of New Orleans. As street vendors faded from cities, calas left people's tables. Now, anyone can easily make calas for breakfast or as a snack.

Vegetable oil, for deep-frying (see Chef's Tips on blended oil, page 309)
2 cups cold cooked long-grain white rice
6 tablespoons all-purpose flour
3 heaping tablespoons sugar
2 teaspoons baking powder
¼ teaspoon salt
Dash nutmeg
2 large eggs, beaten
¼ teaspoon pure vanilla extract
Confectioners' sugar

Fill a heavy, deep, straight-sided pan no more than halfway with oil (oil expands when hot, so leave plenty of room from the top of the pan). Then heat up the oil over medium-low heat. Warm the oil while you are making the batter.

Separate the grains of rice in a large bowl with your fingers or a spoon so there are no clumps. Add all the dry ingredients to the rice and toss well to coat. Add the eggs and vanilla, and then mix them in thoroughly so there are no dry spots.

Use a thermometer to check the temperature of the oil (it should be approximately 360°F). Once the oil is the right temperature, turn the heat to medium.

Form the calas into quenelles (egg-shaped dumpling) using two large tablespoons. Scoop the calas with one tablespoon, and angle the top of the spoon toward the oil; with the other tablespoon, shape the calas, and carefully slide the quenelle of calas into the hot oil.

As an alternative, you can form the calas into balls using a mini ice cream scoop. Spray the scoop with baking spray; then scoop the calas, and carefully drop the calas directly into the hot oil (make sure not to splash).

Drop in a few calas at a time. Do not crowd the pan.

When the calas hit the oil, they will immediately sink to the bottom. Do not stir or fetch them, as the heat from the stove top will push the calas back to the top, where they will begin to float. Once one side has puffed and browned, they will roll themselves over to puff and brown the other side. If they do not, give them a gentle nudge with a spider or slotted spoon until they do.

Fry the calas until they are golden brown. Remove them with a spider or a slotted spoon or tongs. Drain well on several sheets of paper towel, and continue to fry batches of calas until completed. Dust them generously with confectioners' sugar.

Savory Calas

Elizabeth Pearce *(The Cocktail Tour, New Orleans, Louisiana)*
Serves 4

This savory option is a modern twist on an old traditional favorite, and can now be found on many menus in New Orleans.

Vegetable oil, for deep-frying
2 cups cold cooked long-grain white rice
6 tablespoons all-purpose flour
2 teaspoons baking powder
¼ teaspoon salt
3 tablespoons diced ham or cooked smoked sausage
3 green onions or scallions, thinly sliced
1 teaspoon hot sauce
2 eggs, beaten

Fill a heavy, deep, straight-sided pan no more than halfway with oil (oil expands when hot, so leave plenty of room from the top of the pan). Then heat up the oil over medium-low heat. Warm the oil while you are making the batter.

Separate the grains of rice in a large bowl with your fingers or a spoon so there are no clumps. Add all the dry ingredients to the rice, and toss well to coat.

Add the ham, green onions, hot sauce, and eggs, and mix them in thoroughly so there are no dry spots.

Follow the Sweet Calas recipe (page 79) for procedure and technique to form and fry.

Serve savory calas with grainy mustard or a remoulade.

Multigrain Bread

Amber Robertson-Smith *(Nashville, Tennessee)*
Makes 1 loaf

> One of Tennessee's top crops is wheat; try this warm bread slathered with a compound butter. As an added bonus, this delicious bread requires no kneading.

2 cups lukewarm water
1 teaspoon active dry yeast
2 tablespoons honey
1 cup whole-wheat flour
2 cups all-purpose or bread flour
1 cup light rye flour
1 tablespoon salt
2 tablespoons sesame seeds, plus more for sprinkling (see Chef's Tips on nuts and seeds, page 318)
¼ cup sunflower seeds, plus more for sprinkling
2 tablespoons flaxseeds, plus more for sprinkling
1 tablespoon canola oil

To bloom the yeast, combine lukewarm water (105°F), yeast, and honey in a large bowl. Allow the mixture to rest for 5 to 10 minutes (yeast may bubble). In the meantime, in another bowl, combine the flours with the salt and seeds. Add the dry ingredients to the bowl with the liquids, and stir with a wooden spoon until well blended. Cover the bowl with plastic wrap and let it rest for 12 to 20 hours at room temperature.

Transfer the dough to well-floured parchment paper or Silpat® on a sheet pan, and shape into a log. Loosely cover with another piece of parchment paper. Let the dough rest at room temperature for 1½ hours or until it has doubled in size. After an hour, place a small Dutch oven in your oven, and preheat to 475°F. Once the oven is preheated, carefully remove the Dutch oven.

Working quickly, carefully pour a tablespoon of canola oil into the Dutch oven. Using a pastry brush, spread oil on the bottom and sides. Take the dough out of the parchment paper and drop it into the Dutch oven. Sprinkle with additional seeds. Cover with the lid and place in the oven. Reduce the heat to 450°F and cook for 30 minutes. Remove the lid and bake for an additional 20 to 30 minutes until the loaf is brown. Cool on a wire rack before slicing.

Baked Potato Soup

Kath Younger *(Charlottesville, Virginia)*
Serves 3–4

2 thick slices bacon
2 big Russet potatoes, chopped into cubes (peeled if desired)
⅓ cup all-purpose flour
2 cups milk
2 cups vegetable broth
2 teaspoons kosher salt
¼ teaspoon smoked paprika
¼ cup sherry, preferably cream sherry
⅓ cup cheddar cheese, grated
Greek yogurt, for garnish (may substitute sour cream)

Heat a large pot on medium-high and brown the bacon until crispy. Remove the bacon slices and reserve. Add potatoes to the rendered bacon fat and sauté until they begin to soften (about 7 minutes). In a separate bowl, whisk flour into milk. Add the milk mixture to the pot, and then whisk in broth, salt, and paprika. Cover and simmer, stirring occasionally so the bottom does not brown (about 20 minutes).

Stir in sherry. Serve in bowls topped with bacon, cheese, and a sprinkle of paprika. Garnish with Greek yogurt.

Iceberg Lettuce with Chutney Dressing

Ursula Knaeusel *(Ursula's Cooking School, Atlanta, Georgia)*

Serves 4–6

> If you are ever driving in the gorgeous state of Georgia during the month of July, you will see roadside stands overflowing with large, sweet, golden-colored Vidalia onions.
>
> *Story by Mary Elizabeth*

¼ cup heavy cream

½ cup mayonnaise

¾ cup sour cream

½ cup mango chutney

2 teaspoons curry powder

1 teaspoon lemon pepper

½ teaspoon salt

1 head iceberg lettuce, washed and torn into pieces

1 cup red grapes, halved

½ Vidalia onion, thinly sliced

½ cup walnuts, coarsely chopped (see Chef's Tips on nuts and seeds, page 318)

Put the first seven ingredients in a mixing bowl and blend together with a whisk. Keep refrigerated until ready to serve.

Toss the lettuce with grapes and onions. Fold in the chutney dressing and sprinkle with walnuts before serving.

Curried Chicken and Virginia Grape Salad

Kath Younger *(Charlottesville, Virginia)*
Serves 2

> Sweet grapes are indigenous to Virginia, but you can replace them with your favorite local vine-ripened beauties for this recipe. If you enjoy a savory chicken salad that combines sweet, earthy, creamy, and spicy flavors, then you must try this one.
>
> *Story by Chef Nicole*

2 skinless, boneless chicken breasts, cooked and shredded
1 stalk celery, thinly sliced
10 grapes, halved
⅓ cup diced Golden Delicious apple
1½ tablespoons chopped pecan (see Chef's Tips on nuts and seeds, page 318)
1 tablespoon dried cranberries
2 tablespoons Greek yogurt
½ tablespoon light mayonnaise
½ teaspoon curry powder
¼ teaspoon cinnamon
¼ teaspoon mustard seeds
Crushed red pepper flakes, salt, and freshly cracked black pepper, to taste

Combine all the ingredients in a bowl. Refrigerate before serving. Serve on bread or a bed of lettuce.

Grilled Peaches Wrapped in Proscuitto di Parma with Basil and Goat Cheese

Chef Marc Suennemann *(Chateau Elan Inn, Braselton, Georgia)*
Yield 16 pieces

Blended oil (see Chef's Tips on blended oil, page 309)

4 Georgia peaches, halved and pitted

8 thin slices prosciutto di Parma

16 fresh basil leaves

½ pound fresh chevre goat cheese

4 tablespoons aged balsamic vinegar (see Chef's Tips on reduction, page 310)

Preheat a grill on high. Use a pastry brush to lightly coat the peach halves, cut-side only, with blended oil. Once the grill is extremely hot and clean, grill the peaches, cut-side-down, for about 2 to 3 minutes until the peaches have dark grill marks. Remove from the grill, cut each in half, again, and reserve. Slice the prosciutto into 16 strips, each about 2 inches wide and approximately 6 inches long. To assemble, secure the basil leaf and ½ ounce of goat cheese on top of a peach quarter, and wrap with one strip of prosciutto. Before serving, drizzle some fine, aged balsamic vinegar or balsamic reduction over the top.

Vidalia Onion Dip

Sabrina Toole *(Vidalia, Georgia)*

Serves 6–8

1 cup Swiss cheese, grated
1 (8 oz.) bar cream cheese, softened
¾ cup mayonnaise
2 large Vidalia onions, peeled and finely diced
1 cup brown sugar
2 cups butter-flavored, crackers
2 cups bacon, cooked until crisp, and crumbled

Combine the Swiss cheese, cream cheese, mayonnaise, and onions. Place in a large enough casserole dish to hold the mixture. Mix the brown sugar, crackers, and bacon. Top the cheese mixture with the cracker mixture. Bake at 350°F for 15 minutes. Serve warm with crackers.

Spinach-Artichoke Tofu Dip

Amber Robertson-Smith *(Nashville, Tennessee)*
Makes 2–3 cups

This recipe features tofu, a bi-product of soy, which is one of Tennessee's top crops. Tofu often acts as a sponge, absorbing the flavors that surround it. Therefore, the taste of this classic recipe will be quite recognizable to most, although the silky, white tofu will put a twist on the dip's texture.

10 ounces frozen spinach, thawed, squeezed, and well-drained
1 (14 oz.) can artichoke hearts, drained
4 ounces silken tofu
3 cloves garlic, smashed (see Chef's Tips on garlic, page 314)
⅓ cup grated Parmesan cheese, plus additional for sprinkling on top
⅔ cup Greek yogurt
¼ teaspoon sea salt
Cayenne pepper, to taste

Preheat an oven to 350°F. Puree the spinach, artichokes, tofu, and garlic in the bowl of a food processor. In a separate bowl, mix together the cheese, yogurt, salt, and pepper. Add the pureed mixture, and mix well. Transfer to a 4- by 6-inch baking dish, sprinkle additional cheese on top, and bake for 45 minutes or until the cheese is golden brown.

Sassy Shrimp

Chef Sandra Mannaravalappil *(The South Charlotte Chef, Charlotte, North Carolina)*
Serves 6

> When I moved to North Carolina and started working as a personal chef, I tried to incorporate my Italian heritage with Southern ingredients. This recipe seems to satisfy both. Traditionally, when it comes to North Carolina, we all think of the same things—barbecue, pork, coastal shrimp, and grits. In tribute to my Italian heritage, I serve this with grilled polenta cakes.

½ cup barbecue sauce (see recipe for Texas BBQ Sauce on page 300)
¼ cup canola oil
3 tablespoons lemon juice, freshly squeezed
½ ounces Dijon mustard
½ teaspoon red chile flake or crushed red pepper flakes
¼ teaspoon cayenne pepper or smoked paprika
¼ teaspoon freshly cracked black pepper
20 (18–20 count) Red Carolina shrimp, peeled and deveined
½ pound maple-smoked bacon
5–8 bamboo skewers or barbecue stakes
1 roll or log polenta (located in the Italian section)
Blended oil, for grilling (see Chef's Tips on blended oil, page 309)

Sauce

Combine the first seven ingredients in a blender or food processor (or mix well by hand). Separate the sauce into thirds: one-third for marinating, one-third for basting, and one-third for dipping.

Place the shrimp in a plastic food storage bag, and add one-third of the sauce; let marinate in a refrigerator for 2 hours to overnight. Prepare the skewers by soaking them in water for 2 hours to overnight (to keep from burning on the grill).

If grilling outdoors, prepare a charcoal grill, making sure that it is extremely hot and clean.

If grilling indoors, preheat the broiler.

Bacon

Cut each slice of bacon in half, and lay in one flat layer on a sheet pan. Place in a broiler and cook the bacon no more than halfway through; it should still be soft and pliable. Remove from the broiler and transfer to another pan lined with paper towel to cool. Once cool enough to handle, wrap the bacon around the shrimp, and place three to four bacon-wrapped shrimp on each skewer, making sure that the bacon ends are securely fastened with the skewer (to keep from unraveling).

Shrimp

Cook the bacon-wrapped shrimp on the hot outdoor grill or on a sheet pan in the broiler until the shrimp begin to turn pink (approximately 2 to 3 minutes). Baste with one-third of the barbecue sauce mixture using a brush until well-coated. Be careful that excess sauce does not fall through the grill grates and begin to smoke and burn. If this occurs, immediately remove the shrimp, and continue cooking on a hot stove-top grill pan. Turn the shrimp, and grill on the other side until the bacon is crisp and the shrimp is firm and fully cooked (approximately 2 to 3 minutes more). Remove from the grill and reserve.

Polenta

Heat a dry grill pan on your stove top until it begins to smoke. Paint slices of polenta with blended oil using a pastry brush. Carefully lay them flat on the pan. Do not move the polenta around until you achieve nice grill marks (about 3 minutes); then flip with a heat-resistant spatula and repeat.

Serve

Place two skewers of the shrimp crisscrossed over the polenta. Drizzle with the final one-third of barbecue sauce to finish.

Shrimp and Grits

Executive Chef Gregg McCarthy *(The Grand Marlin, Pensacola, Florida)*

Serves 4

I found the most wonderful grits for this recipe by accident. My wife and I were at a local festival in Pensacola, Florida, and heard this odd sound around the corner. We went over to investigate the noise, and, much to my delight, it was a local couple who had an old stone-wheel grinder and were milling grits. I went home and cooked the grits, and they were absolutely the freshest tasting grits that I ever had. They have a great buttery corn flavor. You really do not need to add too much to them, but, of course, I do.

Grits
1 quart (4 cups) water
1 stick (½ cup) unsalted butter
2 ounces heavy cream
1¼ pounds C & D Mill grits
5 ounces Boursin® cheese
½ cup Parmesan cheese, grated
2 teaspoons salt
1 teaspoon freshly cracked black pepper

Andouille Tomato Stew
1 ounce olive oil
1 pound andouille sausage
¼ cup chopped garlic
1 large onion, diced
1 large green pepper, diced
3 ribs celery, diced
1 cup white wine
4 (16 oz.) cans chopped tomatoes (see Chef's Tips on tomato concasse, page 321)
8 ounces chicken stock
1 bay leaf

1 teaspoon each dried thyme, dried basil, and sugar

1½ ounces dark roux (see Note on page 94)

1 teaspoon salt

¼ teaspoon red chile flakes

¼ ounce Tabasco® sauce

1 ounce Worcestershire sauce

Marinade

3½ ounces chipotle chiles, finely chopped

¼ cup Old Bay® seasoning

1 tablespoon blackening seasoning

¼ cup finely minced garlic

2½ cups canola oil

1 teaspoon cayenne pepper

1 bunch fresh thyme, finely chopped

1 teaspoon Worcestershire sauce

Shrimp

20 jumbo fresh Gulf shrimp, peeled and deveined

Salt and freshly cracked black pepper, to taste

1 bunch scallions, chopped, for garnish

Grits

Bring water, butter, and cream to a boil. While stirring, slowly add grits. When all the water is absorbed and the grits are thick, add cheeses, salt, and pepper.

Andouille Tomato Stew

Heat oil and brown the sausages until the fat is rendered out. Remove the sausages from the pan and reserve. Sauté garlic in the rendered fat until golden brown. Add fresh vegetables, and sauté for 10 minutes. Add white wine, and reduce until almost dry. Put the browned sausages back into the pan, and add the remaining ingredients. Simmer for 20 to 30 minutes. Yields 3 quarts.

Marinade

Mix all the ingredients in a bowl. Pour 2 cups of marinade into a separate bowl and add shrimp. Marinate for 1 to 2 hours. Store the remaining marinade for 5 days in an airtight container in the refrigerator or for 3 months in the freezer. Yields enough marinade for 5 pounds of shrimp.

Shrimp

Heat a large sauté pan over medium heat. Remove the shrimp from the marinade, and sauté until just cooked through (approximately 7 to 9 minutes). Season with salt and pepper to taste. Remove from the heat.

Place 6 ounces of stew in the bottom of a bowl; spoon the grits in the center of the stew. Place the shrimp around the grits in an even pattern. Top with scallions and serve immediately.

To Make a Dark Roux

Using equal parts liquid fat (oil or melted butter) and all-purpose flour, melt butter in a sauté pan over low heat. Whisk in the all-purpose flour; while continuously whisking, the flour begins to color from white to blonde to brown to dark (approximately 8 to 10 minutes). Dark roux will smell nutty and look like a dark peanut butter. Immediately pour the hot dark roux into a heatproof bowl and set aside.

Shrimp with White Grits, Chanterelle Mushrooms, Cheddar, and Black Truffles

Executive Chef Andrew Matthews *(BLT PRIME, New York, New York; inspired by Florida)*
Serves 3

Executive Chef Andrew's inspiration behind this recipe was to "add modern technique and restaurant-style presentation to a classic Southern dish." The addition of earthy chanterelles and irresistible black truffles catapults the flavor of these grits to a new level of excellence.
Story by Chef Nicole

Shrimp
1 pound shrimp, peeled and deveined

Butter Sauce
1 shallot, finely diced
1 teaspoon oil
¾ cup white wine
1 tablespoon unsalted butter, diced
Salt and freshly cracked black pepper, to taste

Grits
4 cups vegetable stock (see Index, page 343)
1 cup white grits
1 tablespoon unsalted butter
6 ounces cheddar cheese, grated
6 ounces Parmesan cheese, microplained
Chives, finely chopped, for garnish
Salt and freshly cracked black pepper, to taste

Garnish

½ teaspoon canola oil

15 small chanterelle mushroom

1 small black truffle (substitute a drizzle of truffle oil)

Micro radish greens

Smoked paprika oil

Shrimp

Peel and devein the shrimp, and set aside in the refrigerator.

Butter Sauce

In a medium saucepan, sweat the shallots in oil over medium-high heat. When the shallots become transparent, add the wine and reduce by half. At this stage, remove the pan from the heat and whisk in the diced butter, a little at a time. Whisk continuously until all of the butter is fully melted. Add salt and pepper to taste, and set aside in a warm spot.

Grits

In a large saucepan, bring the vegetable stock to a boil. Add the grits, reduce the heat to low, and stir in very well. Leave the grits to cook for 1 hour or until it becomes very soft (it should look almost like a puree). When you have achieved this consistency, add the butter and cheese, and stir well until fully melted in. Season with salt and pepper, and set aside.

Garnish

Over low heat, slowly start to reheat the grits with a little more vegetable stock and a pat of butter.

In a small frying pan, heat canola oil over medium heat; then start to sauté the chanterelles.

In a medium-sized frying pan, put enough butter sauce to cover the bottom by a ¼-inch and bring to a boil.

At this stage, season the shrimp well with salt and pepper. Add the shrimp to the butter sauce. Add a pat of butter to the chanterelles, and add chives to the grits. Cook everything for another 1½ minutes.

Remove the shrimp and chanterelles from their pans, and place onto paper towels. In the middle of each serving bowl, put two large spoonfuls of grits, then five pieces of chanterelles on top of each plate of grits, and evenly scatter the shrimp over all three bowls. Sprinkle the micro radish greens over each, and then slice some black truffles or drizzle some truffle oil over each. Finish each bowl with a few drips of smoked paprika oil, and you ready to eat.

Shrimp Creole

Melanie Foster *(Inspired by New Orleans; resides in Blaine, Minnesota)*
Serves 4–6

> I could eat shrimp every day, and this is a quick and easy way
> to get my quota. I love how the sweet shrimp combines with the
> tangy sauce. Like many Creole or Cajun recipes, this dish begins
> with the "holy trinity" of onions, celery, and green peppers.

1 tablespoon olive oil
1 green pepper, diced
1 onion, diced
2 celery stalks with leaves, sliced
2 garlic cloves, minced (see Chef's Tips on garlic, page 314)
1 teaspoon salt
¼ teaspoon cayenne pepper, adjust to taste
1 (15 oz.) can tomato sauce
1 (15 oz.) can diced tomatoes, un-drained (see Chef's Tips on tomato
concasse, page 321)
1 teaspoon fresh thyme leaves
1 bay leaf
1 pound shrimp, peeled and deveined
1 cup long-grain rice

Heat the oil in a saucepan or skillet to medium heat. Add the vegetables, garlic, and salt, and cook for about 5 to 10 minutes until almost tender, stirring occasionally. Add cayenne pepper, tomato sauce,
diced tomatoes, thyme, and bay leaf. Bring to a boil, lower the heat,
and simmer for 20 minutes until reduced slightly and the vegetables
are tender. Add shrimp, stir, and simmer for another 2 minutes or so
until the shrimp are firm and pink. Remove from the heat. Discard the
bay leaf. Cook the rice according to the package directions. Serve the
shrimp and sauce over the rice.

Cajun Delight

Kath Younger *(Charlottesville, Virginia)*
Serves 2

10 jumbo wild-caught shrimp, peeled and deveined
Canola or coconut oil, as needed
20 okra pods, cut into bite-sized pieces
1 ear corn, decobbed (See Chef's Tips on corn, page 322)
1 cup frozen lima beans, thawed
1 large heirloom tomato, diced
1 zucchini, diced
2 cups cooked grits or rice
Cajun seasoning, to taste

Pan-sear the shrimp in oil, leaving them alone so they form a crust. Remove from the pan and set aside.

Add more oil, and sauté the vegetables until they are cooked (about 5 minutes).

Sprinkle on Cajun seasoning to taste, being careful not to over-season, since it is very salty.

To serve, spoon the grits or rice into two bowls, top with vegetables, and garnish with shrimp.

Low-Country Boil

Kath Younger *(Charlottesville, Virginia)*
Serves 4

> For Kath, nothing says beach vacation more than a low-country
> boil—and it pairs well with cold beer.

4 lemons, sliced
½ bag (1½-ounce) Zatarain's® Crab Boil mix
¼ cup Old Bay® seasoning
5 red potatoes, cut into quarters
1 pound kielbasa, chopped into 1-inch pieces (may substitute turkey kielbasa)
3 ears corn, halved
1 pound each rock shrimp and Gulf shrimp

Fill an extra-large pot with water, sliced lemons, Zatarain's® mix, and
Old Bay® seasoning. Bring to a boil. Add potatoes and kielbasa. Cook
for 20 minutes. Add corn. Cook for 2 minutes. Add shrimp. Cook until
pink (3 to 5 minutes; be careful not to overcook). Drain and eat.

Gumbo

Alison Blondeau *(The New Orleans School of Cooking, New Orleans, Louisiana)*
Serves 15–20

Gumbo has been named the official Louisiana state cuisine. The "trinity" used in this recipe is a quintessential combination of onions, celery, and green peppers that is found in most Cajun recipes.

1 chicken, cut into 8 pieces
1 cup blended oil (may also use lard or bacon drippings)
1½ pounds andouille sausage

Trinity
1 cup all-purpose flour
4 cups chopped onions
2 cups chopped celery
2 cups chopped green peppers
1 tablespoon minced garlic (see Chef's Tips on garlic, page 314)
8 cups stock or flavored water (see Index, page 343)
2 cups chopped green onions or scallions
8 cups rice, prepared according to package directions
Gumbo filé (see note below)
Cajun seasoning blend, to taste

Season and brown the chicken in oil over medium heat. Add sausage to the pot, and sauté with the chicken. Remove the chicken and sausage from the pot, and reserve.

Trinity

Make a dark roux using the flour and remaining oil in the pot (see page 94). Add onions, celery, and green pepper. Add garlic to the mixture, and stir continuously.

After the vegetables reach the desired tenderness, return the chicken and sausage to the pot, and cook with the vegetables, continuing to stir frequently. Gradually stir in the liquid and bring to a boil. Reduce the heat to a simmer and cook for an hour or more. Season to taste with Cajun seasoning.

Approximately 10 minutes before serving, add green onions. Serve the gumbo with or without rice, accompanied by French bread and filé.

Chef's Tip

Filé is a fine green powder of young, dried ground sassafras leaves. It is commonly used in gumbo for flavor and thickening. It may be placed on the table for individuals to add to their gumbo, if they wish (¼ to ½ teaspoon per serving is recommended).

Pecan-Crusted Trout

A Silverware Affair *(Birmingham, Alabama)*
Serves 6

> Pecans (Alabama's state nut) and freshwater trout (found in
> the rivers and streams of the Southeast) are highlighted in this
> recipe.

1 cup all-purpose flour
4 eggs, beaten
1 tablespoon water
½ cup panko (Japanese) breadcrumbs
½ cup pecans, toasted and finely chopped (see Chef's Tips on nuts
and seeds, page 318)
6 large trout fillets, deboned
1 tablespoon blended oil, more as needed (see Chef's Tips on blended
oil, page 309)
Salt and freshly cracked black pepper, to taste

Bread the fish using the Chef's Tips instructions for standard breading procedure (page 319).

Place each of the following mixtures into separate shallow pans, wide
enough to hold the trout. Make a dry flour mixture by combining the
flour, salt, and pepper. Make a wet egg mixture by combining the eggs
and water. Make a dry breadcrumb mixture by combining the panko
breadcrumbs and pecans.

Heat the pan with blended oil. Place the trout, fillet-side-down, in the
flour mixture, then in the egg wash, and, lastly, firmly pressed into
the panko-pecan mixture. Sauté the trout, pecan-side-down, for about
2 minutes or until golden brown. Flip and sauté for 1 more minute or
until firm.

Red Snapper Milanese with Spicy Roasted Cherry Tomatoes, Arugula, and Orange-Caper Mayonnaise

Head Chef Paul Niedermann *(BLT Steak, New York, New York; inspired by Florida)*

Serves 4

Growing up in Florida, all I ever did was fish. It was something that my grandfather did with my brother Chris and I ever since I could remember, and we always had a fish-fry when we got back. Even as we got older, our love of fishing remained. My brother turned his love for fishing into a career and, whenever I have a day off, I spend it on his boat. After fishing all day, we take what we have caught, and have dinner together.

Now, working as a chef in Florida, and having an Italian background, I came up with this dish. Having such easy access to fresh fish and amazing citrus all year-round, naturally, I found a way to combine the two into something great.

Spicy Roasted Cherry Tomatoes
1 pint cherry red tomatoes, washed and cut in half
2 teaspoons sugar
4 sprigs thyme, leaves only
½ clove garlic, minced
1 teaspoon white balsamic vinegar
1 teaspoon red pepper flakes, lightly chopped
1 ounce extra-virgin olive oil
Salt and freshly cracked black pepper, to taste

Orange-Caper Mayonnaise
3 cups mayonnaise
½ cup minced capers
½ bunch parsley, chopped

½ bunch chives, chopped

¼ bunch tarragon, picked and chopped

¼ bunch oregano, picked and chopped

Juice and zest of 1 orange (see Chef's Tips on citrus zest, page 311)

Salt and freshly cracked black pepper, to taste

Fish

4 (10 oz.) skinless red snapper fillets, pin bones and bloodline removed

2 cups all-purpose flour

6 eggs, beaten

1 clove garlic, minced

1 cup Parmesan cheese, finely grated

3 ounces water

½ bunch Italian flat-leaf parsley, finely chopped and divided

6 cups panko (Japanese) breadcrumbs

1 tablespoon dried oregano

¼ bunch cilantro, finely chopped

1 cup extra-virgin olive oil

4 cups baby arugula

1 cup Spicy Roasted Cherry Tomatoes

2 cups Orange-Caper Mayonnaise

2 lemons (1 juiced and 1 cut into wedges)

Kosher salt and freshly cracked black pepper, to taste

Spicy Roasted Cherry Tomatoes

Combine all the ingredients in a bowl.

Place the tomato mixture in a baking pan lined with a piece of parchment paper.

Bake in a 250°F oven until the tomatoes are soft and blistered (about 30 minutes).

Orange-Caper Mayonnaise

Combine all the ingredients in a bowl. Season to taste. Yields 1 quart.

Fish

Place a piece of plastic wrap on the cutting board, and then place the fish, flesh-side-up, onto the plastic. Cover with another piece of plastic.

Carefully and lightly pound the fish until the entire fillet is $\frac{1}{8}$-inch thick. Repeat this process until all the fish is pounded. Place the fish on a baking sheet and reserve in the refrigerator until you are ready to bread.

Bread the fish using the Chef's Tips instructions for standard breading procedure (page 319).

Place each of the following mixtures into separate shallow pans, wide enough to hold the snapper.

Make a dry flour mixture by combining the flour, salt, and pepper.

Make a wet egg mixture by combining the eggs, garlic, cheese, water, and half of the parsley. Make a dry breadcrumb mixture by combining the breadcrumbs, oregano, half of the parsley, and cilantro.

To cook, heat up the oil in a large sauté pan on medium heat until the oil begins to smoke. Carefully place the fish into the pan and cook until golden brown (about 3 minutes). Flip the fish and cook the other side until it is also brown.

To serve, place the fish onto plates or one platter, and dress the arugula with the juice of one lemon and a drizzle of olive oil. Garnish with Spicy Roasted Cherry Tomatoes, and serve with Orange-Caper Mayonnaise and slices of lemon on the side.

Chicken and Dumplings

Annette Brandes *(Cape Coral, Florida)*
Serves 6–8

> This is Annette's husband's favorite Southern comfort meal. His mother cooked a meal that was similar to this one.

House Seasoning

1 cup salt
¼ cup black pepper
¼ cup garlic powder

Chicken

1 (2½ lb.) chicken, cut into 8 pieces
3 ribs celery, chopped
1 large onion, chopped
2 bay leaves
2 chicken bouillon cubes
1 teaspoon House Seasoning (see above)
4 quarts water
1 (10¾ oz.) can condensed cream of celery or cream of chicken soup

Dumplings

2 cups all-purpose flour
1 teaspoon salt
Ice water

House Seasoning

Mix the ingredients together and store in an airtight container for up to 6 months. Yields 1½ cups.

Chicken

Place the chicken, celery, onion, bay leaves, bouillon, and House Seasoning in a large pot. Add 4 quarts of water, and bring to a simmer over medium heat. Simmer the chicken until it is tender and the thigh juices run clear (about 40 minutes). Remove the chicken from the pot, and, when it is cool enough to handle, remove the skin and separate the meat from the bones. Return the chicken meat to the pot. Add the cream of celery soup to the pot with the chicken, and simmer gently over medium-low heat.

Dumplings

Mix the flour with the salt and mound together in a mixing bowl. Beginning at the center of the mound, drizzle a small amount of ice water over the flour. Using your fingers, and moving from the center to the sides of the bowl, gradually incorporate about ¾ cup of ice water. Knead the dough and form it into a ball.

Dust a good amount of flour onto a clean work surface. Roll out the dough (it will be firm), working from the center to ⅛-inch thick. Let the dough relax for several minutes.

Cut the dough into 1-inch pieces. Pull a piece in half and drop the halves into the simmering soup. Repeat. Do not stir the chicken once the dumplings have been added. Gently move the pot in a circular motion so the dumplings become submerged and cook evenly. Cook until the dumplings float and are no longer doughy (3 to 4 minutes).

To serve, ladle the chicken, gravy, and dumplings into warm bowls.

Chef's Tip

If the chicken stew is too thin, it can be thickened before the dumplings are added. Simply mix together a slurry of 2 tablespoons of cornstarch and ¼ cup of cold water in a separate container. Then whisk this mixture into the stew and bring to a boil. Once boiling, stew should come to desired consistency. If still thin, add another slurry.

Marinated Grilled Chicken

Kaya Hard *(Elephant Seasoning, Gulf Breeze, Florida)*
Serves 3–5

> One of my favorite dishes at every family cookout was the marinated, char-grilled chicken that my dad Chef Carlo would make using his Elephant® seasoning blend. The aroma of chicken sizzling on the charcoal grill is a scent that I will never forget, and the first bite of Dad's grilled chicken was like heaven on earth. This dish would bring everyone together around the grill. It was always story time when my dad started grilling. Friends and neighbors would come by to see what that wonderful aroma was, and, once they found out where it was coming from, my Dad would always offer a piece of his chicken, along with one of his famous stories.

¼ cup soy sauce
¼ cup Worcestershire sauce
⅛ cup Dale's® marinade
⅛ cup vegetable oil
10 chicken thighs or wings (with or without the drum separated)
2 tablespoons Elephant® all-purpose seasoning blend (plus 1 tablespoon liquid smoke if using a gas grill)

Mix together the soy sauce, Worcestershire sauce, marinade, and oil. Pour over the chicken and marinate for 4 hours, rotating every hour.

Lay the chicken on a flat tray, and then generously sprinkle each piece with Elephant® seasoning until every piece is well-coated and seasoned.

Heat the grill and clean. Grill, turning occasionally, until fully cooked (and the internal temperature reaches 165°F). For chicken thighs, grill for approximately 15 minutes. For chicken wings, grill for approximately 10 minutes.

Southern Fried Chicken

Chef Nicole *(Inspired by St. Augustine, Florida)*
Serves 4

> One of the most valuable culinary lessons I took with me after having the pleasure of living and working down South was how to "properly" fry chicken. The cooks at the Aviles Restaurant at the Hilton Historic Bayfront in St. Augustine, Florida told me the secret to achieving the characteristic crunch of fried chicken—"It's all in the cornstarch!" I've added the rice flour for the same effect and found that this recipe "yields" happy customers every time!
>
> *Story by Nicole Roarke*

1 whole chicken (cut into 8 pieces)
1 quart buttermilk
2 cups all-purpose flour
½ cup rice flour
1 cup cornstarch
1 tablespoon kosher salt
1 teaspoon freshly cracked black pepper
1 teaspoon garlic powder (optional)
1 teaspoon onion powder (optional)
1 teaspoon cayenne (optional)
1 teaspoon paprika (optional)
2 eggs
Fryer oil (See Chef's Tips on blended oil, page 309)
Salt and freshly cracked black pepper, to taste

Place chicken parts into a large bowl and cover with buttermilk. Cover bowl with plastic wrap and place on the bottom shelf of the refrigerator. Refrigerate overnight.

Mix all dry ingredients in a large bowl and set aside. Remove chicken from buttermilk, reserve buttermilk, and place chicken into a separate container.

Begin dredging the chicken by coating one piece at a time in the dry flour mixture, making sure to fully coat each piece. Shake off any additional flour and lay chicken onto a sheet tray. Whisk eggs into reserved buttermilk. One at a time, dip chicken pieces into the buttermilk and egg mixture then dredge the chicken pieces, one at a time, into the dry flour mixture for a second time. Lay fully coated/battered chicken on a sheet tray. Place chicken into the refrigerator for 20–30 minutes so coating adheres.

While chicken is resting in the refrigerator, pour the fryer oil into a deep fryer (or deep sauce pot on the stove top), then heat over medium-high heat. After 30 minutes remove the chicken from the refrigerator and set aside. Once the fryer oil has reached 350°F to 375°F, begin frying the chicken a few pieces at a time (be sure not to overcrowd the pot). The fried chicken should be golden brown and crunchy on the surface before removing from the oil with a fryer basket, spider, or slotted spoon. Lay each piece onto a sheet tray. Be sure the internal temperature of the chicken is 165°F; if not, then bake in a 400°F oven until fully cooked. Season with additional salt and pepper, to taste.

Spice Rub Pulled Pork

Chef Nicole *(Inspired by St. Augustine, Florida)*

Serves 8–10

A custom-made spice rub is an ingenious way to add a tremendous amount of flavor to any tough cut of meat. The almost excessive amount of dried herbs and spices are necessary to penetrate through the fatty exterior of this otherwise tasteless piece of pork. The touches of sweet apple and cinnamon help to create an overall depth of flavor while balancing well with the other spicy ingredients.

Story by Nicole Roarke

Dry Spice Rub

3 tablespoons kosher salt

2 tablespoons freshly cracked black pepper

1 tablespoon each whole cloves, yellow and/or brown mustard seeds, cumin seeds, and coriander seeds (see Chef's Tips on nuts and seeds, page 318)

3 tablespoons paprika

2 tablespoons ground chili powder

½ tablespoon cayenne pepper

½ tablespoon ground allspice

1 tablespoon ground ginger

½ tablespoon ground garlic

Pork

5 pounds pork shoulder or butt (cut in half)

2 tablespoons blended oil (see Chef's Tips on blended oil, page 309)

1 large yellow onion, peeled and sliced

½ gallon apple cider

4–6 cups chicken stock (see Index, page 343)

3 whole bay leaves

4 sprigs fresh thyme

1 whole cinnamon stick

¼ cup each cornstarch and water (optional; see Chef's Tips on slurry, page 322)

Salt and freshly cracked black pepper, to taste

Dry Spice Rub

Mix all of the dry spice rub ingredients into a large container. Set aside.

Pork

Remove pork from package and pat dry with a clean paper towel; cut in half and set aside. Score the pork by using a knife to make shallow cuts (½-inch deep) in a cross hatch pattern on the top of each piece. Place pork into the container with the dry spice rub and begin coating each piece with the rub. Continue to coat each piece with as much spice rub as possible, being sure to rub the spice mix into the scores. Cover the container with plastic wrap and refrigerate for at least 8 hours or overnight.

Preheat an oven to 350°F.

Remove pork from refrigerator, pat off any excess spice rub, and set aside. Rest the pork on a counter top for 30 minutes to allow it to acclimate to room temperature.

Heat a large roasting pan or sauce pan over a medium-high flame for 2 minutes. Add oil and begin searing each piece of pork for approximately 1 minute per side or until the pork has a golden brown crust (be sure not to blacken or char the pork; if this begins to happen, immediately lower the flame and remove the pork until the pan has cooled). Once cool, begin searing again. Remove pork and allow to rest on a sheet tray.

Add yellow onion and stir for approximately 3 minutes or until onions begin to brown and soften or caramelize. Return pork to the pan and place over the bed of sautéed onions. Add the apple cider and simmer for 2 minutes. Add the chicken stock until it reaches ½ inch from the top of the pork. Add remaining ingredients (except cornstarch and water), turn off the flame, and cover the pan with foil or a lid.

Place the pan on the middle rack of a preheated oven for 2 hours. After 2 hours, check if the pork is fork tender and if the surrounding liquid has reduced by half. If pork is still tough or if more than half of the liquid has reduced, add more chicken stock, cover, and return to oven for an additional hour. Check the pork every 30 minutes for desired doneness (fully cooked pork should be fork tender all the way through and can be easily pulled by hand).

Once the pork is fully cooked, remove it from the pan, loosely cover with foil, and set aside. Once cool enough to handle, pull the pork by hand or cut into pieces. Strain remaining liquid through a mesh strainer (to remove large spices and herbs) into a sauce pan and simmer on the stovetop until it has reduced to a thick sauce, or add a slurry. Add salt and freshly cracked black pepper to taste.

Mix pulled pork with the sauce from the pan or with additional barbecue sauce (see page 300 for recipe).

New Orleans Red Beans and Rice

Melanie Foster *(Inspired by New Orleans; resides in Blaine, Minnesota)*
Serves 6–8

My mom grew up in New Orleans, where this dish is traditionally served on Mondays (also known as "wash day," when washing clothes took a lot more effort and time, often occupying an entire day). It would simmer all day on the stove while the wash was being done. Now, it just reminds me of Mom, who absolutely cannot eat this without fresh French bread slathered with butter and plenty of yellow mustard. I cannot help but agree. It tastes so good with the creamy beans and sausage. I suspect you could easily adjust this recipe, and make this in your slow cooker; just add water to barely cover the beans, as the vegetables will produce a lot of liquid as well.

2 cups dried small red beans
1 pound smoked kielbasa, cut into 1-inch slices
4 cloves garlic, minced
1 large onion, minced
1 green pepper, minced
1 cup celery, minced
2 bay leaves
1 tablespoons Tabasco® sauce
¾ teaspoon ground cloves
1 tablespoon parsley
Salt and freshly cracked black pepper, to taste

Put the beans in a large pot; cover by at least 2 inches with water. Soak overnight. In the morning, add more water until it comes to an inch above the beans, and bring to a boil. Boil hard for 10 minutes, drain, and return to the pot with the remaining ingredients. Pour in enough water to just cover everything and bring to a simmer. Simmer for 4 to 5 hours or until the beans are tender, stirring occasionally. If the liquid starts to evaporate, cover with a lid. It should not be too soupy, but have the consistency of chili. Discard the bay leaves. Serve over hot rice with more Tabasco® sauce.

Summer Succotash

Amber Robertson-Smith *(Nashville, Tennessee)*
Serves 4

3 tablespoons salted butter
2 cups Vidalia onions, diced small
2 cups fresh sweet corn kernels (see Chef's Tips on corn, page 322)
1 pound shelled edamame
2 tablespoons fig vinegar
½ teaspoon freshly cracked black pepper
3 small tomatoes, diced
1 yellow bell pepper, seeded and diced
3 tablespoons fresh basil, chopped

Melt butter in a skillet over medium-high heat. Add onion, and sauté for 2 to 3 minutes. Add corn, and sauté for another 2 to 3 minutes. Add edamame, and sauté for another 2 to 3 minutes. Add vinegar, pepper, tomatoes, and yellow pepper, and sauté for another minute; then remove from the heat. Transfer to the succotash serving bowl, decorate with basil, and serve.

Herb-Buttered Corn

Amber Robertson-Smith *(Nashville, Tennessee)*
Serves 4

1 stick (½ cup) unsalted butter, room temperature
1 tablespoon garlic, minced
1 tablespoon chives, finely chopped
1 tablespoon basil, finely chopped
1 tablespoon parsley, finely chopped
1 tablespoon oregano, finely chopped
1 tablespoon thyme, finely chopped
4 ears Tennessee sweet corn, shucked (see Chef Tips on corn, page 322)

In a small bowl, mix together the butter, garlic, and herbs. Set aside. Fill the pot halfway with water, and place the corn inside. Bring to a boil and remove the corn. Serve the corn slathered with 1 tablespoon of herbed butter.

Chef's Tip

See Chef's Tips on compound butter (page 312). Leftover herb butter keeps well in the refrigerator for 5 days or in the freezer for 3 months.

Pralines

Alison Blondeau *(The New Orleans School of Cooking, New Orleans, Louisiana)*
Makes 1–50 pralines, depending on size

Creole confections occupy a unique position in the United States, the most popular of these being the praline. Their name is derived from Marshal Luplesis-Praslin and his butler's recipe for almonds coated in sugar used as a digestive aid. When French colonists settled in Louisiana, native pecans were substituted for almonds.

No lengths were spared by the Creoles to achieve perfection in candy-making. Along with their vast collection of Creole recipes, cooks had their own secret method for making the best pralines, which they guarded carefully, and handed down from generation to generation.

Today, pralines are as many and varied as they were in the very beginning. We hope your memories of New Orleans are as sweet as these pralines.

1½ cups pecans, roasted (see Chef's Tips on nuts and seeds, page 318)
1½ cups sugar
¾ stick (6 tablespoons) butter
¾ cup light brown sugar, packed
½ cup milk
1 teaspoon pure vanilla

Bake the pecans on a sheet pan at 275°F for 20 to 25 minutes until slightly browned and fragrant. Let cool and combine all the ingredients; bring to a "soft ball stage" (238 to 240°F), stirring constantly. Remove from the heat.

Stir until the mixture thickens and becomes creamy and cloudy, and the pecans stay suspended in the mixture.

Spoon out on buttered waxed paper, aluminum foil, or parchment paper. (When using waxed paper, be sure to buffer with newspaper underneath, as hot wax will transfer to whatever is beneath.)

To make praline sauce, add ½ cup of corn syrup to the mixture. Pralines can be flavored with chocolate, coffee, or brandy.

Carolina Sour Cream Pound Cake

Chef Sherri Beauchamp *(The Seasonal Kitchen, Fort Mill, South Carolina)*
Serves 8

> Since moving to South Carolina, I feel that the most Southern
> item that I have had the privilege to enjoy (besides great barbecue)
> is pound cake. Pound cake is everywhere in the South, and this
> recipe is from a dear friend, whom I have had the honor to meet
> since moving here. The top and side crust on this pound cake is
> crisp and crunchy—it is the perfect balance to the moist crumb
> of the cake. It is delicious and very different from my grandma's
> Northern pound cake.

2 sticks (½ pound) unsalted butter, room temperature
3 cups sugar
1 cup sour cream
3 cups all-purpose flour
½ teaspoon baking powder
6 eggs
½ teaspoon pure vanilla extract
1 teaspoon pure almond extract

Preheat an oven to 325°F. Cream butter and sugar together, and then
add sour cream. Sift the flour and baking powder together. Alternate
adding the dry mixture and eggs, one at a time, to the cream mixture,
beating after each one. Add vanilla and almond extracts. Pour into a
greased and floured tube pan, and bake for 1 hour and 20 minutes.

Georgia Peach Pound Cake

Cindy Dickey *(Dickey Farms, Musella, Georgia)*
Serves 16

1 cup plus 2 tablespoons butter, divided
2¼ cups sugar, divided
4 eggs, room temperature
1 teaspoon pure vanilla
3 cups all-purpose flour, divided
1 teaspoon baking powder
½ teaspoon salt
2 cups fresh Georgia peaches, chopped

Preheat an oven to 325°F. Grease a 10-inch tube pan with 2 tablespoons of butter. Sprinkle the pan with ¼ cup of sugar. Cream 1 cup of butter; gradually add 2 cups of sugar, beating well. Add eggs one at a time, beating well after each addition. Add vanilla, and mix well. Combine 2¾ cups of flour, baking powder, and salt; gradually add to creamed mixture, beating until well blended. Dredge the peaches with the remaining ¼ cup of flour. Fold the peaches into the batter. Pour the batter into a prepared pan. Bake at 325°F for 1 hour and 10 minutes. Remove from the pan and cool completely.

Bananas Foster

Serves 4

> When visiting Louisiana one year, my husband and I tried the state specialty, bananas foster. This popular dessert was created at Brennan's Restaurant. It became one of our favorite desserts to make as a young married couple.
>
> *Story by Mary Elizabeth*

½ stick (¼ cup) unsalted butter
¼ cup brown sugar
2 tablespoons fresh lemon juice
1 teaspoon cinnamon (prefer Vietnamese cinnamon)
3 tablespoons fresh orange juice
¼ cup triple sec
1 tablespoon dark rum
2 very ripe bananas, cut in half lengthwise, then halved

Combine all the ingredients (except the liquors and bananas) Place in a skillet over low heat on top of the stove, and cook, stirring, until the sugar dissolves and the butter melts. Stir in the liquors, and then place the bananas in the pan. When the banana sections soften and begin to brown, carefully lift the bananas out of the pan and evenly distribute over ice cream. Generously spoon warm sauce over the top of the ice cream, and serve immediately.

Warm Pineapple Crisp with Honey Streusel, Rosemary Syrup, and Bourbon Ice Cream

Pastry Chef Anastazia Carter *(Miami, Florida)*
Serves 12–14

After eating dinner at a restaurant in Miami, the server recommended this pineapple crisp. Who could ever resist ordering it after hearing the description? The unique pairing of rosemary and pineapple proves to be a delicious flavor combination. I asked if I could meet the pastry chef, who sat with me and told me her story. After receiving a business degree, Chef Ana started working in a church daycare. Eventually, they asked her to start cooking for the students. It was then that she realized her passion, and she decided to follow her dream and attend culinary school. She describes her desserts as part of her ministry of love and a way of nurturing others.
Story by Mary Elizabeth

Honey Streusel

1¼ cups all-purpose flour
1 teaspoon cinnamon
½ cup brown sugar
1½ teaspoons pure vanilla extract
½ teaspoon salt
½ cup honey (preferably light amber honey)
6 tablespoons unsalted butter, chilled and cut into cubes

Pineapple Filling

2 tablespoons unsalted butter
1 sprig rosemary, needles removed
1½ pounds fresh pineapple, cut into ½-inch cubes
1 teaspoon freshly grated lemon zest
½ vanilla bean
5 tablespoons brown sugar

1 tablespoon all-purpose flour

1 teaspoon salt

1 tablespoon cinnamon

½ teaspoon freshly grated nutmeg

Rosemary Syrup

2 sprigs rosemary

2½ cups simple syrup (see Chef's Tips on simple syrup, page 321)

Garnish

Confectioners' sugar

Bourbon ice cream

Honey Streusel

Combine the flour, cinnamon, and brown sugar; whisk. Place in a mixer with a paddle attachment. Combine the vanilla, salt, and honey. While the mixer is on low speed, scrape these ingredients into the dry mix. Increase to medium speed. Mix until blended. Gradually add butter. Mix on medium speed just until the butter is broken into the mix (this stage is a short mix; do not over-mix). Spread the dough over the sheet pan. Bake at 350°F for 5 minutes; then rotate and bake for 4 minutes. When still warm, crumble the streusel and set aside.

Pineapple Filling

Heat the butter and rosemary over low heat in a covered pot for approximately 6 minutes. Strain the butter. Discard the rosemary leaves. Set aside. Toss the pineapple with the rosemary-infused butter, and zest in a rectangle pan (4 inches deep by 12¾ inches wide by 20¾ inches long). Set aside.

Split the vanilla bean, and scrape out the seeds; using your fingers, break the seeds into brown sugar. Add flour, salt, cinnamon, and nutmeg. Whisk together and pour onto the pineapple cubes. Toss until evenly coated.

Bake uncovered at 375°F for 5 minutes. Rotate the pan, stir the pineapples, and bake for an additional 3 minutes. Allow to cool.

Rosemary Syrup

Combine the rosemary leaves and simple syrup into a pot, and bring to a boil. Allow the rosemary to steep in the syrup until cool.

Pour the streusel on top of the pineapple filling, and top with 1½ tablespoons of rosemary syrup. Heat at 375°F until warm. Sprinkle with confectioners' sugar and a scoop of bourbon ice cream.

White Chocolate Bread Pudding

Executive Chef Nick Fawal *(Vic & Ike's, Pensacola, Florida)*
Serves 8

> An inviting and delicious twist on this popular Southern dessert, bread pudding is often called the "apple pie of Louisiana."

3 cups whipping cream
10 ounces white chocolate
1 cup milk
½ cup sugar
2 eggs
8 egg yolks
1 loaf French bread, sliced into ¼-inch pieces and dried in the oven
2 tablespoons white chocolate shavings, for garnish

Heat the cream in a double boiler, and add the white chocolate; when the chocolate is melted, remove from the heat.

In a double boiler, heat the milk, sugar, eggs, and egg yolks until warm. Blend the egg mixture into the cream and chocolate mixture.

Spray the bottom of a pan with baking spray. Place the bread slices in a 9- by 13-inch baking pan. Pour half of the mixture over the bread, and let it settle for awhile, making sure that the bread soaks up all the mixture. Cover with aluminum foil and bake at 275°F for 1 hour. Remove the foil, and bake for an additional 15 minutes until the top is golden brown. If desired, sprinkle with chocolate shavings prior to serving.

Kentucky Derby Pie

Yields 1 (9-inch) pie

> This original pie recipe was given to me by a friend who was
> born and raised in Kentucky. The Kentucky derby is so popular
> that locals celebrate by preparing this pie and the specialty
> drink, mint julep, in its honor.
> *Story by Mary Elizabeth*

½ cup melted unsalted butter
1 cup sugar
1 cup light corn syrup
4 eggs, beaten
1–2 tablespoons bourbon (optional)
½ cup semisweet chocolate morsels
1 cup pecans, chopped
1 unbaked 9-inch pie crust (see Index, page 339)

Preheat an oven to 350°F. Combine first seven ingredients in a large
bowl, mixing well with a wooden spoon. Pour into the unbaked pie
crust, and bake for 40 to 45 minutes or until firm.

Moon Pie

A Silverware Affair *(Chattanooga, Tennessee)*
Yields 2 (9-inch) cheesecakes

A Silverware Affair is a catering company with several locations, but their headquarters is in Chattanooga, Tennessee, where Moon Pies are popular. They suggested pairing this with a Coca-Cola, which was first bottled in their city, too. Both are Southern favorites. The recipe also works well with other add-ins, such as Oreos®, Twix® pieces, and various candies.

Graham cracker crust, for 2 9-inch spring-form pans
1 quart heavy cream
1¾ cups sugar
1 package (1 tablespoon) gelatin
1½ teaspoons pure vanilla
4 pounds cream cheese, softened
5 Moon Pies®, diced into ⅛-inch chunks

Prepare the graham cracker crust using the directions on page xxx. Mix the cream, sugar, gelatin, and vanilla over medium heat until the gelatin is dissolved. Cool for 10 minutes and add cream cheese. Mix together. Gently fold in the Moon Pies® and pour into the graham cracker crust shells. Cool for a minimum of 2 hours to set; then cut, serve, and enjoy.

Kim's Key Lime Pie

Amy Pawliw *(Inspired by Key West, Florida; resides in Plainview, New York)*
Yields 1 (9-inch) pie

> Every spring, my closest friends and I visit a new city in
> Florida. One year, we visited the Keys, and were determined to
> try Florida's famous dessert. Since then, my friends and I have
> tried to replicate the flavors that we remember so fondly, and,
> out of all of them, this recipe is the best. It was shared with Amy
> from her sister's friend Kim.
> *Story by Mary Elizabeth*

Crust

1½ cups crushed graham cracker crumbs (about 16 crackers)
3 tablespoons sugar
1 stick (½ cup) unsalted butter, melted

Filling

4 large egg yolks
1 (14 oz.) can sweetened condensed milk
½ cup fresh Key lime juice (approximately 12 Key limes or 5 large
limes)
2 teaspoons grated lime zest (see Chef's Tips on citrus zest, page
311)

Crust

Mix the crumbs and sugar, and then pour in the melted butter. Mix
until combined. Press into a 9-inch pie plate. Bake in a preheated 350°F
oven for 10 to 12 minutes until lightly browned. Place on a rack to
cool.

Filling

Use an electric mixer, and beat the egg yolks until they are thick and turn
to a light yellow; do not over-mix.

Turn the mixer off and add the sweetened condensed milk. Turn the speed
to low and mix in half of the lime juice. Once the juice is incorporated, add
the other half of the juice and the zest, and continue to mix until blended
(just a few seconds). Pour the mixture into the pie shell and bake at 350°F
for 12 minutes to set. Garnish with whipped cream.

Mint Julep

Serves 1

¼ cup water
¼ cup sugar
1 tablespoon fresh mint leaves, roughly chopped
½ cup bourbon
1 sprig fresh mint leaves, for garnish

Make a simple syrup (see Chef's Tips on simple syrup, page 321) by combining water, sugar, and chopped mint leaves in a small saucepan. Bring to a boil over high heat until the sugar is completely dissolved. Allow the syrup to cool (approximately 1 hour). Pour the syrup through a strainer to remove the mint leaves.

Fill a glass with crushed ice and pour in the bourbon and mint syrup. Serve juleps with a mint sprig. For authenticity, serve on a silver platter.

Gluten-Free Red Velvet Cake

Chef Jennifer Franklin *(The Cooking School at Irwin Street, Atlanta, Georgia)*
Serves 6–8

> No one is sure just how this one-of-a-kind cake became known as a Southern confection. American historians confirm the use of shredded red beets and sugar beets in bakery cakes after World War II. During a time when food was rationed, and economic crisis prevailed, bakers would strategically add these secret ingredients. The sugar beets added sweetness to compensate for the scarce supply of sugar, and the surprisingly ruby red center boosted sales.
>
> *Story by Chef Nicole*

Cake
2½ cups gluten-free flour (such as King Arthur® flour)
1½ cups sugar
1 teaspoon baking soda
1 teaspoon iodized salt
2 teaspoons cocoa powder
1½ cups vegetable oil
1 cup buttermilk, room temperature
2 large eggs, room temperature
2 tablespoons (1 ounce) red food coloring
1 teaspoon distilled white vinegar
1 teaspoon pure vanilla extract

Cream Cheese Frosting
1 pound cream cheese, softened
4 cups sifted confectioners' sugar
2 sticks (1 cup) unsalted butter, softened
1 teaspoon pure vanilla extract
Crushed pecans, for garnish (see Chef's Tips on nuts and seeds, page 318)

Cake

Preheat the oven to 350°F. Lightly spray three 9- by 1½-inch round cake pans with baking spray.

In a large bowl, sift together the flour, sugar, baking soda, salt, and cocoa powder. In another large bowl, whisk together the oil, buttermilk, eggs, food coloring, vinegar, and vanilla.

Using a mixer, mix the dry ingredients into the wet ingredients until just combined and a smooth batter is formed.

Divide the cake batter evenly among the prepared cake pans. Place the pans in the oven evenly spaced apart. Bake for about 30 minutes, rotating the pans halfway through the cooking time, until the cake pulls away from the side of the pans, and a toothpick inserted in the center of the cakes comes out clean.

Cream Cheese Frosting

In a stand mixer fitted with a paddle attachment (or with a hand-held electric mixer in a large bowl), mix the cream cheese, sugar, and butter on low speed until incorporated. Increase the speed to high, and mix until light and fluffy (about 5 minutes; occasionally turn the mixer off and scrape down the sides of the bowl with a rubber spatula).

Reduce the speed of the mixer to low. Add the vanilla, raise the speed to high, and mix briefly until fluffy (scrape down the bowl occasionally). Makes enough to frost a three-layer (9-inch) cake. Store in the refrigerator before using until it becomes somewhat stiff. May be stored in the refrigerator for up to 3 days.

Remove the cakes from the oven and run a knife around the edges to loosen them from the sides of the pans. One at a time, invert the cakes onto a plate, and then re-invert them onto a cooling rack, rounded-sides-up. Let it cool completely.

Place 1 layer, rounded-side-down, in the middle of a rotating cake stand. Using a palette knife or offset spatula, spread some of the cream cheese frosting over the top of the cake (spread enough frosting to make a ¼- to ½-inch layer). Carefully set another layer on top, rounded-side-down, and repeat. Top with the remaining layer and cover the entire cake with the remaining frosting. Sprinkle the top with pecans.

King Cake

Melanie Foster *(Inspired by New Orleans, Louisiana; resides in Blaine, Minnesota)*
Yields 1 cake

This is *the* cake of Mardi Gras. A little plastic baby, bean, or coin is hidden in each cake, and the recipient of the lucky piece receives one year of good luck, and hosts the party the following year. I was nine-years-old the first time that I went to Mardi Gras with my parents and brother. I found the baby in the first piece of King Cake that I was ever served, and I am pretty sure that I still have it to this day. (That must be the reason why I have had such an amazing sweet tooth for cinnamon rolls, of which this cake is a festive version.)

Cake
¾ cup warm milk
1 (¼ oz.) package or 2¼ teaspoons active dry yeast
6 tablespoons sugar
½ teaspoon salt
½ teaspoon ground mace
¾ cup unsalted butter, softened
4 eggs
4 cups all-purpose flour, divided
5 tablespoons sugar
1½ teaspoons cinnamon

Glaze
2 cups confectioners' sugar
½ teaspoon pure vanilla extract
4 tablespoons milk, or less as needed

Garnish
3 tablespoons each yellow, green, and purple colored sugars
1 plastic baby or large dried bean

Cake

Pour the warm milk into a large bowl or the bowl of an electric mixer. Sprinkle the yeast and 6 tablespoons of sugar over the milk, and stir until dissolved. Let sit for 5 minutes until foamy. Add the salt, mace, butter, and eggs. Add 3 cups of the flour, and mix on medium speed for 4 minutes. Add the remaining 1 cup of flour, and beat on low until smooth or until the flour is incorporated (about 2 minutes). Cover the bowl with plastic wrap that has been sprayed with baking spray. Let rise in a warm place until doubled in bulk (about 1 hour). Refrigerate, covered, overnight.

In a small bowl, combine the 5 tablespoons of sugar with the cinnamon. Punch down the dough and dump it onto your work surface. Divide into three equal pieces, and, one at a time, roll each piece into a rectangle approximately 24- by 6-inches. Sprinkle with one-third of the cinnamon mixture. Starting on a long side, roll up, pinching the edge to seal. Place the three rolls side by side and loosely braid. Gently transfer to a parchment-lined baking sheet and shape into an oval, pinching the ends to seal. Cover with a clean towel and let rise in a warm place for about 45 minutes.

Preheat an oven to 375°F. Bake for 25 to 30 minutes until golden brown. Cool on a wire rack. Insert the baby (or dried bean) into the cake from the bottom.

Glaze

Mix the confectioners' sugar, vanilla extract, and milk until smooth. Spread on top of the cooled cake.

Garnish

Spoon the colored sugars over the glaze in wide bands, alternating the purple, green, and yellow.

> **Chef's Tip**
>
> When making this cake, be sure to warn your guests about the surprise inside, and supervise small kids while eating this cake.

Part III

Midwest

The "heartland" of the United States is otherwise known as the Midwest. The core of America's states include Ohio, Michigan, Indiana, Illinois, Missouri, Arkansas, Oklahoma, Kansas, Nebraska, Iowa, Wisconsin, Minnesota, North Dakota, and South Dakota.

When visiting these states, you will likely find endless fields of grain and rows of corn, both of which are featured in Oat, Buckwheat, and Flaxseed Waffles (page 144) and Summer Corn Chowder (page 148). Often referred to as the Central Plains, the Midwest is characterized by dry, flat prairie land covered with wild grass and flowers. With very little precipitation available for vegetation to grow, the cuisine of this region typically highlights other valuable resources that the area has to offer. For instance, Braised Beef Ragu (page 177) and Grilled Flank Steak and Roasted Beet Salad (page 175) feature the many cattle raised on this land. Dairy cows, which also have acres to roam on the plains, are the true stars of the Wisconsin cheese show. Midwestern cuisine boasts hearty recipes for one-pot meals such as Kale Hash (page 146) and Tildy Stew (page 174), reminiscent of its historical hearth-cooking.

Although meat is prevalent in these states, the neighboring lakes, streams, and rivers also harbor freshwater fish such as catfish (an Arkansas favorite), which is highlighted in Pistachio Lovers' Catfish (page 159).

Leading crops in this area include soy beans (which are featured in the Native American favorite, Soybean Succotash, on page 188), cherries (used in Chilled Pinot Noir and Door County Cherry Soup on page 154), and morel mushrooms (found in Chicken-Mushroom Mozzarella on page 173). All of these traditional heartland recipes are now making a comeback on the trendy culinary scene.

During the Gold Rush, many of the colonists and settlers from the East began traveling west in search of the "American dream." Northern European immigrants made up of a large population of Germans and Swedes also followed in search of a similar dream, each bringing with them specialties such as German Potato Strudel (page 179) and Grandpa's Blueberry Swedish Pancakes (page 142). With spacious lands full of plentiful resources and strong cultural influences, people who call the heartland of the Midwest home believe that their dream has come true.

Grammie Jayn's Blueberry Coffee Cake

Paul and Jayn Parenti *(A Fare to Remember, Fayetteville, Arkansas)*
Serves 6–8

Cake

2 cups all-purpose flour
2 teaspoons baking powder
½ cup unsalted butter, softened
¾ cup sugar
1 teaspoon lemon zest (see Chef's Tips on citrus zest, page 311)
1 egg, lightly beaten
¾ cup milk
1 teaspoon pure vanilla
1½ cups fresh blueberries

Topping

½ cup brown sugar
¼ cup all-purpose flour
¼ cup chopped pecans (see Chef's Tips on nuts and seeds, page 318)
1 tablespoon cinnamon
½ stick (¼ cup) unsalted butter, melted

Cake

Preheat an oven to 375°F. Sift together the flour and baking powder into a bowl. Set aside. In a mixing bowl, cream together butter, sugar, and lemon zest; beat in the egg.

Blend in the milk, and stir until smooth. Fold the flour mixture into the wet ingredients one-third at a time, just until the dry ingredients are moistened. Fold in the vanilla and blueberries. Batter will be thick; spread in a greased, 9-inch, square baking pan.

Topping

Combine sugar, flour, pecans, and cinnamon. Pour in the melted butter, and mix with a fork or your fingers until mealy or crumbly. Sprinkle this mixture over the batter.

Bake at 375°F for 25 to 30 minutes or until an inserted knife or pick comes out clean.

Grandpa's Blueberry Swedish Pancakes

Melanie Foster *(Blaine, Minnesota)*
Makes 14 pancakes; serves 4–6

I think one of my Grandpa Larson's main goals in life was to feed as many pancakes to as many people as possible. If you were ever lucky enough to spend the weekend with him at his lake cabin near Danbury, Wisconsin, consider yourself blessed. Each night before bed, he could not help setting the table for breakfast, and making this batter to have it resting in the refrigerator, ready and waiting for everyone to roll out of bed and devour platefuls of these thin, delectable goodies. In his younger days, he was even known to hop on his motorcycle and zip through the woods to find the best wild blueberries. I make these often for my family and, while they drizzle on the maple syrup, I can never decide between spreading on butter and homemade strawberry-rhubarb jam, or sprinkling on brown sugar for a sweet, crunchy contrast. I usually end up alternating between the two.

2 eggs
2 cups milk
1 cup all-purpose flour
½ cup Bisquick® (or ½ cup flour and ½ teaspoon baking powder)
2 tablespoons confectioners' sugar
½ teaspoon salt
½ cup blueberries
Baking spray or oil, for cooking

In a medium bowl, beat the eggs, and add milk. Mix well. Add the dry ingredients, and mix with a whisk until fairly smooth. Let stand for 5 minutes. Place a non-stick or cast-iron skillet over medium-high heat. Once pan is very hot, spray with a little non-stick cooking spray or add a bit of oil. Pour about ¼ cup of batter into the hot pan. Sprinkle with a few blueberries. When some of the bubbles on top of the batter have popped, and the edges look brown, flip to the other side and cook for 1 more minute. These pancakes are very thin, and one side should be deep golden brown, and the other side should be speckled with brown. Serve with butter and maple syrup, or rolled up with butter and brown sugar or jelly. (These pancakes can be reheated in foil in the oven or under a paper towel in the microwave.)

Chef's Tip

For a shortcut, mix the dry ingredients together ahead of time and store in a plastic zip-top

Oat, Buckwheat, and Flaxseed Waffles

Julie Smoragiewicz *(Rapid City, South Dakota)*
Yields 9 large waffles

Eating local, healthy foods begins with a hearty breakfast. These waffles contain South Dakota flaxseed, Black Hills honey, and local cage-free eggs. As a shortcut, the grains can be ground in advance, mixed, and stored in the refrigerator or freezer so they are ready when needed.

Whole-Grain Waffle Mix

3 cups old-fashioned rolled oats
2 cups whole buckwheat groats
1 cup flaxseed
2 teaspoons baking powder

Waffles

⅔ cup grain mix
1 whole egg
1 egg white
½ teaspoon pure vanilla
⅓ banana, mashed
1 tablespoon honey

Whole-Grain Waffle Mix

Grind the oats, buckwheat, and flaxseed in a coffee or spice mill. Combine with baking powder, and store in a sealed container in the refrigerator or freezer.

Waffles

Preheat the waffle iron. Whisk the whole egg, egg white, vanilla, banana, and honey. Combine with ⅔ cup of whole-grain waffle mix.

Pour the batter onto a heated and prepared waffle iron. Allow the waffle to bake until lightly browned. Prepare all of the waffles at once, place in a sealed container, and reheat as needed in a toaster oven.

If desired, top with fresh berries, sliced bananas, and maple syrup.

Chef's Tip

For gluten-free waffles, use gluten-free oats, and replace buckwheat with gluten-free waffle baking mix.

For egg-free waffles, replace the egg and egg white with ⅓ cup of plain yogurt.

Kale Hash

Andrea Ratulowski *(Hilliard, Ohio)*
Serves 2

> Most Americans—including myself—have enjoyed a warm helping of breakfast hash, typically made with browned beef, eggs and potatoes. I, however, can honestly say that I have never had a hearty hash made with the nutritious, over-sized, dark green leaves of kale. Full of folic acid and iron, this ingredient will be a great start to anyone's day.
>
> *Story by Chef Nicole*

Potatoes

2 Idaho potatoes, scrubbed and cut into bite-sized cubes
½ tablespoon olive oil (see Chef's Tips on blended oil, page 309)
¼ teaspoon salt and freshly cracked black pepper
½ teaspoon garlic powder
½ teaspoon chile powder

Eggs

1 tablespoon plus 2 teaspoons olive oil, divided
4 eggs, beaten
½ onion, diced
½ green pepper, diced
¼ teaspoon salt and freshly cracked black pepper
1 large bunch kale, stemmed and chopped
¼–½ cup chicken stock (or vegetable stock; see Index, page 343)
½ teaspoon garlic powder
½ teaspoon chile powder

Potatoes

Preheat an oven to 425°F. Line a baking sheet with foil, and spray with nonstick spray or oil. In a large mixing bowl, toss the potatoes, olive oil, salt, pepper, garlic powder, and chile powder. Place the potatoes on the lined (with a silicon mat or aluminum foil) baking sheet in a single layer, and place in the oven. Bake until browned and crispy (about 20 to 25 minutes).

Eggs

In a sauté pan, heat 2 teaspoons of olive oil over medium heat. Add in eggs, and scramble, cooking until just about done. Remove the eggs from the pan and set aside. Add 1 tablespoon of olive oil, and add in the onions and peppers. Sprinkle with salt and pepper, and sauté for about 2 minutes. Add in the kale, and sauté for about 5 minutes. (If the kale still needs to cook, but the pan is getting dry, add in some of the stock a little at a time.) Season the kale mixture with garlic powder and chile powder. When the potatoes are cooked through, remove them from the oven. Add eggs and potatoes in with the kale mixture, and combine. Spoon into large bowls and serve.

Summer Corn Chowder

Andrea Ratulowski *(Hilliard, Ohio)*
Serves 10

One thing that I love is soup. In fact, I love soups, chilis, and stews so much that I could probably eat them every day except perhaps a few really hot summer days, when all that I want to eat are ice cubes).

I have been experimenting with fresh corn a lot this summer. While corn on the cob will always be a favorite, fresh corn can be used in so many other applications, too. I have found it incredibly fun to do different things with the corn that I am getting from the farmers markets this year. Ohio sweet corn is amazing.

Once you remove the corn from the cob, it can be used in salsas, salads, or simply sautéed in a touch of butter. Each experiment always leads to the next one, and then the next one.

My friend Rose had created a corn chowder this summer, and it looked delicious. My husband Scott has had corn chowder as an appetizer on occasion when we have gone out to dinner. I knew that I could create a lovely corn chowder recipe full of vegetables and accentuating the fresh summer corn, and this is the one.

1 large baking potato (Russet or Idaho), cut into bite-sized pieces
Olive oil, for sautéing and roasting potatoes
½ medium onion, diced
2 carrots, diced
1 large zucchini, diced
1 clove garlic
1 green pepper, diced
1 chipotle pepper plus 1 tablespoon adobo sauce
4 ears corn, kernels only (see Chef's Tips on corn, page 322)
1½–2 quarts chicken stock
1 (15 oz.) can white beans (preferably Great Northern or cannellini)

2½ teaspoons garlic powder

1 teaspoon chile powder

Salt and freshly cracked black pepper, to taste

Preheat an oven to 400°F and line a baking sheet with foil. Then spray with olive oil or nonstick spray. Place potatoes on the baking sheet, lightly toss in some light olive oil, and sprinkle with a touch of salt and pepper. Bake until they are crispy on the outside (about 30 minutes). Remove from oven.

In a large soup pot, heat some olive oil (about 2 tablespoons) over medium heat. Add in the onion, carrot, zucchini, garlic, and peppers. Sauté for about 2 to 3 minutes until they start to soften.

Add in half of the corn, and stir. Add the chicken stock and half of the roasted potatoes. Bring to a simmer, and simmer until all the vegetables have cooked and are soft (carrots take the longest). Once all the vegetables have been cooked, turn the heat to low, and use an immersion blender to blend the soup until the vegetables break down and the soup starts to become creamy. Add in the beans along with the rest of the corn and potatoes. Bring back to a simmer, and cook until the potatoes and beans are warmed through. Season with garlic powder, chile powder, and salt and pepper to taste. Ladle into large soup bowls and serve immediately.

Nasturtium-Chive Potato Soup with Herby Croutons

Jamie Stoneham *(Gorman Heritage Farm, Evendale, Ohio)*
Serves 4

Each month at our farm, we teach cooking classes that showcase our produce and meat. We like to include history, nutrition, folklore, cultivation, and storage of all of the main ingredients we use. We always go out into our gardens, harvest the ingredients, and talk about different substitutions that you could use if you do not have specific ingredients. For our November, 2010, session, we taught a "Cooking with Herbs" class. Many people are accustomed to cooking with traditional herbs like basil, thyme, and rosemary, but we wanted to show people that there are many herbs in our gardens that we might not even know are herbs, such as nasturtium (a type of watercress). This is a great recipe for a cool fall or early winter night, when the nasturtium leaves have not frosted yet, and you have potatoes in your root cellar.

Soup

2 tablespoons unsalted butter
½ sweet onion, finely chopped
5 medium potatoes, unpeeled and chopped
30–40 nasturtium leaves, stems removed (harvest only the smaller, younger leaves)
3 cups chicken broth
1 cup water
1¼ cups milk
1 bay leaf
2 tablespoons chopped fresh chives
Salt and freshly cracked black pepper, to taste

Croutons

3 tablespoons olive oil

2 cloves garlic, minced

2 teaspoons chopped fresh thyme

1 teaspoon chopped fresh rosemary leaves

4 cups (¾-inch) whole-wheat bread cubes

Salt and freshly cracked black pepper, to taste

Soup

Melt butter in a preheated soup pan on medium heat, and sauté onions until browned. Add the potatoes and nasturtium leaves to the pan until the leaves wilt (about 5 minutes). Add broth, water, milk, and bay leaf. Add salt and pepper to taste, and bring to a rolling boil.

Cover and simmer gently until the potatoes are tender (about 10 to 15 minutes). Add chives, remove the bay leaf, and puree until smooth. Top with herby croutons and nasturtium blossoms.

Croutons

Preheat an oven to 325°F.

Heat oil in a heavy, medium-sized skillet over medium heat. Add garlic, thyme, and rosemary; sauté until fragrant (about 1 minute). Remove from the heat. Add bread cubes to the skillet, and toss to coat.

Spread out the bread cubes on a rimmed baking sheet. Sprinkle with salt and pepper. Bake just until the croutons are golden, stirring occasionally (about 15 minutes). Makes 4 cups.

Wild Rice-Cranberry Soup

Lynn Elliott *(Way-Cool Cooking School, Eden Prairie, Minnesota)*
Serves 4

> Minnesota is known for being the land of 10,000 lakes. Around those beautiful lakes, wild rice grows and is a favorite to be served as a side dish or in a soup. Wild rice has a wonderful nutty flavor and, when it is paired with cranberries in this delicious soup, the flavors marry together wonderfully to create the perfect combination on a cold Minnesota day.

½ stick (¼ cup) unsalted butter
1 carrot, finely minced
1 celery stalk, finely minced
½ cup finely minced onion
3 tablespoons all-purpose flour
3 cups chicken stock (substitute vegetable stock; see Index, page 343)
1½ cups cooked wild rice
½ cup dried cranberries
1 cup milk or half-and-half
2 tablespoons sherry
Salt and freshly cracked black pepper, to taste

Melt butter in a pan over medium heat. Add carrot, celery, and onion; cook and stir until the carrot is tender (about 8 minutes).

Sprinkle flour over the vegetables, stir until smooth, and gradually add the stock, whisking constantly to prevent lumps. Increase the heat and stir until the soup is thickened (about 5 minutes). Stir in cooked rice and cranberries. Reduce the heat and simmer, stirring occasionally, until the cranberries are soft and plump (about 15 minutes).

Stir in the remaining ingredients. Season with salt and pepper. The soup should keep for 3 days in a refrigerator.

Chef's Tip

To cook wild rice, first rinse in a strainer under cold running water. Bring 2 cups of water, ½ cup of rice, and ½ teaspoon of salt to boil over medium-high heat. Reduce heat, cover, and simmer until the rice kernels open and are slightly chewy (about 45-55 minutes). Drain well. Makes 1½ cups of cooked rice.

Chilled Pinot Noir and Door County Cherry Soup

Chef Terri Milligan *(Inn at Kristofer's, Sister Bay, Wisconsin)*
Serves 8

> Door County cherries are sour cherries, so sweetening is required for this soup. If fresh cherries are not available, substitute with frozen cherries. Be careful when purchasing frozen cherries, as some are frozen with sugar already in them. These presweetened cherries are fine to use in this recipe, but make sure to reduce the additional sugar accordingly.

2½ pounds cherries, pitted (may substitute frozen cherries, thawed)
1¼ cups granulated sugar (or to taste)
Approximately 2½ cups apple or cherry juice
2 cups pinot noir wine
2 tablespoons arrowroot powder or cornstarch (see Chef's Tips on slurry, page 322)
⅓ cup cold water
1 teaspoon ground cloves
½ teaspoon freshly ground nutmeg

Place the pitted cherries and sugar in a medium soup pot. Add enough juice to just cover the cherries. Stir to combine. Add the wine. Bring the soup to a simmer. Simmer for approximately 30 minutes. Taste the soup; if not sweet enough, add additional sugar.

Remove the soup from the heat. Using either an immersion blender or a food processor, puree the soup. (The soup will not be completely pureed; there will be some bits of cherries in the finished soup.)

Place the soup back on the stove and bring to a simmer. To make a slurry, in a separate bowl, dissolve arrowroot or cornstarch in cold water. While slowly pouring the slurry into the soup, continue to whisk until the soup slightly thickens (add additional slurry, if necessary). Add the ground cloves and nutmeg.

Cool the soup to room temperature, and then place in the refrigerator to chill. The soup should chill overnight, if possible.

Serve the soup in a soup bowl or over-sized martini glass.

Chef's Tip

If making this as a chilled soup, use arrowroot powder instead of cornstarch when thickening. Arrowroot creates a soup that is clearer, while cornstarch tends to create a finished soup that is a bit cloudy.

Michigan Cherry Salad with Maple Balsamic Vinaigrette

Eric Blotkamp *(Mirepoix Cooking School, Royal Oak, Michigan)*

Serves 4

Salad

1 (10 oz.) bag spring-mix lettuce
6 ounces Maytag bleu cheese
6 ounces Michigan dried cherries
5 ounces toasted, slivered almonds (see Chef's Tips on nuts and seeds, page 318)

Vinaigrette

⅓ cup Dijon mustard
½ cup maple syrup
¼ cup raspberry balsamic vinegar
¼ cup white balsamic vinegar
1 tablespoon fresh tarragon or 1 teaspoon dried tarragon
¼ teaspoon white pepper
1 teaspoon kosher salt
1 cup blended oil (see Chef's Tips on blended oil, page 309)
Salt and freshly cracked black pepper, to taste

Salad

Combine all the ingredients in a large bowl and set aside. Before serving, drizzle with vinaigrette.

Vinaigrette

To make vinaigrette, see Chef's Tips on emulsification, page 320. Adjust the salt and pepper to taste. Yields 1½ cups.

BLT Bites

Brandon O'Dell *(Friend that Cooks Home Chef Service, Wichita, Kansas)*

Serves 10

> This is a very simple stuffed cherry tomato recipe that resembles the popular flavor of BLT (bacon, lettuce, and tomato) sandwiches. These tomatoes add beauty to any food table, and are incredibly flavorful, while still being very simple.

1 pint cherry tomatoes
¼ pound crisp cooked bacon
1 cup parsley
½ cup mayonnaise

Start by using a sharp paring knife to cut a flat base on the bottom of each cherry tomato (do not cut off too much, but just enough to give the tomato a small, flat base). With the same knife inverted downward, cut out the stem area of the tomato, creating a circular opening ¾ the diameter of the tomato, and hollowing out at least half of the inside of the tomato without cutting to the bottom of the tomato. Place the tomatoes to the side to drain while you prepare the filling.

Break the bacon into pieces by hand and place in a food processor. Add the parsley and mayonnaise. Blend until all the pieces are small enough to be piped through a ⅜-inch opening. If the ingredients seem too dry to pipe, add mayonnaise until the filling is the correct mixture.

Put the filling mixture into a pastry bag, or create a makeshift pastry bag by putting the mixture into a 1-gallon plastic storage bag, and cutting a corner to make an opening a little less than ½ inch. Twist top, pipe the mixture into the openings of the tomatoes, and chill until it is time to serve.

Black Bean and Sweet Corn Salsa

Melanie Foster *(Blaine, Minnesota)*
Makes 8 cups

> One of my favorite food combinations is chips and salsa, and I do not think that I am alone in this. I made four batches of this salsa for my brother's summer wedding, and there was not a bite leftover. In Minnesota, corn is a seasonal delicacy. We eat it off the cob as much as possible, when we can get it fresh at the farm stands in the late summer. I crave this salsa more often than fresh corn, so I am glad that frozen corn works so well in this recipe. Sometimes, I will chop up a fresh mango or peach for a sweet addition. You really do not even need the chips with this—just grab a spoon.

¼ cup fresh lime juice (approximately 2 limes)
¼ cup fresh cilantro, chopped
2 tablespoons olive oil
4 teaspoons canned chipotle chiles in adobo sauce, minced
1 tablespoon red wine vinegar
1 teaspoon cumin
2 (16 oz.) cans black beans, rinsed and drained
1½ cups fresh corn kernels (see Chef's Tips on corn, page 322)
1½ cups red onion, diced (1 medium-small)
1½ cups tomato, diced (3 medium)
1 green bell pepper, seeded and diced
Salt and freshly cracked black pepper, to taste

Whisk the first six ingredients together in a large bowl. Stir in the remaining ingredients, and season to taste with salt and pepper. Chill until serving.

Pistachio Lovers' Catfish

Paul and Jayn Parenti *(A Fare to Remember, Fayetteville, Arkansas)*

Serves 4

½ cup corn meal
½ cup pistachio nuts, toasted and ground (see Chef's Tips on nuts
and seeds, page 318)
4 (6 oz.) skinless, boneless catfish fillets
¼ cup canola or extra-virgin olive oil
Salt and freshly cracked pepper

Mix corn meal and pistachios in a bowl, setting aside. Season catfish
with salt and pepper, rub with olive oil, and dredge in the pistachio
mixture. Heat oil in a heavy sauté pan over high heat. Add the catfish fillets, and cook for 3½ to 4 minutes on the first side and 3 to 4
minutes on the second. Fillets can be held warm in a 200°F oven until
ready to serve. Or, you can place them into a baking dish, pour some
of the remaining olive oil from the pan over them, and cover the dish
with heavy plastic wrap. Then wrap the foil tightly around the plastic
so the fish never becomes dry.

Slightly Spicy and Seared Catfish

Paul and Jayn Parenti *(A Fare to Remember, Fayetteville, Arkansas)*

Serves 4

Seasoning Mix

2 tablespoons paprika

1½ tablespoons salt

1½ tablespoons garlic powder

1 tablespoon coarse ground black pepper

1 tablespoon onion powder

1 tablespoon oregano

1 tablespoon thyme

1½ teaspoons cayenne pepper

Butter Finishing Sauce

1 stick (½ cup) unsalted butter

1 tablespoon Seasoning Mix (see above)

1 lemon, zest and juice (see Chef's Tips on citrus zest, page 311)

1 tablespoon fresh parsley

Salt and freshly cracked pepper, to taste

Catfish

4 (7–8 oz.) skinless, boneless catfish fillets

¼ cup Seasoning Mix (see above)

½ cup extra-virgin olive oil

3 medium lemons, thinly sliced and divided

1 tablespoon fresh parsley, for garnish

Seasoning Mix

Mix together all the ingredients thoroughly. Mix can be stored in an airtight jar for several months.

Butter Finishing Sauce

Preheat an oven to 350°F. In a small saucepan, melt the butter on low heat, and add the seasoning mix, lemon zest and juice, parsley, salt, and pepper to taste. Keep warm on low heat on the stove top.

Catfish

Coat both sides of each fillet with 2 teaspoons of the seasoning mix. Heat the olive oil in a large, heavy-bottomed skillet over medium-high heat, Add the seasoned fillets to the hot skillet, and cook for 1½ minutes on each side to sear the fillets and caramelize the seasoning mix. Line the bottom of a baking dish large enough to fit all four fillets in a single layer with the slices of two lemons, and set aside. Carefully place the seared fish on top of the lemon slices. Pour half of the melted butter finishing sauce into the pan to deglaze the brown bits, stir for about a minute, and top the catfish with the mixture from the pan. Bake until fork-tender (about 10 to 14 minutes). Drizzle the remainder of the melted butter sauce over the fillets. Garnish with slices from one lemon and chopped parsley. Serve with jambalaya and white rice.

Halibut with Asparagus, Yukon Gold Potatoes, and Wild Mushrooms

Chef Terri Milligan *(Inn at Kristofer's, Sister Bay, Wisconsin)*

Serves 6

At the Inn at Kristofer's, we strive to use local ingredients. You cannot get any more local than the use of fresh ramps—I harvest them directly from my backyard. We make pesto and use it on pasta and bruschetta, and we also grill them and add them to a variety of dishes. This is one of my favorite recipes; it incorporates not only ramps, but also locally picked wild morel mushrooms and asparagus. My head chef Eric Thomas is my morel hunter. His locations are secrets even to me, and his "pay" for the morels is a couple of nice bottles of wine. Although I do not grow my own asparagus, I have something even better—a local farmer who comes directly to my back door daily during asparagus season. I buy it directly off his truck. It is picked in the morning, and on our dinner plates at night.

Luckily, morels and ramps coincide with the opening of the halibut season in Alaska. This favorite spring recipe includes wild halibut, ramps, and morels.

Potatoes
6 medium Yukon Gold potatoes, cleaned and skins on
Olive oil, as needed
Salt, to taste

Herb Vinaigrette (optional)
(See Chef's Tips on emulsification, page 320)
2 bunches cilantro and/or basil, cleaned
2 tablespoons rice wine vinegar
1 tablespoon honey
1 teaspoon lemon juice

2 cloves garlic, finely chopped

½-¾ cup blended oil (see Chef's Tips on blended oil, page 309)

Halibut

6 (6–7 oz.) pieces halibut, deboned

Asparagus-Mushroom Mixture

10 morel mushrooms, cleaned and sliced (or shiitake mushrooms)

12 asparagus spears, blanched and sliced into ½-inch pieces on the diagonal (see Note below)

12 ramps wild leeks, roughly chopped, then cleaned, including leaves (see Note below)

1½ pounds spinach, cleaned

Olive oil and/or butter, as needed

Salt and freshly cracked black pepper, to taste

Garnish

Arugula and/or asparagus spears or 6 ramps, grilled

Herb Vinaigrette (see Chef's Tips on emulsification, page 320)

Potatoes

Preheat the oven to 375°F. Line a baking sheet with parchment paper and lightly spray with non-stick cooking spray. Thinly slice the Yukon potatoes with a mandolin slicer, if possible. Place in a large bowl and toss with just enough olive oil to coat. Line the potatoes flat on the baking pan and sprinkle lightly with salt. Roast until lightly browned, but not overly crisp. Remove and cool. Can be made one day ahead and refrigerated.

Herb Vinaigrette (optional)

Bring a pot of water to a boil. Quickly blanch the herbs for about 10 seconds. Remove and rinse under cold water. Squeeze out the excess water (this will keep the herbs bright green).

Place in a blender. Add all the ingredients, except the oil. Pulse to blend. Add the oil in a slow, steady stream through the top of the blender while the blender is going (add just enough oil to create a thick vinaigrette). Taste and adjust the seasoning; then place in a container and refrigerate until ready to use (can be made a day ahead). Bring to room temperature for 10 minutes before using.

Halibut

You can either grill or pan-sear fish (and finish in the oven). If grilling the fish, brush the fish with the olive oil mixture and place, flesh-down-first, on the grill. After a few minutes, move the fish to a slight angle to get a nice grill-mark design. Flip the fish and grill on the other side. If searing on a stove, heat a sauté pan on medium. When hot, add just a small amount of olive oil to cover the bottom of the pan. Place the fish, flesh-side-down, in the pan. When the fish is slightly browned, flip the fish. Finish cooking the fish in a 350°F oven for about 2 to 3 minutes (depending on the size of the fillet).

Asparagus-Mushroom Mixture

While the fish is finishing in the oven or on the grill, finish the Yukon potato mixture. Heat a large sauté pan with just enough olive oil and/or butter to lightly coat the bottom. When hot, add the potatoes, wild mushrooms, asparagus, and half of the ramps. Cover and stir occasionally until the mushrooms are just cooked through (you may need to use two pans if you do not have a pan large enough). Add the spinach, cover, and cook until the spinach is just wilted.

Brush the remaining six ramps with olive oil and grill briefly to char (if you are not grilling the fish, sauté them whole in a sauté pan with a little olive oil).

Divide the potato-asparagus-mushroom mixture among six plates. Top each with a piece of the fish.

Garnish

Garnish with a small arugula bouquet and/or a few pieces of warmed asparagus and the grilled ramps. Garnish the plate with a drizzle of Herb Vinaigrette (optional).

Chef's Tip

The white part of leeks or whole scallions may be substituted for ramps. Cut leeks before washing to expose the center of the stalk. Place them in a colander and rinse well (this removes all of the dirt and grit, which are hidden within the layers of the leek).

To prepare asparagus, hold the stalk by each end and bend until the stalk snaps naturally. The asparagus will always break at the point where the asparagus is no longer tender and becomes extremely fibrous; discard this end. Only use the opposite end with the asparagus tip and tender part of the stalk.

Roasted or Grilled Halibut in a Tomato Jus with Corn Salsa and Morel Mushrooms

Chef Eric W. Lassiter *(Serenade Personal Chefs, Milwaukee, Wisconsin)*
Serves 2

Halibut
2 (6–8 oz.) halibut fillets, skin removed
Fresh lemon juice, to taste
Garlic powder, to taste
Old Bay® seasoning, to taste
Extra-virgin olive oil, to taste
Salt and freshly cracked black pepper, to taste

Corn Salsa
2 cobs sweet corn (see Chef's Tips on corn, page 322)
½ cup red onion, diced
¼-⅓ cup fresh basil, chiffonade
½ cup seeded and diced beefsteak tomato (see Chef's Tips on tomato concasse, page 321)
Honey, to taste
Red pepper flakes, to taste
Salt and freshly cracked black pepper, to taste

Tomato Jus
1 large ripe beefsteak tomato
Extra-virgin olive oil, as needed
½-¾ cup chicken or vegetable stock (see Index, page 343)
2 tablespoons chopped garlic
1 bay leaf (optional)
Unsalted butter, as needed
8 fresh morel mushrooms (dried can be rehydrated and substituted)
White truffle oil (optional)

Halibut

Season the halibut with salt and pepper, lemon juice, garlic powder, Old Bay® seasoning, and olive oil.

Corn Salsa

Steam, and then grill or broil the corn until the kernels begin to char/caramelize. Let cool. Cut the corn off the cob, and toss with the red onion, basil, and ½ cup of diced tomatoes. Drizzle with extra-virgin olive oil. Add honey, red pepper flakes, salt, and pepper to taste. Refrigerate. Adjust the seasonings before serving.

Preheat an oven to 425°F.

Tomato Jus

Rub the beefsteak tomato with olive oil, and roast for 15 to 20 minutes or until the skin begins to blister. Let cool slightly, and then place in a blender or food processor with the stock and garlic. Puree until smooth. Strain into a saucepan and bring it to a hard simmer (you may add a bay leaf at this point). Cover and keep warm.

In an oven-proof skillet, heat olive oil and butter over medium-high heat until the butter begins to brown. Add the halibut, skinned-side-up, and sear until you have a nice golden color (about 5 minutes). Turn the fillets, add the morels, and finish them in the oven (about 5 minutes more).

Ladle the tomato jus into a shallow bowl or soup plate, set the halibut in the center, and scatter the morels around the perimeter. Top with a spoonful of corn salsa. A drizzle of white truffle oil in the soup is also a nice touch.

Cedar Plank Grilled Salmon with Blackberry Wine Reduction and Fresh Blackberries

Julie Smoragiewicz *(Rapid City, South Dakota)*

Serves 4

> Salmon, available in Lake Oahe (Missouri River dam in the center of South Dakota), is perfect for grilling. Try this succulent salmon entrée using cedar planks, which keep the salmon from direct heat and add a smoky flavor to the dish. The cedar planks can be cleaned and used for several grilling sessions. This dish is elegant enough for guests and, if you keep a jar of the wine reduction on hand in your refrigerator, you can prepare this recipe any night of the week for your family—they will thank you.

1 cup blackberry wine (see Chef's Tips on reduction, page 310)
1 (1½ lb.) salmon fillet
1 cup blackberries
Grill seasoning (coarse salt, freshly cracked pepper, crushed coriander seed, and paprika)

Soak the cedar planks by placing them in a pan of water. Weigh down the planks to keep them submerged. Soak for at least 1 to 2 hours.

Pour wine into a shallow sauté pan. Bring the wine to a slow simmer. Simmer until the liquid is reduced to a syrup (this may take 1 to 1½ hours). Remove the reduction from the heat. The reduction can be made in advance and refrigerated until ready to use.

Preheat a grill and clean. Place the salmon fillet, skin-side-down, onto the cedar planks. Pour 2 teaspoons of the wine reduction into a small dish, and brush the salmon with the reduction. Sprinkle the salmon with grill seasoning.

Place the planks onto the hot grill. Close the grill and allow the salmon to cook for 20 to 30 minutes, depending on the grill temperature. Salmon is done when the flesh is flaky, yet still moist, and the temperature registers at 135°F.

Remove the salmon from the plank and place on a serving platter. The salmon can be served with the skin or the skin can be left on the plank. Cover with foil until ready to serve (the salmon will continue to cook, and the temperature will rise another 5 to 10°F).

While the salmon is resting, place the wine reduction in a saucepan over medium heat, and add a handful of berries. Press the berries to release their juices and stir.

Add the remaining berries, stir to heat, and pour over the salmon.

Serve immediately. You can also replace the blackberry wine with loganberry liqueur and the blackberries with loganberries. As an alternative, place the salmon on a bed of greens for a main-course salad.

Springfield-Style Cashew Chicken

Jessica Kohler *(Columbia, Missouri)*
Serves 4

> If you are not familiar with Springfield, Missouri, there are two words that are almost synonymous with it—"Cashew chicken." There are tons of Chinese restaurants in Springfield. It is a running joke that, on every block, you are sure to find a church (being in the Bible Belt), a liquor store, and a Chinese restaurant. Every one of them serves cashew chicken.
>
> Each restaurant has put their own spin on it, so the decision when we visit is not, "Where to go for dinner?," so much as what kind of cashew chicken that we are in the mood for. When we are not in Missouri, we do what any homesick couple would do; we make it ourselves.

4 skinless, boneless chicken breasts

2 cups all-purpose flour (or wheat flour)

1 teaspoon seasoning salt

3 tablespoons cornstarch, divided

1 egg, beaten

2 tablespoons water

2 cups peanut oil, for frying (see Chef's Tips on blended oil, page 309)

2 cups chicken broth (see Index, page 343)

1½ tablespoons oyster sauce

1 tablespoon sugar

2 tablespoons soy sauce

1 teaspoon white pepper

2 cups cashew halves (see Chef's Tips on seeds and nuts, page 318)

2 cups rice, prepared

2 tablespoons chopped chives, for garnish

Wash and cut the chicken breasts into 1-inch pieces. In a shallow dish or bowl, mix together the flour, seasoning salt, and 1 tablespoon of the cornstarch. In another dish or bowl, beat the egg and mix with water. Dip the chicken pieces into the flour mixture, next, the eggs, and then the flour mixture, again. Heat peanut oil in a large skillet and deep-fry the coated chicken in the hot oil for 3 to 4 minutes. Drain on paper towels.

Meanwhile, while frying the chicken, heat broth to boiling in a medium saucepan. Add oyster sauce, sugar, soy sauce, and white pepper, and return to boiling. To make a slurry, mix in a small bowl the remaining cornstarch mixture and a small amount of cold water until well incorporated. Add the cornstarch mixture to the broth a little at a time until the broth thickens, and continue stirring, then cooking for another 5 minutes over medium-low heat.

Preheat an oven to 200°F. Place cashews on a baking sheet, and bake for about 5 minutes. Pour the sauce over the fried chicken and prepared rice, and top with cashews and green onion. Serve with soy sauce.

Michigan Cider-Glazed Chicken Breast

Eric Blotkamp *(Mirepoix Cooking School, Royal Oak, Michigan)*
Serves 4

4 Amish skinless, boneless chicken breasts
Frying oil (see Chef's Tips on blended oil, page 309)
1 quart Michigan apple cider
8 ounces chicken stock (see Index, page 343)
4 ounces cornstarch
4 ounces cold water
Salt and freshly cracked black pepper, to taste

Preheat an oven to 350°F.

Heat a large, straight-sided pan over medium-high heat. Season the chicken breasts with salt and pepper (see Chef's Tips on seasoning, page 320). Pour enough blended oil to coat the bottom of the pan. Sear the chicken, breast-side-down, until golden brown; then flip over and repeat. Remove the chicken and reserve on a sheet pan. Bring the cider and chicken stock to a low boil.

To make a slurry, combine in a separate bowl the cornstarch and cold water until incorporated. Continuously whisk while adding the slurry to the cider and chicken stock until it is the preferred thickness (it should coat the back of a spoon).

Drizzle some sauce over the chicken, and place it in the oven for 15 minutes or until chicken is fully cooked with an internal temperature of 165°F.

Chicken-Mushroom Mozzarella

Melanie Foster *(Blaine, Minnesota)*

Serves 4

This recipe is so easy and delicious; it is one of my family's favorite go-to dinners. Make sure that you pick up some crusty bread to serve alongside for sopping up all the juices. Morel mushrooms, the Minnesota state vegetable, bring this dish to new heights. Yet, as they are extremely seasonal and hard to find, any combination of mushrooms works—even button mushrooms. Just be sure that they are fresh and not canned.

1 tablespoon butter
1 tablespoon olive oil
8 ounces morel mushrooms (any mixture of mushrooms or single variety), wiped clean and sliced
1 pound skinless, boneless chicken breasts
2 cups shredded mozzarella cheese
Salt and freshly cracked black pepper, to taste

Heat butter and oil in a skillet over medium-high heat. Add mushrooms, and quickly toss to coat. Let sizzle without turning until golden on the bottom (about 5 minutes). Toss again and sprinkle with salt and pepper. Place the chicken breasts on top. Sprinkle generously with more salt and pepper, lower the heat to medium-low, and cover. Cook for about 8 minutes, turn chicken over, season the other side, cover, and cook for another 8 minutes or so until the juices run clear when pierced with a knife or fork. Spread cheese over the top and cover until melted.

Tildy Stew

Susan Gordy *(Cincinnati, Ohio)*
Serves 6–8

> The name for Tildy Stew comes from Abraham Lincoln's stepsister Matilda Johnson Hall. While working at Lincoln Log Cabin, I created this stew after being inspired from several 1840s-era cookbooks. The stew was very popular with the staff and volunteers at the living history site, and, after time, just became known as "Tildy Stew."

1 pound bulk pork sausage
5–6 white potatoes, sliced
2–3 yellow onions, sliced
2–3 green or yellow peppers, sliced
1 pound sauerkraut
½ cup water

Brown and drain the sausage. In a covered Dutch oven or casserole dish, layer half of the ground sausage, half of the potatoes, half of the onions, half of the peppers, and half of the sauerkraut. Continue layering until you run out of fillings, ending with the sauerkraut. Add water, cover, and bake at 325°F until the potatoes are done (approximately 1 hour).

Grilled Flank Steak and Roasted Beet Salad

Julie Smoragiewicz *(Rapid City, South Dakota)*
Serves 4

> This dish features our local producers and retailers, who provide us with lean and natural grass-fed beef, golden beets, and fresh greens. These are all available locally during the winter. Not only do our local producers offer the freshest foods possible, but their success helps to strengthen our local economy. Farm-to-table eating is a win-win for everyone.

3 medium golden beets, diced
1 pound flank steak
2–3 teaspoons grill seasoning (coarse salt, freshly cracked pepper, crushed coriander seed, and paprika)
1 pint cherry tomatoes
8 cups fresh greens
¼ red onion, thinly sliced
2–3 tablespoons balsamic glaze (see Chef's Tips on reduction, page 310) or balsamic vinaigrette (see Chef's Tips on emulsification, page 320)
Olive oil, as needed
Sea salt and freshly cracked pepper, to taste

Preheat the oven to 425°F.

Wash the beets, leaving them whole. Toss the beets with olive oil, and sprinkle with sea salt and pepper. Place each beet into a pouch of foil, and then place the pouches onto a shallow sheet pan and roast for 30 to 35 minutes until fork-tender. When ready, remove from the oven and set aside.

Sprinkle both sides of the steak with grill seasoning. Grill the steak for 2 minutes on each side to sear the meat. Lower the coals and cook until the steak is medium-rare to medium. Remove the steak from the grill, cover, and allow the meat to rest for 10 minutes.

Remove the beets from the foil (be sure to wear gloves and wipe off the beet skins). Dice or slice as desired.

While the steak rests, place a handful of cherry tomatoes over 2 cups of greens. Top with diced beets. Thinly slice the steak across the grain. Place the steak slices over the salad. Top with red onion slices, and drizzle with balsamic glaze.

Chef's Tip

As an alternative, consider adding bleu cheese crumbles, hard-boiled egg wedges, and sliced avocado.

Braised Beef Ragu

Brandon O'Dell *(Friend that Cooks Home Chef Service, Wichita, Kansas)*
Serves 4–6

Here in the Midwest, we love beef. While the flavor of beef can be best showcased with simple preparations like grilling with a light amount of salt and pepper, this recipe uses a braising technique that will allow you to cook any cut of meat—even the toughest of the tough—and have it turn out as tender as can be.

My Beef Ragu is a one-pot wonder that wows every time. The flavors are sophisticated enough for the toughest critic, and basic enough for any meat-and-potato eater.

1 teaspoon salt
1 teaspoon freshly cracked black pepper
½ cup all-purpose flour
1½ pounds beef roast, cut into 1½- by 1½-inch chunks (any cut will do)
2 tablespoons extra-virgin olive oil
1 (375 ml.) bottle burgundy cooking wine
10 ounces mushrooms, sliced
1 large white onion, diced large
6 cloves garlic, finely chopped
10 ripe roma tomatoes, cored, peeled, seeded, and cut into chunks (see Chef's Tips on tomato concasse, page 321)
2 sprigs fresh rosemary
2 sprigs fresh thyme
¼ cup chopped fresh parsley

Preheat a 4-quart pot or Dutch oven on medium heat. In a large mixing bowl, combine the salt, pepper, and flour. Lightly coat your beef chunks, one by one, in the flour mixture. Shake off the excess flour and set aside. Add the olive oil to the pot, and then crank the heat up to high. Sear a few pieces of beef at a time, set them aside on a plate, and continue the process until each piece is well-browned. Return them to the pot and add wine.

Bring the wine to a simmer, and then add the mushrooms, onions, garlic, tomatoes, and herbs, and cover (you can either strip the herbs from their stems and chop them before adding, or add them whole and remove the stems when it is finished cooking).

Cover and simmer for 2½ hours. Be sure that the liquid is not boiling and you have a tight-fitting lid. If your lid does not fit tight enough or your heat is too high, you may have to add water to the pot part-way through the cooking process. When the meat is nice and tender, remove the pot from the heat and stir in parsley.

Serve over pasta, egg noodles, potatoes, or any type of rice.

German Potato Strudel

Julie Smoragiewicz *(Rapid City, South Dakota)*
Serves 4

This hearty Dakota Territory dish has been a family tradition for generations. My grandmother Olivia prepared this hearty meal for the neighboring farmers and friends who helped my grandfather with crops each harvest season. Whenever I visited the vast, open prairie, strudel with German sausage was one of my favorite meals. Shortly after I had married, we visited my grandmother, and she patiently taught me to make strudel and many other traditional family recipes. Those lessons were a wonderful gift.

1⅛ cups milk
1 egg
2 teaspoons sugar
½ teaspoons salt
2½ teaspoons yeast
1½ sticks unsalted butter, softened and divided
3 cups all-purpose flour
1 large onion, sliced
2 large potatoes, chopped into bite-sized pieces

Warm milk in a saucepan. The milk should be comfortable to touch, but still warm.

Pour the milk into the bowl of a stand mixer fitted with a dough hook or into a bread machine. Add egg, sugar, salt, and yeast. Add 4 tablespoons of butter, and mix for 1 minute.

Add flour. Knead for 10 minutes until the dough begins to form. Place the dough in a buttered bowl, and cover loosely with plastic wrap or a kitchen towel. Set aside in a warm location for 1 hour or until the dough has doubled in size.

Butter a clean counter top. Using buttered hands, spread the dough into a large rectangle. Pick up the dough at each corner and stretch to thin the dough. Repeat until the dough is approximately 20- by 20-inches and ¼-inch thick.

Spread the additional 4 tablespoons of butter over the dough. Cut the dough in half horizontally so you have two pieces, each approximately 10- by 20-inches. Roll dough toward you, and stretch the dough roll so the dough is no thicker than 1½ inches. Cut the dough roll into 1-inch pieces.

Place 2 tablespoons of butter in each of two (10- to 12-inch) lidded pans, and melt over low heat.

Add half of the onions and half of the potatoes to each pan. Add 1 to 1½ cups of water to each pan, just enough to cover most of the onions and potatoes.

Place the dough slices, cut-end-up, on top of the onions and potatoes, cover tightly, and cook over medium heat for approximately 25 minutes. The lid must stay on until the strudel is finished; resist the temptation to open the lid. Opening the lid will cause the steam to escape, and the strudel will become dry and tough.

You will know that the strudel is done when the sound of cooking potatoes and onions will change as they finish cooking. The sound of bubbling water will be replaced with butter sizzling on the bottom of the pan, and the strudel and potatoes beginning to brown. If you are using a glass lid, look for the absence of simmering water.

Serve with German sausage such as bratwurst and brown gravy. If there are any leftovers, cut each piece of strudel in 2 to 3 pieces and fry in butter until golden brown.

Wild Mushroom Pasta

Chef Eric W. Lassiter *(Serenade Personal Chefs, Milwaukee, Wisconsin)*
Serves 4

> Wisconsin's parkland and temperate climate make it a wonderful place to go mushroom hunting.

½ cup yellow onion, diced
2 tablespoons garlic, minced (see Chef's Tips on garlic, page 314)
Extra-virgin olive oil, as needed
4 cups chicken stock, divided (see Index, page 343)
6 ounces dried porcini mushrooms
6 ounces dried shitake mushrooms
2 cups baby portobello mushrooms, chopped
2 teaspoons herbs de Provence
¼-⅓ cup chicken demi-glace
1 pound fusilli pasta, cooked
Feta and Parmesan cheese, to garnish
Crushed red pepper flakes, to taste
Dry red wine, to taste
Salt and freshly cracked black pepper, to taste

Lightly sauté onion and garlic in olive oil over medium heat until the onion is translucent. Bring 2 cups of chicken stock to a boil, reduce to a simmer, and add dried mushrooms. Allow to reconstitute. Drain and reserve the liquid. Add baby portobellos to the onion-garlic mixture, and sauté until soft. Add the reconstituted mushrooms, and toss to combine. Add the remaining 2 cups of chicken stock/mushroom broth, ½ cup at a time, until you get the volume that you want (for more intense mushroom flavor, cook the portobellos less, add stock/mushroom broth, and reduce). Adjust the flavor with salt and pepper, herbs de Provence, chicken demi-glace, red pepper flakes, and dry red wine. Combine with pasta and serve, garnished with feta and Parmesan cheese.

Sweet Potato Dumplings (Gnocchi) with Sage-Buttered Apples

Julie Smoragiewicz *(Rapid City, South Dakota)*
Serves 8–10

These hearty and savory dumplings reflect the flavors of the prairie and harvest ingredients. This recipe was developed for young ranch families.

2 pounds sweet potatoes
1 egg plus 1 egg yolk, whisked
4 tablespoons unsalted butter, softened
½ teaspoon salt
½ teaspoon freshly ground black pepper
3 cups plus ½ cup all-purpose flour
1 stick (½ cup) unsalted butter
4 shallots or 1 medium-sized mild onion, finely chopped
4–5 leaves fresh sage
4 apples, peeled, cored, and sliced

Bake the sweet potatoes at 425°F for an hour or until fork-tender. Remove the potatoes from the oven and cool to room temperature. Peel the potatoes and press through a potato ricer or medium sieve.

Place egg and egg yolk in a food processor that is fitted with a dough blade. Add softened butter, salt, pepper, and sweet potatoes, and combine. Add flour, ¾ cup at a time, and pulse just enough to incorporate (over-processing can result in tough dumplings/gnocchi).

Remove the dough from the processor and form into a large ball. Dust in flour as needed. Allow the dough to rest for 30 minutes.

Divide the dough into baseball-sized pieces and roll into a rope about ½-inch in diameter. Cut the rope into ½-inch-long pieces. Dust in flour. Using the tines of a fork, press down on the small pieces of dough, pulling the fork toward you as you press down. The dough will curl with the fork marks inside the curl. Fold the curl backward so the curl is on the outside. This step deviates from traditional eastern European dumplings and follows the Italian gnocchi preparation to create more surface area on the dumplings, allowing them to cook more quickly and absorb more of the sage-butter sauce.

At this point, the dumplings can be placed in a single layer on a large sheet pan and frozen. Place the frozen dumplings in a zip bag and return to the freezer.

Melt one stick of butter in a large frying pan. Add shallots, and sauté until translucent. Add chopped sage leaves (reserve a few for garnish), either whole or in thin slices, and apple slices. Sauté until the apples are tender.

While the apples are sautéing, bring water and ½ teaspoon of salt to a rapid boil. Add the dumplings. Once they have floated to the surface, cook for another 3 to 4 minutes. Remove the dumplings with a slotted spoon and stir into the sautéed apples. Garnish with the remaining sage leaves.

Roasted Vegetable Polenta Pie

Emily Segal *(Inspired by Indiana; resides in Israel)*
Serves 8

Polenta

5 cups vegetable stock (see Index, page 343)
1 teaspoon salt
½ teaspoon black pepper
2 teaspoons dried oregano
1¾ cups corn meal
1 tablespoon barley malt syrup (optional)

Topping

½ cup tomato sauce (see "Marinara Sauce" in Index, page 337)
2 teaspoons minced olives, green or black
2 tablespoons minced garlic
¼ cup minced fresh herbs (such as basil and oregano)
1 teaspoon sweet paprika
1 teaspoon sumac (optional)
½ eggplant, sliced in thin rounds
1 tomato, sliced in thin rounds
4 mushrooms, thinly sliced
1–2 tablespoons olive oil

Polenta

Bring the broth and spices to a boil. Slowly stir in the cornmeal and syrup. Whisk over low heat for about 8 minutes. The mixture will become thick and aromatic. Remove from the heat. Lightly oil a 10-inch spring-form pan, and press the polenta smoothly and evenly across the bottom. Set aside.

Preheat the broiler to high.

Topping

On top of the polenta base, spread the tomato sauce, and then sprinkle the olives, fresh herbs, and garlic. Layer the vegetables in a circular fashion, and sprinkle with the spices, if using. Drizzle with olive oil, place in the oven, and broil for 10 to 12 minutes until the top is browning. Let cool for a few minutes, and then release the outer ring, slice, and serve.

Chef's Tip

This can also be made ahead and served cold.

Maple Balsamic-Glazed Squash

Jamie Stoneham *(Gorman Heritage Farm, Evendale, Ohio)*
Serves 6

Butternut squash is a hard-shell squash similar to pumpkins and gourds. Commonly, these cool weather gems have a tender, sweet center that is delightful when roasted. We like to pair our Nasturtium-Chive Potato Soup (page 150) with this dish, because the bite of the nasturtium and the starch of the potatoes blend beautifully.

Squash

2 tablespoons unsalted butter
2 medium-sized butternut squash, sliced and cubed ½-inch thick
6-8 ounces bleu cheese, crumbled

Glaze

⅓ cup balsamic vinegar
¼ cup maple syrup
1 tablespoon minced fresh rosemary leaves
2 teaspoons Dijon mustard
½ teaspoon salt
½ teaspoon freshly cracked black pepper
2 cloves garlic, paste or minced (see Chef's Tips on garlic, page 314)
2½ tablespoons blended oil (see Chef's Tips on blended oil, page 309)

Butternut Squash

Melt butter in a preheated, stainless steel saucepan on medium heat just until it starts to brown and smells nutty (be careful, because the butter will very easily burn during this stage).

Add in cubed butternut squash, and sauté, covered, for 15 minutes or until it is beginning to become fork-tender.

Glaze

Mix together all the ingredients and whisk until combined.

Mix the glaze into the saucepan with the squash, and sauté for 10 more minutes or until soft, but not mushy. Stir occasionally. Serve on top of a bed of pasta, couscous, or rice. Top with bleu cheese crumbles.

Soybean Succotash

Emily Segal *(Inspired by Indiana; resides in Israel)*
Serves 6

> Although Indiana soy is not generally grown for use as edamame, these healthy green soybeans add a wonderful and protein-rich twist on traditional Indiana succotash.

2½ cups shelled edamame
3 ears fresh corn on the cob or 2½ cups frozen corn, thawed (see Chef's Tips on corn, page 322)
1 red pepper, diced
3 stalks celery, diced
¼ cup fresh dill, finely chopped
1 cup minced fresh chives

Dressing
3 tablespoons white wine vinegar
2 tablespoons olive oil
1 teaspoon sugar
½ teaspoon salt
1 teaspoon paprika
Pinch cayenne pepper
Freshly cracked black pepper, to taste

Bring a large pot of water to a boil on the stove. Drop in edamame and corn kernels. Boil for 5 minutes to lightly blanch. Drain and cool. Toss together with the remaining ingredients. Make the dressing in a separate bowl and toss together. Serve at room temperature.

Marinated Soybeans

Melanie Foster *(Blaine, Minnesota)*
Serves 6

I have not met anyone who does not love the pleasant crunch and satisfying fun of shelling cooked and salted edamame pods and popping them in their mouth one by one. Even my kids will happily eat this healthy favorite. Yet, if you want something different, try this simple vinaigrette to marinate the cooked, shelled soybeans. It will keep a long time in the refrigerator, and can be ready to add to any other salad or just as a refreshing, cold side dish.

1 (16 oz.) bag frozen, shelled soybeans
1 tablespoon white vinegar
1 tablespoon lime juice
1 teaspoon sugar
1 teaspoon soy sauce
¼ teaspoon dry mustard
¼ teaspoon garlic powder
¼ teaspoon freshly cracked black pepper
2 tablespoons blended oil (see Chef's Tips on blended oil, page 309)
6 scallions, chopped

Cook the soybeans according to the package directions. Drain and shock in ice water to cool. Set aside. In a mason jar, add the rest of the ingredients. Screw the lid onto the jar and shake until combined. Add the cooked and cooled soybeans to the jar, and shake gently to mix. Place in the refrigerator to chill until serving.

Risotto Napoleon with Dried Door County Cherries

Chef Terri Milligan *(Inn at Kristofer's, Sister Bay, Wisconsin)*
Serves 6

One of the most popular harvests in Door County is our local cherries. With over 100 acres of cherry trees, our little county ranks fourth in cherry production in the United States. These tart Montmorency cherry trees provide beautiful blossoms throughout May, and a terrific crop of cherries in mid-July. Since they are sour, they are used mainly in pies and jams; they, however, can also be dried and used throughout the years. Chef Milligan has created this unusual rice pudding dessert that incorporates dried Door County cherries with a sweet risotto, flavored with fresh vanilla bean and a touch of Grand Marnier®. For a gourmet touch, she serves it between layers of phyllo dough that have been sprinkled with coarse sugar and a garnish of caramel sauce and cream anglaise.

Phyllo Triangles
1 stick (½ cup) unsalted butter, melted
6 sheets phyllo dough, thawed according to directions
Crystal sugar or other coarse-sanding sugar

Risotto Rice Pudding
3 cups half-and-half
3 cups heavy whipping cream
1½ cups sugar
1¼ cups arborio rice
1 teaspoon ground cinnamon
1 vanilla bean, split, or 1 teaspoon vanilla extract
¼ cup dried cherries or cranberries
3 tablespoons Grand Marnier® (or orange-flavored liqueur)
2 egg yolks
2 tablespoons unsalted butter
1 tablespoon orange or lemon zest (see Chef's Tips on citrus zest, page 311)

Phyllo Triangles

Melt the butter in a small saucepan. Unwrap the phyllo dough, and loosely cover with a piece of plastic wrap. Then place a damp and rung-out towel over dough to avoid drying out the edges. Preheat an oven to 350°F.

Line a baking pan with parchment paper or a silicon/silpat® mat. Carefully lift one of the phyllo sheets, and place on a work area. Use a pastry brush to brush the dough completely with butter. Sprinkle the dough with some coarse sugar. Place another sheet on top of the phyllo. Brush with butter. Continue with a third piece, brush with butter, and sprinkle with sugar.

Cut the phyllo into equal-size triangles. Place the cut phyllo on the prepared baking sheet. Place another piece of parchment paper over the phyllo. Place a clean baking sheet of the same size on top of the parchment to "weigh down" the triangles. Make another set of triangles using the remaining three pieces of phyllo. You may need another pan, depending on the size of your baking sheets. (You will have more phyllo dough than needed. You can make additional triangles and store them in an airtight container for future use, or re-roll the dough and wrap in Saran™ wrap. Refreeze for future use.)

Place the phyllo pan(s) in the oven on the middle rack. Bake for 7 to 8 minutes. Pick up the top pan and check the dough. The phyllo should be lightly brown. If needed, bake for an additional 2 minutes. Remove the pan. Carefully lift off the top pan. Let the phyllo cool. Remove the parchment paper. Store in an airtight container with clean parchment paper separating the phyllo pieces. The pieces can be stored for several days in a cool, dry place.

Risotto Pudding

Spray an 8- by 8-inch square baking pan with 1-inch sides with non-stick food spray.

In a large pot, place the half-and-half, cream, sugar, rice, cinnamon, and vanilla. If using a vanilla bean, scrape the "seeds" out of the vanilla bean, and put in the mixture. You can put the actual bean in the mixture as well; tie the bean with kitchen string, however, so you can remove it after the risotto is done. Place on a medium burner and bring to a boil.

Reduce the heat to a simmer. Stir on and off for approximately 35 to 40 minutes. The rice should absorb most of the liquid, and the rice should be slightly chewy, but not too soft. Remove the vanilla bean if using.

While the rice is cooking, prepare the cherries. Place the dried cherries in a bowl. Sprinkle with Grand Marnier®. Let it sit in the liquid while the rice is cooking. Remove from the heat, and stir in the egg yolks, butter, and zest.

Add the cherries with the liquid. Stir to combine. Place the rice pudding in the prepared pan. Let cool. Then cover with plastic wrap and refrigerate until ready to use. Can be made several days ahead of time.

Place one triangle piece on a serving plate. Using an ice cream scoop, scoop out a generous portion of the rice pudding. Sprinkle the top of the pudding with some granulated sugar.

Carefully caramelize the top of the pudding by using a kitchen butane torch, being careful not to burn the phyllo dough.

Top with another piece of phyllo, placing it slightly on a diagonal.

Continue with the remaining dessert plates. If desired, garnish the plate with a splash of caramel sauce.

Persimmon Pudding

Jan Bulla-Baker *(Bloomington, Indiana)*
Serves 12

> Here is a recipe that uses local ingredients and is certainly a
> Midwest favorite. Persimmons can be tart, but this recipe adds
> an element of sweetness that creates an overall well-balanced
> bite.

1–2 cups sugar
2–3 cups persimmon pulp
1 teaspoon baking soda
1½ cups buttermilk
3 eggs
1 teaspoon pure vanilla
⅓ cup light cream
1½ cups unbleached white flour
1 teaspoon baking powder
⅛ teaspoon sea salt
1 teaspoon cinnamon
½ cup unsalted butter

Preheat an oven to 325°F.

Mix the sugar and pulp together in a large bowl. Mix the baking soda
and buttermilk in a separate bowl, and stir until the foaming stops;
add to the pulp mixture. Add the eggs, vanilla, and light cream. Sift
the flour, baking powder, salt, and cinnamon.

Pour melted butter in a 13- by 9-inch baking pan, and grease the sides.
Pour any excess butter into the pudding mixture, and then back into
the pan. Bake for 45 to 50 minutes or until set in the middle. Serve
with whipped cream (see Baking Tips on whipped cream, page 326).

Grandma's Rhubarb Kuchen

Julie Smoragiewicz *(Rapid City, South Dakota)*
Serves 6

Rhubarb is one of the first spring harvests to be enjoyed from the Dakota garden. This recipe is based on my grandmother Olivia's kuchen, which is South Dakota's state dessert. Grandma was an amazing cook, and I loved everything that she made. We could always count on Grandma having plenty of kuchen whenever we came to visit her. Kuchen is not only prepared with rhubarb, but also dried apricots, prunes, and even cottage cheese. This recipe produces enough to enjoy today, and have some left over to freeze for the days and weeks ahead. *Kuchen* is the German word for cake, and is perfect for breakfast or dessert.

Dough

4 teaspoons fresh yeast
4 teaspoons sugar
½ cup warm water (105°F)
⅓ cup unsalted butter, softened
⅜ cup sugar
1⅔ cups warm water
½ teaspoon baking soda
½ teaspoon baking powder
½ teaspoon salt
5⅔ cups all-purpose flour

Filling

4 cups fresh rhubarb, chopped
2 cups sweet or sour cream
1 cup sugar
4 eggs
2 tablespoons all-purpose flour

Cinnamon-Sugar Topping

4 tablespoons sugar

1 teaspoon cinnamon

Dough

Dissolve the yeast and 4 teaspoons of sugar in ½ cup of warm water (105°F). Melt butter in a small saucepan over low heat. Add the melted butter and ⅜ cup of the sugar and 1⅔ cups warm water to the yeast mixture.

Add baking soda, baking powder, and salt; stir to combine.

Add flour one cup at a time until incorporated.

Knead for 3 to 5 minutes until the dough is smooth (the dough will keep for up to 1 week if stored in an airtight container in the refrigerator). Remove from the refrigerator for at least 20 minutes prior to using the refrigerated dough.

Form dough into a ball, place it in a buttered bowl, and cover with a clean, dry kitchen towel.

Let the dough rise for 30 minutes or until doubled in size.

Spread dough into four buttered 9-inch pie pans.

Filling

Slice the rhubarb into bite-sized pieces. Mix the cream, sugar, eggs, and flour. Pour over the dough.

Top with rhubarb and distribute evenly. Combine the remaining sugar and cinnamon.

Sprinkle with the sugar and cinnamon mixture. Bake at 350°F for 30 to 35 minutes.

Remove from the oven and cool. Cover and store in the refrigerator, or freeze individually in zip bags.

Quick Old-Fashioned Pie Crust

Paul and Jayn Parenti *(A Fare to Remember, Fayetteville, Arkansas)*
Makes 1 (10-inch) crust or 2 (8–9-inch) crusts

> This pie crust has a minimal amount of sugar, so, in addition to providing a flaky exterior for sweet pies, this is also perfect for hearty and savory dishes like pot pie.

2¼ cups all-purpose flour
1 tablespoon sugar
1 teaspoon salt
1½ teaspoons baking powder
⅓ cup plus 1 tablespoon boiling water
⅓ cup plus 1 tablespoon vegetable oil

Sift together flour, sugar, salt, and baking powder into a bowl with a tight cover. Add boiling water and vegetable oil. Cover the bowl, and shake together until thoroughly mixed.

Turn dough out into a pie plate, coating your hands with flour and quickly pressing to the bottom and sides of the plate. If you want to roll it out, add flour to the board and roll quickly. Continue as the recipe calls.

Super-Flaky Pie Dough

Paul and Jayn Parenti *(A Fare to Remember, Fayetteville, Arkansas)*
Makes 2 (9–10-inch) unbaked pie crusts

This recipe for old-fashioned pie crust is over 110 years old, and is the only one that I use for pies. The shortening is considered a solid fat, which melts while baking in the oven. As the fat heats up, it changes form from solid to liquid, and then to a gas or vapor, otherwise known as steam. While baking in the hot oven, the steam creates pockets. These pockets of steam allow layers of the dough to rise, which gives this pie dough its flaky quality.

4 cups all-purpose flour
1 teaspoon salt
2 cups vegetable shortening
1 cup water

Into a large bowl, sift the flour with the salt. Using a pastry blender, cut the shortening into the flour until small balls form. Add the water, and toss gently with a fork (do this quickly). It may look like the dough is too wet, but this is normal. Wrap in foil and refrigerate for 8 hours. When you are ready to use, turn the pastry out on a well-floured board, cut in half, and place in a pie plate. If using only one crust, tightly wrap the other half and return to the refrigerator. Continue as the pie recipe indicates (dough can be refrigerated for up to 2 weeks, if wrapped tightly).

Bumbleberry Pie

Chef Terri Milligan *(Inn at Kristofer's, Sister Bay, Wisconsin)*
Makes 1 pie

> Bumbleberry is a mixture of cherries from Door County, Wisconsin, and other fresh seasonal berries.

Egg Wash

3 tablespoons milk or heavy cream

1 large egg

Pie

1½ pounds tart cherries, pitted, or 3 cups frozen tart cherries, pitted

3 cups assorted berries (such as blueberries, raspberries, and blackberries)

¼ cup cornstarch

1 cup plus 2 teaspoons sugar

2 tablespoons all-purpose flour

2 tablespoons coarse-sanding sugar or raw sugar

2 unbaked pie crusts (see Index, page 339)

Egg Wash

Mix together all the ingredients. Set aside.

Pie

Toss the cherries and berries with the cornstarch, 1 cup of sugar, and 2 tablespoons of flour.

Roll out half of the pie dough. Lightly spray a pie tin with non-stick spray. Gently place the dough in the tin, making sure that there is at least 1 inch of pastry overlapping the edge. Place fruit in the pie.

Roll out the remaining dough. With a pastry brush, lightly brush the egg glaze on the rim of the pie. Place the top dough layer on the pie. Press around the pie to adhere to the edges. Trim and crimp edges.

With the remaining dough, make seven cookie-cutter decorations for the top of the pie. With a pastry brush, brush the top of the pie with the egg wash. Place the decorations evenly around the pie. Make two slits with a knife in the middle of the pie to release steam. Sprinkle sanding sugar or raw sugar on top of the pie.

Place pie in the refrigerator for 30 minutes before baking. This will harden the crust so it has less of a tendency to shrink when baking. Bake in a 375°F preheated oven for 1 hour or until the top of the pie is nicely browned. Make sure to place the pie on a baking sheet in case some of the mixture comes out of the edge. Cool for 1 hour before serving.

Chef's Tip

This pie can be frozen and saved for future use. Place the unbaked pie on a baking pan in the freezer. Freeze for 3 hours, and then wrap in foil and label. Take directly out of the freezer and bake as directed above. Additional baking time is not necessary. Do not thaw prior to baking.

Shaker Lemon Pie

Susan Gordy *(Cincinnati, Ohio)*
Yields 1 (9-inch) pie

> This pie was the all-time favorite and best-seller at the annual
> Fourth of July pie auction, which we have held every year at the
> Lincoln Log Cabin State Historic Site. The highest bid for one
> pie was $40!

2 large lemons
2 cups sugar
¼ teaspoon salt
4 eggs
4 tablespoons unsalted butter, melted
3 tablespoons all-purpose flour
1 (9-inch) unbaked pie crust (see Index, page 339)

Thoroughly wash the lemons, and then dry with paper towels. Using
a mandolin or a sharp knife, slice the lemons very thin; remove and
discard the seeds. Toss the slices with sugar and salt. Cover and set
aside at room temperature for 24 hours.

Preheat an oven to 425°F. Whisk eggs in a bowl until frothy. Add butter and flour, whisking until smooth. Stir into the lemon mixture.

On a lightly floured surface, roll out the dough into one (12-inch)
round. Fit one round into a 9-inch pie plate, and pour in the filling.
Bake until the edges begin to brown and the pie starts to set up (about
30 minutes). Reduce the heat to 350°F, and bake until the crust is
golden brown (25 to 30 minutes more). Remove from the oven and let
cool for at least 30 minutes before slicing.

Bavarian Blueberry Tart

Paul and Jayn Parenti *(A Fare to Remember, Fayetteville, Arkansas)*
Serves 12

> Nestled within the Ozark National Forrest, Fayetteville—as
> well as most of northwestern Arkansas—is beautiful. We have
> an abundance of fresh blueberry and grape orchards. Being
> very close to the Oklahoma, Missouri, and Kansas boarders,
> northwestern Arkansas also has an interesting fusion of many
> different culinary backgrounds.

Crust
1 cup all-purpose flour
½ cup unsalted butter
⅓ cup sugar
½ teaspoon almond (or pure vanilla) extract

Filling
½ cup sugar
16 ounces cream cheese, room temperature
2 large eggs
1 teaspoon almond (or pure vanilla) extract

Topping
2½ cups fresh blueberries (divided, saving ½ cup for garnish)
⅓ cup sugar
½ teaspoon cinnamon
½ teaspoon nutmeg, freshly ground
¼ teaspoon cardamom
¼ cup almonds, sliced
½ pint heavy cream, whipped (optional) (see Baking Tips on
whipped cream, page 326)

Crust

Preheat an oven to 375°F. Combine all the crust ingredients in a mixing bowl, and beat on medium speed. Scrape down the sides until the dough is soft and can be formed into a ball. Press into the bottom of your 10-inch spring-form pan.

Filling

In a separate mixing bowl, beat sugar and cream cheese until smooth. Add eggs one at a time, scraping the bowl often, until very smooth. Add extract until just incorporated. Spread the filling over the unbaked crust.

Topping

Place blueberries in a large bowl and lightly spray with baking spray. Combine sugar, cinnamon, nutmeg, and cardamom, and sprinkle over the berries. Gently toss until the berries are nicely coated with the sugar mixture, but still firm.

Bake for 35 minutes, sprinkle with almonds, and continue baking for another 15 to 20 minutes until the filling is set. Cool, keep in a refrigerator, and serve cold. This can be served with a dollop of whipped cream and a few fresh blueberries for garnish.

Gooey Butter Cupcakes

Holly Cunningham *(Hollyberry Baking Company, Saint Louis, Missouri)*

Yields 2½ dozen standard-size cupcakes

Here is the "legend" of the gooey butter cake, which is gaining popularity across the country. Two families claim that their bakery created the cake, but, essentially, it was in a bakery in Saint Louis where a "mistake" was made, and that was how the gooey butter cake was born. Here is our version in a cupcake; it has become a huge favorite at events, and it is like nothing you have ever had.

Layer 1
1 (18¼ oz.) package yellow cake mix
1 stick (½ cup) unsalted butter, melted
1 egg

Layer 2
½ stick (¼ cup) unsalted butter, softened
¼ cup cream cheese, room temperature/softened
1 (18¼ oz.) package yellow cake mix
½ cup sweetened, condensed milk
1 egg
⅓ cup water

Gooey Butter Cupcake Frosting
1 (8 oz.) package cream cheese, softened
1 stick (½ cup) butter, softened
¼ cup sweetened condensed milk
2 cups powdered sugar, sifted
1 teaspoon pure vanilla extract

Preheat an oven to 350°F. Fill a standard-size cupcake pan with cupcake liners.

Layer 1

Combine the first three ingredients, and blend on low speed until the mixture comes together completely and pulls away from the sides of the bowl. Scoop a level tablespoon of the mixture into the bottom of each cupcake liner, and press down with your fingers to form the first layer.

Layer 2

Cream together softened butter and cream cheese in a bowl until completely smooth and free of lumps. Add the cake mix, sweetened condensed milk, and egg, and blend on low speed for 30 seconds. Lastly, gradually add the water while mixing. Continue mixing the layer for about 1 minute on medium speed or until completely combined. Scrape down the sides and bottom of the bowl, and mix, again, for 10 seconds until the second layer is completely blended.

Fill the liners with about 2 tablespoons of this second layer. Bake in a 350°F oven for 15 minutes until the cupcakes are a light golden brown. Remove from the oven and allow to cool. At this point, the cupcakes will "fall" and form a crater. Cool for 10 minutes in the pan, and then remove to cool completely on a wire rack.

Frosting

Cream together the cream cheese and butter in a mixing bowl on low speed until completely smooth and free of lumps. Add the sweetened condensed milk and blend. Then add the powdered sugar one cup at a time, and blend on low speed to avoid a "powder shower." When completely combined, scrape down the sides of the bowl, and add the vanilla. Blend in the vanilla completely.

Once the cupcakes are completely cool, fill the crater of the cupcakes with the gooey butter cupcake frosting. Sprinkle with powdered sugar and serve.

Frying Pan Fudge Cake

Ron Popp *(Wheat Fields Catering, Omaha, Nebraska)*
Serves 6–8

Cake
⅔ cup white sugar
2 sticks (1 cup) butter, room temperature
1 cup all-purpose flour
½ cup milk
3 ounces unsweetened chocolate, melted

Topping
½ cup brown sugar, firmly packed
⅔ cup white sugar
3 rounded tablespoons cocoa
1½ cups boiling water
1 tablespoon pure vanilla

Cake

Preheat an oven to 350°F. In a mixing bowl, mix the sugar and butter thoroughly. Then add flour and milk, and mix, again. Fold in chocolate and mix thoroughly. Place this mixture evenly in the bottom of a well-greased, deep, iron frying pan with iron handle for baking.

Topping

In a small bowl, mix together sugars and cocoa. Place this mixture atop the first mixture.

Mix water with vanilla, and pour atop the second mixture. Place in the preheated 350°F oven. Bake for about 40 minutes or until the top mixture sets up like a stiff pudding. Cool. Top with whipped cream and cherry sauce.

Part IV

NORTHWEST

The Northwest region contains the Rocky Mountain states of Colorado, Idaho, Montana, Utah, and Wyoming, as well as the Pacific states of Oregon, Washington, Alaska, and parts of Northern California.

The Rocky Mountain states have access to all that nature has to offer—from fresh-caught fish (see Lakeside Trout, page 225) to wild berries (see Marion Berry Crème Brule French Toast, page 210) and hunted game such as elk (Brown Rice Flour-Crusted Grilled Elk or Venison, page 233). The sheepherders and ranchers who settled the valleys and prairies of Idaho and Wyoming centuries ago began farming a variety of potatoes. Presently, it continues to be Idaho's number-one crop, which chefs now enjoy using in a multitude of ways (see French Red Wine-Infused Potato Salad with Chives and Chervil, page 238). Popular rustic food such as artisan bread, baked beans, and pork stew were once known as "traveling cowboy food," although many of the locals now use updated ingredients.

The building of the railroads through the Northwest offered work to many Chinese immigrants, who eventually resided together in areas referred to as "Chinatowns." After a series of natural disasters struck Japan, even more Asian immigrants arrived in the Northwest, bringing with them the unique ingredients and cooking styles of their homeland. The heavy Asian influence on Northwestern cuisine still reigns supreme, lending itself to terms such as "Pacific Rim cooking" (see Panko-Battered Hon Shimeji Mushrooms, page 239) and "fusion cuisine" (see Kim-Chee Burgers, page 232).

Mary Elizabeth recalls strolling through Pike Place Market while on a trip to Seattle, Washington, in hopes of purchasing a souvenir from her trip. She inquired of one of the locals as to what she should choose, and she was told that Washington state is known for its Honey Crisp apples, which are featured in Apple Pie (page 243). Being from the Northeast, where apples are readily available, she wondered what could be so special about this Washington variety. To be polite, she purchased the apples anyway and found that the flavor was so delectable and so different from any apple that she had ever eaten.

Marion Berry Crème Brule French Toast

Chef John Paulk *(Mezzaluna Fine Catering, Portland, Oregon)*
Serves 6–8

1 stick (½ cup) unsalted butter
1 cup packed brown sugar
2 tablespoons corn syrup
1 (9-inch) round-loaf country-style bread
5 large eggs
1½ cups half-and-half
1 teaspoon vanilla
1 teaspoon Grand Marnier® (or orange-flavored liqueur)
¼ teaspoon salt
2 pints Oregon Marion berries or blackberries

In a small, heavy saucepan, melt butter with brown sugar and corn syrup over moderate heat, stirring until smooth, and pour into a 13- by 9- by 2-inch baking dish.

Cut six (1-inch-thick) slices from the center portion of the bread, reserving the ends for another use, and trim the crusts. Arrange the bread slices in one layer in the baking dish, squeezing them slightly to fit.

In a bowl, whisk together eggs, half-and-half, vanilla, Grand Marnier®, and salt until combined well, and pour evenly over the bread. Chill the bread mixture, covered, for 8 to 24 hours.

Preheat an oven to 350°F, and bring the bread mixture to room temperature.

Sprinkle with berries.

Bake the casserole, uncovered, in the middle of the oven until puffed and the edges are pale (35 to 40 minutes). Serve hot French toast immediately.

Smoked Salmon Cheesecake

Chef Darnell Harness *(Simply Dine Catering, influenced by Alaska; resides in Henderson, Nevada)*
Serves 10

> I go fishing every two years in Sitka, Alaska, and salmon is always my favorite catch. When cooked right, it is a show-stopper. This savory cheesecake is a great alternative to serving quiche at your next brunch. Serving this dish with an assortment of gourmet crackers and grapes makes for a great presentation.

½ cup panko (Japanese) breadcrumbs
4 large eggs
3 (8 oz.) bars cream cheese, room temperature
⅓ cup heavy cream
¼ cup red bell pepper, chopped
1 tablespoon extra-light olive oil
¾ teaspoon dill weed
1 tablespoon shallot, chopped
¼ teaspoon white pepper
4 ounces smoked salmon, finely chopped
½ cup gruyere cheese, grated

Preheat an oven to 300°F. Butter the sides of an 8-inch spring-form pan and sprinkle the bottom with the breadcrumbs. Chill the pan in the refrigerator while preparing the batter. In a mixing bowl, beat together the eggs, cream cheese, and heavy cream until smooth.

In a saucepan, sauté the bell pepper in olive oil over medium-high heat until softened.

Fold the pepper and remaining ingredients into the cream cheese mixture.

Pour the batter into the prepared spring-form pan. Wrap foil around the pan, and place in a roasting pan. Pour hot water into the roasting pan to about halfway up. Carefully place in the preheated oven and cook for 90 minutes. Turn the oven off and crack open the door to let the cheesecake cool for 1 hour in the oven. Move to a rack until completely cool, and then refrigerate overnight. Run a knife around the pan and remove the spring-form sides.

Ham and Cheese Herb Puff Pastry Squares

Marguerite M. Henderson *(Salt Lake City, Utah)*

Yields 16 appetizer bites

In Utah, we are fortunate to have two artisan companies that provide the best in salami and cheeses. Award-winning Creminelli Fine Meats and Beehive Cheese Co. have products sold around the country in the finest food shops. Prosciutto cotto is an Italian ham. If not available, substitute with your favorite ham. SeaHive cheese is made with Utah salt, and, since we are the "beehive" state, the word "SeaHive" is a combination of sea salt and beehive.

1 (17⅓ oz.) package 2 frozen puff pastry sheets, thawed at room temperature immediately before use

2 tablespoons coarse ground mustard

½ pound Creminelli prosciutto cotto, thinly sliced

½ pound Beehive SeaHive cheese, shredded

2 tablespoons chopped fresh rosemary

2 tablespoons chopped fresh sage

1 egg

1 tablespoon heavy cream

2 tablespoons sesame seeds (see Chef's Tips on nuts and seeds, page 318)

Lay one sheet of puff pastry on a baking sheet lined with either parchment paper or Silpat®.

Brush the sheet with the mustard, leaving about ½-inch border without the mustard.

Place the prosciutto on the mustard, laying it evenly with about ½-inch border without the ham.

Sprinkle the prosciutto evenly with the shredded cheese, leaving about ½-inch border without the cheese.

Sprinkle the cheese with rosemary and sage. Place the second sheet of pastry on top, pressing the edges together.

Using a fork, crimp the edges. Beat egg with heavy cream to make an egg wash. Brush this on top of the pastry, and then sprinkle with sesame seeds.

Bake the pastry on the middle rack of a preheated 425°F oven for 18 to 20 minutes or until puffed and golden.

Remove from the oven and allow to cool for 5 minutes. Using a pizza cutter, cut the pastry into 16 squares. Serve warm.

California Apple, Raisin, and Almond Chicken Salad

Corrie Fukuda *(Resides in Riverside, California; inspired by Berkeley, California)*

Serves 2

A restaurant's sweet and salty chicken salad sandwich inspired me to make this for myself one day. I tried to keep it as simple as possible. It is best to use fresh ingredients, such as Golden Delicious apples and local sun-soaked grapes or raisins, which are plentiful in Northern California.

1 cup chicken (rotisserie-style), cooked and chopped
1½ tablespoons mayonnaise
¼ cup fresh Golden Delicious apple, chopped
2 tablespoons California raisins
1–2 tablespoons almonds, slivered

Mix the chicken with mayonnaise, apple, raisins, and almonds. Refrigerate the mixture for 20 to 30 minutes before serving.

Kamut Wheat Salad

Emily Seitz *(Good Food Store, Missoula, Montana)*
Serves 4–6

I have selected a recipe that we feature in our store that represents Montana. Kamut is a grain grown in Eastern Montana, and has a rather interesting history. It was first brought to the states by a Montana farmer, and is originally from Egypt.

Kamut

1½ cups Kamut® brand khorasan wheat kernels (may substitute wheat berries)
3 cups water
½ tablespoon minced garlic (see Chef's Tips on garlic, page 314)

Dressing

¼ cup balsamic vinegar
1 tablespoon Dijon mustard
¼ cup olive oil (see Chef's Tips on blended oil, page 309, and emulsification, page 320)
½ cup safflower oil
2 tablespoons white wine vinegar
Salt and freshly cracked black pepper, to taste

Salad

1 red bell pepper, diced small
½ cup feta cheese crumbles
¼ cup chopped cilantro
⅓ cup kalamata olives, pitted and roughly chopped

Kamut

Add the Kamut® wheat kernels and garlic to the water, and bring to a boil. Reduce the heat and simmer until the wheat is tender (about ½ hour or perhaps more). Add more water, if needed. Drain and cool.

Dressing

Whisk together all of the dressing ingredients until thoroughly combined (you will have extra dressing from this recipe, which you can use in other dishes).

Salad

Toss the cooled wheat with the salad ingredients and top with ⅓ cup of dressing.

Kale and Hazelnut Salad with Sesame-Citrus Vinaigrette

Serves 2; yields 1 cup dressing

Per her sister Liz's request for a healthy lunch, Chef Nicole created a salad inspired by Oregon's state nut, the hazelnut, also known as a filbert.

Dressing

¼ cup sesame oil
½ cup blended oil (see Chef's Tips on blended oil, page 309)
Paste from 1 clove garlic
Zest of ½ orange
Zest of ½ lemon
¼ cup segments and juice of 1–2 oranges
½ teaspoon fresh ginger, peeled and minced
½ teaspoon Dijon mustard
1 teaspoon honey
1 teaspoon turmeric
Kosher salt and freshly cracked black pepper, to taste

Salad

1 head kale, washed, ribs removed and discarded, and leaves sliced into bite-sized pieces
1 cup broccoli florets
⅛ cup thinly sliced red onion
¼ cup hazelnuts, toasted (see Chef's Tips on nuts and seeds, page 318) and roughly chopped
¼ cup golden raisins

Dressing

Combine both oils in a pourable liquid measuring cup, and set aside. Combine the remaining ingredients in a mixing bowl. To emulsify the dressing, vigorously whisk the mixture while slowly pouring the oils in a constant, steady stream (see Chef's Tips on emulsification, page 320).

Salad

Toss all the salad ingredients in a large bowl. Prior to serving, add dressing to taste.

Oysters Hangtown

Chef George Schneider *(Inspired by Lake Tahoe, California; resides in Bayville, New York)*
Serves 1

> While working in Lake Tahoe, California, there were many local dishes with wonderful old stories. Legend has it that, during the 1800s in Reno, Nevada, a doomed man facing the hangman's gallows was asked what he wanted for his last meal. Thinking about it for a while, he decided that oysters were his choice, knowing very well that there were none available in the Sierra Nevada Mountains. The sheriff granted his prisoner's request, and was able to arrange getting oysters from the San Francisco Bay area through the trading post in Hangtown, California. Hence, the clever prisoner was able to extend his life.

6 Pine Island oysters
2 ounces seasoned flour, for dredging
3 slices bacon, chopped
2 scallions, sliced
2 eggs, beaten
1 ounce baby field greens, washed
1 lemon, cut into 8 wedges
Salt and freshly cracked black pepper, to taste

Shuck the oysters, saving any juice in a small bowl. Make the seasoned flour in a separate bowl by adding the salt and pepper to the flour, setting aside. Heat a sauté pan, and place the diced bacon in it, cooking over medium heat until golden brown. Add the scallions, and cook for 1 minute (do not remove the bacon fat). Pass the shucked oysters through the seasoned flour, pat off the excess, and then place them in the egg wash. Arrange the bacon and scallion mixture evenly in the sauté pan, and place the egg-dipped oysters on top of the mixture so it will stick to the egg. Cook the first side until golden brown (about 2 minutes), and then turn to and finish the second side (about 1 minute).

To serve, place the baby greens in the center of a plate, and arrange the cooked oysters around the greens (bacon/scallion-side-up). Add any remaining oyster liquid to the pan, deglaze, and then pour over the top of the plated oysters. Garnish with the lemon wedges.

Oregon Rock Shrimp on Grit Griddle Cakes

Chef John Paulk *(Mezzaluna Fine Catering, Portland, Oregon)*
Serves 8

Shrimp

2 pounds Oregon rock shrimp in their shells (about 42), peeled and shells reserved
2 tablespoons creole seasoning, divided
½ teaspoon freshly cracked black pepper
2 tablespoons olive oil, divided
¼ cup diced yellow onions
2 tablespoons minced garlic
3 bay leaves
3 lemons, peeled and sectioned
2 cups water
½ cup Worcestershire sauce
¼ cup dry white wine
¼ teaspoon salt
2 cups heavy cream
2 tablespoons unsalted butter

Grit Cakes

2 tablespoons canola oil, plus more for grilling
1 medium yellow onion, finely diced
2 cloves garlic, finely minced
1 cup dry white wine
4 cups shrimp stock (chicken or vegetable stock can be substituted)
1 cup yellow stone-ground corn meal
2 ears grilled corn, kernels removed (see Chef's Tips on corn, page 322)
Salt and freshly cracked black pepper, to taste

Shrimp

Season the shrimp with 1 tablespoon of Creole seasoning and freshly cracked black pepper.

Heat 1 tablespoon of the oil in a large pot over high heat. When the oil is hot, add the onions and garlic, and sauté for 1 minute.

Add the reserved shrimp shells, remaining Creole seasoning, bay leaves, lemons, water, Worcestershire sauce, wine, salt, and freshly cracked black pepper. Stir well and bring to a boil.

Reduce the heat and simmer for 30 minutes. Remove from the heat. Allow to cool for about 15 minutes, and strain into a small saucepan (there should be about 1½ cups).

Place over high heat, bring to a boil, and cook until thick, syrupy, and dark brown (about 15 minutes). Makes about 4 to 5 tablespoons of barbecue base.

Heat the remaining 1 tablespoon of oil in a large skillet over high heat. When the oil is hot, add the seasoned shrimp, and sauté them, occasionally shaking the skillet, for 2 minutes.

Add the cream, butter, and barbecue base. Stir and simmer for 3 minutes. Remove the shrimp and set aside.

Grit Cakes

Butter the bottom and sides of a 9- by 11-inch baking pan, and set aside.

Heat the oil in a medium saucepan over high heat. Add the onion, and cook until soft (about 3 minutes). Add the garlic, and cook for 30 seconds. Add the wine, and cook until completely reduced.

Add the stock, and bring to a boil. Slowly whisk in the corn meal, stirring until it begins to thicken. Season with salt and pepper, reduce the heat to medium, switch to a wooden spoon, and continue cooking, stirring until the mixture is smooth and soft (about 20 minutes). If the mixture becomes too thick, stir in some water (it should be a pourable consistency).

Stir in the corn kernels, and pour the mixture into the prepared pan, spreading evenly. Cover and refrigerate until firm (2 to 24 hours). Cut the corn meal mixture into even squares or any shape that you desire.

Heat a sauté pan on medium-high heat. Using a pastry brush, paint the cakes on both sides with some of the canola oil, and season with salt and pepper. Pan-sear the cakes until golden brown on each side (about 1½ minutes per side). Remove to a plate and top each cake with the shrimp mixture.

Scallops with Mushrooms in Whiskey Sauce

Laraine Derr *(Chez Alaska Cooking School, Juneau, Alaska)*

Serves 4

Scallops are becoming more of a luxury in Alaska, as more people discover the wonderful qualities of scallops grown in our cold, clean waters. Our best scallops come either from Yakutat or Kodiak. This is a wonderful quick recipe that draws "ooh's" and "ah's" from people.

1 tablespoon blended oil (see Chef's Tips on blended oil, page 309)
1½ pounds diver's/sea scallops, cleaned and muscles removed
1 pound mushrooms
1 tablespoon fresh lemon juice
1½ tablespoons unsalted butter
4 scallions, thinly sliced
¼ cup heavy cream
½ cup whiskey
Salt and freshly cracked black pepper, to taste

Heat a 10-inch sauté pan until very hot. Add blended oil. Sear the scallops on the flat side in the hot pan, leaving at least 1 inch between each scallop. As soon as you finish putting the scallops in the pan, start turning the first ones. Cook, undisturbed, until they begin to brown (about 2 minutes). Remove to a bowl. Toss mushrooms with lemon juice. Melt butter in the pan that the scallops have been sautéed in, and add mushrooms. Season and cook for 2 minutes. Reduce the heat, and cook until the mushrooms are deeply browned. Add scallions, and lightly sauté. Add cream to the pan, and heat. Add whiskey. Ignite very carefully. Cook until the cream is reduced. Add scallops and juice back to the pan. Season with salt and pepper. Serve with pasta or rice.

Lakeside Trout

Chef Eric Wilson *(Jackson Hole, Wyoming)*
Serves 4

Good morning, Wyoming! There is nothing better than waking in the state of Wyoming, and delving into any of its back-country waters and wild lands. For me, it starts early every May. The rain soaks the earth, prompting morel mushroom season. I start in the morning by catching several lake trout. I then proceed to the bank, where the morel mushrooms flourish. In the rainy spring, it does not take long to find the mushrooms. After I have picked a half-dozen mushrooms, I build a small fire, and cook my trout using this recipe. After eating your lakeside trout, sit back, relax, and enjoy the best nap on earth.

2 tablespoons olive oil
4 tablespoons salted butter, divided
4 de-boned fillets lake trout
½ dozen morel mushrooms, sliced
2 tablespoons white wine
Juice of 1 lemon
1 tablespoon chopped chives
Salt and freshly cracked black pepper, to taste

Place a cast-iron pan on the fire. Add olive oil and 1 tablespoon of butter. Cook the boned-out fillet of trout seasoned with salt and pepper, flesh-side-down, until brown. Invert the trout browned-side-up on a plate. Add mushrooms to the pan. Cook for 4 minutes until soft. Add white wine. Let the wine reduce by half. Add 3 tablespoons of butter in small chunks, and swirl the pan until the butter and wine are married and thick. Now, pour the morel sauce over the trout, and sprinkle with lemon and chives.

Zucchini-Basil-Wrapped Wild Alaskan Salmon

Chef Sharon Barton *(Chez Alaska Cooking School, Juneau, Alaska)*
Serves 4

> As in other parts of the United States, zucchini grows well in southeast Alaska. Wild Alaskan salmon also grows wonderfully well in our part of the country; therefore, a marriage of great resources has resulted in the following recipe.

Salmon

2 medium zucchini (each 6–7 inches long)
4 wild Alaskan salmon fillets, skinned
4 tablespoons blended oil, plus additional for brushing (see Chef's Tips on blended oil, page 309)
16 fresh basil leaves
Salt and freshly cracked black pepper, to taste

Mustard Mayonnaise

1 teaspoon Dijon mustard
¼ cup mayonnaise
1 lemon, freshly squeezed
Salt and freshly cracked black pepper, to taste

Salmon

Shave the zucchini lengthwise with a potato peeler into 20 thin strips. For each piece of fish, arrange five strips of the zucchini to overlap one another; brush with blended oil, and lightly season with salt and pepper. Place two basil leaves on each arrangement of zucchini. Season the salmon with salt and pepper, and place on top of the basil leaves. Top each fish with two basil leaves. Roll the zucchini around the salmon, overlapping the ends (similar to wrapping a pancake around a sausage). Heat a 12-inch skillet over medium heat, and add blended oil. When hot, carefully add the wrapped salmon, placing seam-side-down. Cover the skillet, and cook without turning for about 5 minutes until just opaque.

Mustard Mayonnaise

Mix mustard, mayonnaise, salt, and pepper in a small bowl.

Serve the fish over rice with a small dollop of mustard-mayonnaise and a squeeze of fresh lemon juice. This dish can also be served by adding a little butter and white wine to deglaze the skillet, and a tablespoon of the sauce over the salmon.

Seafood Pasta with Garlic Sauce

Chef Derrick Snyder *(Chez Alaska Cooking School, Juneau, Alaska)*
Serves 4

> Alaskan favorites such as rock cod, smoked salmon, and halibut work wonderfully in this garlicky pasta. Fresh shrimp from your local fishery always makes a delicious addition.

4 anchovy fillets
6 tablespoons olive oil
½ cup finely minced garlic
1 cup white wine
24 ounces seafood
1 pound dry pasta, cooked and drained
¼ cup minced parsley
6 tablespoons unsalted butter
Juice of ½ lemon
Parmesan and lemon slices, for garnish
Salt and freshly cracked black pepper, to taste

In a very large pan, sauté the anchovies in olive oil over medium heat. While stirring, mash the anchovies with a wooden spoon until they dissolve into the oil. Add garlic, and continue sautéing, stirring constantly, over medium heat until the garlic begins to turn golden brown and gives off a toasty smell. Deglaze the pan with white wine. Bring to a boil and reduce by half. Stir in the seafood and cook briefly until the seafood is opaque. Add cooked pasta and parsley to the sauce. Season with salt and pepper to taste, and heat through. Finish by adding butter and lemon. Serve with Parmesan cheese and lemon slices.

Red Grape and BBQ Chicken Pizza with Mozzarella and Fresh Basil

Culinary Institute of America *(Saint Helena, California)*
Yields 2 (9-inch) pizzas

Recently, I had the pleasure of visiting and eating at the Culinary Institute of America (CIA). If you have never had the opportunity to tour the majestic building overlooking the Napa Valley in California, I suggest that you do so. My dear friend Lorraine and I dined on exceptional food prepared by the culinary students themselves. The enthusiastic waitress proudly exclaimed that she was a month from graduation. In fact, all of the CIA students were required to work the "front of the house" in order to earn their culinary degrees. We were so impressed by the entire experience. This recipe was featured on their luncheon menu that day.

Story by Mary Elizabeth

12 ounces chicken breasts, skinless
¾ cup BBQ sauce, divided (see recipe for Texas BBQ Sauce on page 300)
2 (6 oz.) pizza dough balls (see recipe below)
Flour or corn meal, for dusting
¼ cup olive oil
¼ pound mozzarella cheese, preferably fresh, sliced into rounds
2 cups red grapes, sliced
16 fresh basil leaves, torn (just before use)
2 tablespoons pecorino romano, grated

BBQ Chicken

Preheat a grill to medium. In a small bowl, toss the chicken breasts with ½ cup of the BBQ sauce. Grill the chicken over medium heat until nicely charred and cooked through (about 10 minutes). Cool and cut into bite-sized pieces.

Pizza

Preheat an oven to 450°F. Place a baking stone on the middle shelf of the oven for at least 30 minutes. Then make one pizza at a time. Roll the dough ball out on a floured counter, and transfer it to a pizza peel or inverted sheet pan that has been dusted with flour or corn meal.

Mix the olive oil with the remaining ¼ cup of BBQ sauce, and spread 2 tablespoons of the sauce over the surface of the dough, leaving a ¼-inch border uncovered. Arrange half of the mozzarella over the top of the pizza, and then place half of the diced BBQ chicken evenly over the pizza. Top with 1 cup of the red grapes.

Carefully slide the pizza from the peel to the baking stone or sheet pan. Bake for 10 to 12 minutes. The crust should be puffy and thin in the center.

Remove from the oven and top with basil and pecorino romano cheese. Repeat with the remaining ingredients to make the second pizza.

Pizza Dough

Yields 2 (9-inch) pizzas

1 cup warm water (105°F)
¼ ounce yeast
¼ ounce olive oil
1 teaspoon salt
2 teaspoons honey
¾ pound bread flour
1 tablespoon olive oil

Mix the first five ingredients in a mixer with a dough hook. Blend for 2 to 3 minutes, and then slowly add the flour. Mix until a smooth, elastic dough forms, and knead for 12 minutes. Allow to proof by placing the dough into a greased, large metal mixing bowl, and cover loosely with plastic wrap or a dry towel in a warm area (80°F) until double in size. Punch down the dough, and scale by removing the dough from the bowl and cutting it in half, yielding two (6-ounce) balls. Brush with oil, cover, and place in a cool place until ready to cook.

Chicken with Artichokes

Chef J.D. McDonald *(Food by Hand, Corte Madera, California)*

Serves 4

California supplies the United States with artichokes, the majority of which are grown along the coast.

1 free-range broiler or fryer chicken, cut into pieces
2 tablespoons all-purpose flour
1 tablespoon olive or canola oil
2 small celery stalks, thinly sliced
2 small carrots, thinly sliced
1 medium yellow onion, thinly sliced
½–¾ cup white wine
2 small cloves garlic (see Chef's Tips on garlic, page 314)
3–4 sprigs fresh thyme
1 sprig fresh marjoram
2 dozen baby artichokes, trimmed and halved
2 cups chicken broth or stock
1 handful shelled peas, for garnish
1 pound cooked pappardelle pasta
1 tablespoon chopped flat-leaf parsley
Salt and freshly cracked black pepper, to taste

Season the chicken with salt and pepper. Dust lightly with flour. In a wide, shallow pan with a lid, heat the oil over medium-high heat. Pan-sear the chicken until golden brown on both sides. Remove the chicken and reserve. Add the celery, carrot, and onion to the pan; add a pinch of salt, and toss to combine. Cover the pan, and lower the heat to sweat the vegetables (approximately 15 to 20 minutes) or until the vegetables cook into a soft and somewhat creamy consistency. Then increase the heat, and deglaze with wine. Simmer the wine until reduced to a syrupy consistency. Add garlic, thyme, and marjoram, and stir until the garlic becomes aromatic. Add the artichokes, and stir until they begin to brown. Return the chicken to the pan, and add enough broth to cover the chicken by two-thirds. Bring to a boil, and then immediately drop to a simmer and cover. Cook until the chicken reaches an internal temperature of 165°F. Serve over pappardelle pasta, garnishing with peas and parsley.

Kim-Chee Burgers

Chef J.D. McDonald *(Food by Hand, Corte Madera, California)*
Serves 4

This is a recipe that was born on a hot summer day when we wanted a burger with a pan-Asian taste. It has become a favorite around here. The ingredients listed below are readily available at your local Asian market.

1 pound ground pork
2 tablespoons huli-huli sauce (sweet Thai chile glaze may be substituted)
1 tablespoon hoisin sauce
4 hamburger buns
4 tablespoons mayonnaise
1 (16 oz.) jar kimchi
Fresh cilantro, chopped, for garnish
Freshly cracked black pepper, to taste

Season the pork with the huli-huli sauce and black pepper. Mix the hoisin sauce and mayonnaise, and set aside. Grill the burgers until just done. Grill or toast the buns. Spread the mayonnaise mixture on the buns. Dress the burgers with kimchi and cilantro.

Brown Rice Flour-Crusted Grilled Elk or Venison

Executive Chef Dale Van Sky *(Red Mountain Resort, Ivins, Utah)*
Serves 1

> This is one of my favorite recipes for elk or venison, which are indigenous to our area. Elk and venison are considered game meats, which are commonly described as strong-flavored and rich. This preparation includes a garnish of refreshing and crunchy vegetables to balance the flavor.

Prickly Pear Sauce

2 tablespoons apple cider vinegar

¼ cup prickly pear syrup

Meat

4 ounces elk (or venison) tenderloin or sirloin

Brown rice flour, as needed

Olive oil, as needed

Kosher salt and cayenne pepper, to taste

Garnish

¼ cup jicama

¼ cup chayote squash

¼ cup napolito cactus pad

¼ cup roma tomato, seeded and sliced (see Chef's Tips on tomato concasse, page 321)

2 tablespoons shallots, minced

¼ cup fresh blueberries, split

Olive oil, as needed

Prickly Pear Sauce

Mix all the ingredients and set aside.

Meat

Cut the elk into two medallions; dip the elk in prickly pear sauce. Lightly sprinkle the elk steaks with kosher salt and cayenne pepper. Dredge in brown rice flour. Spray the elk with olive oil. Grill for 2 to 3 minutes per side.

Garnish

Spray olive oil on the jicama, chayote, and napolito. After grilling, slice into julienned or matchstick pieces. Combine with the remaining ingredients. Serve over the elk medallions.

Buffalo Chili Sauce

Chef J.D. McDonald *(Food by Hand, Corte Madera, California)*
Yields 3 cups

> Sometimes, you really want a good chili-cheese dog. The chili
> sauce that I came up with has a smooth, pourable texture that
> makes it perfect for a garnish on hot dogs or fries, with the added
> benefit of clean-tasting ingredients such as lean buffalo meat.
> This is not an everyday food, but rather, a healthy alternative to
> an otherwise guilty pleasure.

1 medium yellow onion, finely chopped

4 cloves garlic, smashed (see Chef's Tips on garlic, page 314)

1 teaspoon olive oil

1 pound ground buffalo

1 (15 oz.) can tomato sauce (see "Marinara Sauce" in Index, page 337)

1 tablespoon ancho chile powder

1 tablespoon California chile powder

2 teaspoons Indian cayenne powder

1 teaspoon cumin

1 pinch cinnamon

1 pinch ground cloves

2 tablespoons bottled chile sauce

Water or beer, to achieve consistency

Salt and freshly cracked black pepper, to taste

Sauté the onions and garlic in olive oil (or bacon fat). When soft, add
the meat, and cook until just no longer pink. Put the meat mixture
into a food processor, and pulse until fine in order to give your sauce
the proper consistency.

Return the meat mixture to the saucepan and add the remaining ingredients. Add enough water or beer to achieve a loose, but not soupy
consistency.

Simmer gently for 2 or 3 hours, stirring occasionally. Taste and adjust the seasoning to your liking. You can bottle the chili in airtight
containers, and store in the freezer for 3 months or in the refrigerator
for 3 days.

Fingerling Potatoes in Smoked Gouda Cheese Sauce

Executive Chef Kristin Trevino *(Cooking with Kristen, Heyburn, Idaho)*
Serves 6

Idaho is famous for growing potatoes of all varieties. Fingerling potatoes are named for their distinct shape and size, which look just like fingers. Their soft skins are sand or rose-colored, and their creamy, off-white flesh holds up to just about any cooking preparation.
Story by Chef Nicole

Cream Sauce
½ onion, chopped
1 tablespoon olive oil
1 pint (2 cups) heavy cream
1 cup grated Parmesan cheese
4 ounces cream cheese, softened
2 cups shredded smoked gouda
2 teaspoons smoked paprika
½ teaspoon cayenne pepper, optional
Salt and freshly cracked black pepper, to taste

Potatoes
4 cups assorted Idaho fingerlings, washed
1 tablespoon olive oil
2 cloves garlic, minced (see Chef's Tips on garlic, page 314)
1 tablespoon fresh flat-leaf parsley

Cream Sauce

Sweat onions in olive oil over medium heat until the onions have lightly caramelized or browned. Place in a blender with the remaining ingredients. Blend the ingredients well and set aside.

Potatoes

Precook the fingerlings either in a steam bag, by boiling in salt water until tender, or by roasting in the oven with olive oil, salt, and pepper. In a large sauté pan, add olive oil, garlic, and parsley, and sauté for about 1 minute. Add the potatoes, and sauté on medium-high heat until lightly browned. Add 2 cups of cream sauce to the pan of potatoes, simmer, and reduce until thickened.

Chef's Tip

This recipe will yield more cream sauce than needed for the potatoes, but it will keep in the refrigerator for 3 days or in the freezer for 3 months. It also goes great over thinly sliced potatoes; in a casserole dish, cover with sauce and top with additional cheese, and then bake for approximately 1 hour at 400°F or until the potatoes are fork-tender.

French Red Wine-Infused Potato Salad with Chives and Chervil

Executive Chef Kristin Trevino (*Cooking with Kristin, Heyburn, Idaho*)

Serves 4–6

1½ pounds small, assorted fingerlings
2 tablespoons red wine vinegar
1 tablespoon Dijon mustard
3 tablespoons olive oil (see Chef's Tips on emulsification, page 320)
½ cup celery heart, thinly sliced
¼ cup chopped fresh chervil
2 tablespoons chopped fresh chives
Salt and freshly cracked black pepper, to taste

Place the potatoes in a large saucepan with water to cover. Bring to a boil over high heat, reduce to medium, and cover. Let simmer until the potatoes are fork-tender, drain, and set aside to cool. Using a food processor, add vinegar, mustard, salt, and pepper. Slowly add in olive oil to create an emulsion.

When the potatoes are fully cooled, add all the remaining ingredients, and cover with dressing. Season with salt and pepper to taste.

Panko-Battered Hon Shimeji Mushrooms

Corrie Fukuda *(Resides in Riverside, California; inspired by Berkeley, California)*
Serves 4–6

> These mushrooms have a meaty, buttery taste, with some pieces being soft, but firm, and others being strong and crunchy. They make an excellent replacement for fried chicken or calamari.

1½ cups all-purpose flour
1 teaspoon salt
2 eggs
1 (3½ oz.) box panko (Japanese) breadcrumbs
5-8 uncooked large hon-shimeji mushroom stalks, sliced ¼-inch-thick lengthwise (or portobello mushrooms)
Blended oil (see Chef's Tips on blended oil, page 309)

Bread the mushrooms using the Chef's Tips instructions for standard breading procedure (page 319).

Place each of the following mixtures into separate shallow pans wide enough to hold the mushrooms.

Make a dry flour mixture by combining the flour and salt.

Make a wet egg mixture by combining the beaten eggs.

Make a dry breadcrumb mixture using the panko breadcrumbs.

Proceed by dredging the mushrooms one at a time into the flour mixture; pat the mushrooms to remove any excess flour. Then dip into the egg mixture; be sure to fully coat. Then dredge into the breadcrumbs until fully coated. Continue this process until all the mushrooms are breaded. Lay each mushroom onto a sheet pan, being careful not to overcrowd them or lay on top of one another.

Pour blended oil into a 12-inch skillet so the oil is ½-inch high. Heat on medium-high until the oil sizzles when a piece of panko is dropped in. When the oil is hot enough to shallow/pan-fry, begin by carefully placing the mushrooms into the skillet, being careful not to over-crowd the pan. Flip the mushrooms when the bottom sides are golden brown (1 to 2 minutes on each side). Take the cooked mushrooms out of the skillet using a metal spatula or tongs. Place them on a large, paper towel-covered platter or sheet pan. Cool slightly.

Baked Pears

Chef Andrea Beaman *(Inspired by Northern California, Washington, and Oregon; resides in New York, New York)*
Serves 4

> Bosc pears are native to the Northwestern states. These large, long-necked, squat-bottomed, and dark-skinned delicacies are both sweet and tart. Not only are they incredible to consume out of hand, but they are especially flavorful when fresh-baked.

4 Bosc pears
2 cups apple juice
1 cinnamon stick
6–8 cloves

Preheat an oven to 400°F. Cut a thin slice off the bottom of each pear to help keep them standing upright in a baking dish. Pour fruit juice into the pan. Add cinnamon stick and cloves. Roast the pears, basting every 15 minutes, until tender, browned, and puckered. Remove the pears and place on a serving plate. Drizzle the liquid from the bottom of the baking pan on top of the pears.

Asian Pear-tini

Corrie Fukuda *(Resides in Riverside, California; inspired by Berkley, California)*
Serves 2

California pioneered the popular food trend known as fusion. It is a blending of cuisines from more than one cultural background. Northern California has a library of recipes influenced by the many Japanese-American families living there. Many of them are farmers. I have relatives who are still farming and selling their fruit at farmers markets. My dad and I have created this very special blended drink made of Asian pears from a local farm.

1 medium-sized Asian pear, peeled and chopped (about 2 cups)
$1/2$ cup vodka
1 cup De Kuyper® Sour Apple liqueur
4 cups ice
Fresh mint leaves, for garnish (optional)

Pour everything in a blender. Blend well. Pour into individual glasses. Top each drink with a mint leaf.

Bosc Pear Sauce

Ellen L. Madison *(Woody Hill Bed & Breakfast, Westerly, Rhode Island)*
Yields 1¼ cups

> Bosc pears are indigenous to the Northwest Coasts of California, Washington, and Oregon.

½ stick (¼ cup) unsalted butter
3 tablespoons brown sugar
2 Bosc pears, peeled, cored, and chopped
½ cup sugar
½ teaspoon cinnamon
¾ cup water, divided
1 teaspoon cornstarch

Melt butter in a small saucepan. Add brown sugar, and stir until the brown sugar dissolves. Stir in the pears, sugar, and cinnamon, and cook over a low heat until the pears are softened. Add ½ cup of water, and bring to a boil.

In a separate bowl, mix the remaining ¼ cup of water with cornstarch, and mix well until combined. Whisk this mixture into the pears, and simmer until thick. Serve warm over waffles or ice cream.

Apple Pie

Tim McGuire *(Inspired by Washington; resides in Rhinebeck, New York)*

Serves 6–8

> Although Tim lives and works in upstate New York, when asked what kind of apples he prefers, he emphatically answers, "Honey Crisp apples from Washington State, of course."

6–7 Honey Crisp apples, sliced (moderately chunky)
4 tablespoons sugar
1 (9-inch) Pâte Sucrée (unbaked sweet pie dough/crust; see recipe on page 244)
2–3 tablespoons cornstarch
1 teaspoon cinnamon
½ teaspoon nutmeg, freshly grated
2 tablespoons unsalted butter, cut into cubes
Egg wash (see below) and turbinado (raw) sugar

Toss the apples and sugar in a large bowl, and let them sit for at least 30 minutes, but preferably for 1½ hours. While waiting, prepare the crust, drain the apples, and reserve. Toss the apples with cornstarch and spices; set aside.

Reduce the apple juices over a medium flame just until they thicken and darken. Pour this over the apple filling and toss, again. Put the apples in the bottom of the crust, top with the cubes of butter, and then cover with the top crust. Brush the top with egg wash and sprinkle with turbinado sugar.

Bake in a hot oven at 400°F for 45 to 50 minutes. The crust should be brown, and the filling should be bubbly. Cool on your windowsill (or counter top) for about an hour before serving.

Pâte Sucrée

Yields 1 (9-inch) crust

Crust

2 sticks (1 cup) unsalted butter, room temperature
½ cup sugar
1 egg
1 tablespoon heavy cream
3 cups all-purpose flour

Egg Wash

1 tablespoon heavy cream, half-and-half, or milk
1 large egg yolk

Crust

Combine the butter and sugar by creaming until well blended. Add the egg, heavy cream, and flour; combine until all the ingredients are well blended and form a ball.

Egg Wash

Beat the egg yolk with the selected liquid, and brush on the pie crust with a pastry brush.

Chef's Tip

One variation is to reduce the flour by 1 ounce and add 1½ ounces of cocoa powder. Or, you can reduce the flour by 4 ounces and add 4 ounces of ground nuts to produce a tender, flavorful pie crust known as a torte dough.

Sautéed Strawberries in Wine-Pepper Sauce with Vanilla Ice Cream

Chef Sharon Barton *(Chez Alaska Cooking School, Juneau, Alaska)*
Serves 4–6

Strawberries are not indigenous to Alaska; therefore, we have recipes that prepare fruit in various ways other than fresh. This recipe is one that we have prepared at the cooking school that continues to astound visitors.

3 cups strawberries, fresh or frozen
1 cup hearty red wine, divided
6 tablespoons sugar
¼ teaspoon freshly cracked black pepper
1 (1½-inch) piece vanilla bean, split
¾ tablespoon cornstarch
1½ tablespoons unsalted butter
6 sprigs mint
Vanilla ice cream, as needed
Freshly ground black pepper, to taste

Wash, stem, and quarter the strawberries; set aside. If using frozen berries, place them in a colander and run cold water over them until they defrost.

Combine ¾ cup of wine, sugar, and ¼ teaspoon pepper in a heavy, medium-sized saucepan. Scrape in seeds from the vanilla bean; add the bean. Stir over medium heat until the sugar dissolves. Whisk ¼ cup of wine with cornstarch in a small bowl to blend. Add the cornstarch mix to the sauce, and whisk constantly until the mixture boils and thickens (about 2 minutes; see Chef's Tips on slurries, page 322). Remove the vanilla bean pieces. Set aside.

Melt butter in a large skillet over high heat. Add berries, and sauté for 1 minute. Add the sauce and additional pepper, to taste, to the mixture; bring to a boil. Divide the berries and sauce among four to six martini glasses; top with ice cream and garnish with mint sprigs.

Banana Hazelnut Upside-Down Cake

Chef John Paulk *(Mezzaluna Fine Catering, Portland, Oregon)*
Serves 8

This cake, featuring locally grown Oregon hazelnuts, can be served as a formal dessert with softly whipped cream, or would also be perfect as a sweet brunch dish.

Hazelnut Spread
¾ cup unsalted butter
½ pound dark brown sugar
½ cup chopped toasted hazelnuts (see Chef's Tips on nuts and seeds, page 318)

Cake
⅓ pound hazelnuts, toasted, skinned, and coarsely chopped (see Chef's Tips on nuts and seeds, page 318)
1 cup sugar
1 stick (½ cup) unsalted butter
2 eggs
1 cup sour cream
2 teaspoons pure vanilla extract
½ cup banana puree, from 1 or 2 bananas
1¾ cups all-purpose flour
2 teaspoons baking powder
1 teaspoon salt
Hazelnut Spread
1–2 whole bananas, very ripe

Hazelnut Spread

Melt the butter. Remove from the heat, and whisk in the brown sugar and nuts. Store in the refrigerator.

Cake

Preheat the oven to 375°F. Butter a 9-inch cake pan or 8 (1-cup) ramekins. Toast the nuts, and let them cool completely.

In a food processor, grind the nuts with the 1 cup of white sugar until very fine.

In a mixer, cream the butter; then add the sugar mixture. Remove from the mixer.

Add the eggs one at a time, and combine thoroughly. Add the sour cream and vanilla, and stir. Mix in the banana puree.

Stir in the flour, baking powder, and salt to make a smooth batter (do not over-mix, or the cake will be tough).

To bake, cover the bottom of the prepared cake pan or ramekins with some of the warmed Hazelnut Spread (microwave for 40 seconds or so). Fan the banana slices over it until the bottom is covered. Spoon in the batter.

Bake until just set (about 35 to 40 minutes, or 15 to 20 minutes for smaller ramekins). Keep warm in a low oven, and turn it out at the last minute.

Peppermint Semifreddo

Chef John Paulk *(Mezzaluna Fine Catering, Portland, Oregon)*
Serves 6

This recipe was inspired by peppermint grown and harvested in the Northwestern state of Oregon.

½ cup crushed candy canes, separated
1½ cups heavy cream
3 large eggs, separated
9 tablespoons sugar, separated
6 tablespoons peppermint-flavored liqueur

Crush candy canes in a food processor. Place heavy cream in a mixer bowl, add 5 tablespoons of crushed candy, and whip until stiff peaks form. Chill until ready to use.

Place a large metal bowl over a pan of simmering water; whisk egg yolks and 3 tablespoons of sugar until pale in color. Add liqueur; whisk vigorously until the mixture is thick (3 to 5 minutes). Cool in a refrigerator.

Set the heat-proof bowl of an electric mixer over a pan of simmering water. In this bowl, whisk the egg whites and remaining 6 tablespoons of sugar until the sugar dissolves and the mixture is warm to the touch (about 2 minutes). Attach the bowl to the mixer, and beat until stiff and glossy peaks form.

Fold the egg white mixture into the egg yolk mixture one-third at a time. Fold in the whipped cream mixture.

Spoon the mixture into six serving dishes (such as martini goblets), layering it with reserved candy cane. Freeze until firm (at least 2 hours to overnight).

Garnish with crushed candy cane and warmed hot fudge on the side.

Eggnog Bread Pudding with Cookie Butter Crème Anglaise Sauce

Chef Darnell Harness *(Simply Dine Catering, Henderson, Nevada)*
Serves 10

2 pounds Krispy Kreme® doughnuts
2 cups eggnog
2 cups half-and-half
6 large eggs
1½ cups sugar
1 teaspoon nutmeg
1 teaspoon cinnamon
½ cup coffee-flavored or white chocolate liqueur
1 teaspoon sea salt
1 teaspoon pure vanilla extract
1 tablespoon sugar
3 tablespoons unsalted butter, melted

Cookie Butter Crème Anglaise Sauce
6 large egg yolks
¾ cup sugar
½ teaspoon ground ginger
½ teaspoon cinnamon
¼ cup cookie butter
3 cups heavy cream
Pinch salt

Take the doughnuts and leave them out for 4 days until they are hard. In a large bowl, add the eggnog, half-and-half, eggs, sugar, nutmeg, cinnamon, liqueur, salt, and vanilla. With a wire whisk, beat the ingredients until the mixture is smooth. In the same bowl, add the cut-up doughnuts, and refrigerate overnight. In a greased 9- by 13-inch pan, pour the doughnut and custard mixture in, and sprinkle 1 tablespoon of sugar over the top. Place the pan in a preheated 350°F oven, cook for 30 minutes, and remove.

Drizzle melted butter over the mixture, return to the oven, and cook for another 30 minutes or until the custard looks set and is golden brown.

Cookie Butter Crème Anglaise Sauce

In a bowl, whisk together the egg yolks, sugar, and spices until smooth and creamy. In a saucepan place the heavy cream, cookie butter, and salt, and whisk until the mixture is smooth and combined.

Bring the mixture to a simmer. Ladle some of the warm heavy cream-cookie butter mixture into the bowl with the egg mixture to temper it. Pour the mixture back into the heavy cream, and bring the heat back up to simmer.

Cook the mixture until the temperature is 170°F or the mixture coats the back of a spoon. Strain the mixture twice, and let it cool at room temperature for 30 minutes. Pour the mixture in a squirt bottle and refrigerate until ready to use.

Part V

SOUTHWEST

The great Southwest region of America includes California, Nevada, Arizona, New Mexico, Texas, and Hawaii. Throughout the region, locals enjoy the year-round availability of an abundance of indigenous vegetables and fruits. The farmers' markets and street carts are filled with avocados, chiles, corn, jicama, and mangos, as well as spices such as cumin, cayenne, and coriander and fresh herbs such as Mexican oregano and cilantro.

Mexico's proximity to this region has most definitely influenced its cooking style. The first time Nicole was introduced to Southwest cuisine was as a young line cook in San Diego, California. The resort where she worked was as busy as it was beautiful. Each morning, they fired close to 350 orders of Huevos Rancheros (page 259), a popular Mexican-inspired breakfast dish, which she came to love as she did so many other traditional Southwest dishes.

In the following pages, you will find many cherished recipes from kitchens across the region, each highlighting authentic Southwestern flavors such as the sweetness of mango in recipes like Hawaiian Island Summer Gazpacho (page 260) and Arizona Mango Salsa (page 287).

Another key flavor element in Southwestern cuisine is spice. Just as apples are prevalent in the Northeast, chiles are a favorite in the Southwest, and the varieties are seemingly endless. Hawaii and California prefer to add the heat of a jalapeño to their signature dishes. Meanwhile, New Mexico is home to a true Western showdown between red and green chiles. Both are predominant in their state's dishes, but the locals are divided on which they favor. You can decide for yourself after trying Carne Adovada (page 295) and Hatch Green Chile-Chicken Stew (page 283). Chipotle chiles are also a common ingredient that incorporates a smoky flavor to the region's traditional spicy fare.

Corn, in its many forms, is almost always present in a Southwestern meal, from hominy used to make New Mexican Posole (page 264) to ground corn found in the soft-pressed tortillas used to hold the famous California Fish Taco (page 278).

There is no better way to highlight fresh fish caught off the Hawaiian coast than to feature it in the Ceviche of the Big Island (page 277). This citrusy dish offers the most refreshing and palatable way to enjoy the island's bounty.

Texas represents not only the big and bold taste of Texas BBQ Sauce (page 300), but also the Mexican-influenced cuisine known as Tex-Mex, found in dishes such as Ricardo's Stacked Red Chile Cheese Enchiladas (page 292). Finally, what is a trip to the Southwest without indulging in dessert? Our favorite is the Mexican Chocolate Cheesecake (page 308), laced with the flavor of cinnamon and the warmth of cayenne.

Parfaits with Ginger-Infused Melon and Honeyed Yogurt

Chef Michelle Moore *(South Pasadena, California)*

Serves 4–6

¾ cup water (see Chef's Tips on simple syrup, page 321)

½ cup sugar

2–3 tablespoons chopped fresh ginger

5–6 cups 1-inch diced assorted melon pieces (about 3 pounds)

2 cups plain yogurt

2–4 tablespoons honey or agave nectar, or to taste

Mint sprigs, optional

¼ cup coconut, toasted, optional (see Chef's Tips on nuts and seeds, page 318)

Make a simple syrup by heating water in a saucepan to boiling. Reduce the heat, and stir in the sugar and ginger. Carefully stir the mixture until the sugar has completely dissolved. Allow the mixture to gently simmer for about 5 minutes until it thickens slightly. Remove from the heat, and strain the liquid into a container. Allow to cool completely before use.

Place the diced melon in a large bowl, and pour ½ cup of the syrup over the melon. Gently toss and set aside.

Make the sauce by combining the yogurt and honey or agave nectar, and adjust the sweetness to taste.

Using four to six clear decorative glasses, spoon the melon, extra syrup, and yogurt in layers, dividing the mixtures equally. If desired, top each off with a mint sprig and a bit of toasted coconut.

Chef's Tip

You can use one type of melon instead of an assortment. Instead of dicing the melon, try making small melon balls.

You can also use different flavorings for the syrup, like citrus (use the peels or oranges or lemons), two to three sticks of cinnamon, or one split vanilla bean.

You can also flavor the yogurt by adding finely chopped bits of candied ginger or ⅛ teaspoon of cinnamon.

Almond Pancakes

Andrea Garro *(Vista, California)*
Serves 4

½ cup almond flour or meal
1¾ cups oat (for a wheat-free option) or whole-wheat pastry flour
1 tablespoon baking powder (non-aluminum)
½ teaspoon sea salt
1 egg
1 tablespoon pure vanilla extract
1½ cups almond, rice, or soy milk
¼ cup grapeseed oil

Mix the dry ingredients in a bowl. Mix the wet ingredients in a separate bowl, and then pour into the dry ingredients, combining. Cook on a lightly oiled skillet until golden brown. Serve warm with maple syrup or honey.

Chef's Tip

Try substituting ½ cup of shredded coconut or ¼ cup of malt-sweetened chocolate chips for almond flour or meal. Add lemon zest, the juice of one lemon (add a little less milk), and ½ cup of poppy seeds for lemon-poppy seed pancakes.

Baked Blueberry-Pecan French Toast

Susie Davis West *(Inspired by Texas; resides in Lynbrook, New York)*
Serves 6

> This recipe was sent to me from our childhood friend Susie. Her dear mom, Mrs. Davis, grew up in Texas, where the state nut is pecans.

1 (24-inch) baguette, cut into 20 (1-inch) slices
6 large eggs
3 cups whole milk
½ teaspoon freshly ground nutmeg
1 teaspoon vanilla extract
1 cup packed brown sugar, divided
1 cup pecans, chopped (see Chef's Tips on nuts and seeds, page 318)
½ stick plus 1 teaspoon unsalted butter, softened
¼ teaspoon salt
2 cups fresh blueberries
½ stick (¼ cup) unsalted butter

Spray a 13- by 9-inch, oven-proof dish with baking spray. Layer baguette slices in the baking dish. In a large bowl, whisk together eggs, milk, nutmeg, vanilla, and ¾ cup of brown sugar. Pour evenly over the bread. Pat the bread down with the back of a wooden spoon. Cover with plastic wrap, and place in a refrigerator for at least 8 hours or until all the liquid is absorbed.

Preheat an oven to 350°F. Spread the pecans evenly over a jelly-roll pan, place the pan on the middle oven rack, and bake for 8 minutes until fragrant. Toss the pecans with 1 teaspoon of butter and salt. Increase the temperature to 400°F. Sprinkle pecans and blueberries over the top of the bread mixture. Cut ½ stick of butter into pieces, place in a saucepan with the remaining ¼ cup of brown sugar, and heat on low until the butter is melted. Drizzle the butter mixture over the bread, and bake for 20 minutes or until the liquid from the blueberries is bubbling.

Huevos Rancheros

Andrea Garro *(Vista, California)*
Serves 2

4 corn tortillas
½ cup medium salsa
½ cup chopped onions
1 tablespoon chipotle chiles in adobo sauce
½ cup cooked black beans
4 eggs

Optional Toppings
Cheddar cheese, grated
Scallions, parsley, or cilantro, chopped
Tofu or almond milk cheese, as desired

Heat the tortillas in an oven or toaster just until soft. Warm the salsa, onions, and chipotle chiles in adobo sauce, and heat the black beans in a non-stick pan. Move to one side. Crack the eggs, and cook for 3 to 5 minutes to the desired firmness. Place two warm tortillas side by side on a warmed plate, and slide the eggs, half of the salsa, and the beans onto the tortillas. Repeat with the remaining eggs. Garnish with your choice of toppings.

Island Summer Gazpacho

Chef Aline Steiner *(À Table Hawaii, Honolulu, Hawaii)*
Serves 6–8 as a first course or 12–14 as an appetizer

> Although we are lucky to have sun and warmth year-round in the Hawaiian Islands, summer also brings even warmer temperatures and, most importantly, beautiful sweet and tasty mangoes. Here is a cool recipe for a mango-cucumber cold soup or a play on traditional gazpacho.

2 ripe Hawaiian mangos, peeled and coarsely chopped
1½ Japanese cucumbers, seeds removed
1½–2 cups cold water
2 teaspoons sherry or rice vinegar
3 tablespoons olive oil (see Chef's Tips on emulsification, page 320)
1 teaspoon sea salt

Place all the ingredients (except the olive oil and sea salt) into a blender. While the blender's motor is running, add in the olive oil. The consistency should be a bit thicker than cream soup, so add in some water, if necessary. It should not be overly sweet, so taste for seasoning and add a pinch of sea salt, if necessary.

Place in the refrigerator until ready to serve, and serve cold.

Almost-Meatless Butternut Squash and Black Bean Chili

Chef and Dr. Sonali Ruder *(Resides in New York, New York; inspired by San Diego, California)*
Serves 6

> This hearty and nutritious chili recipe is perfect to prepare in the fall, when butternut squash is in season all throughout the United States. Chipotles are canned smoked jalapeño peppers, which complement the sweet butternut squash. By incorporating healthy vegetables and black beans in this dish, only a small amount of ground beef is added. This cuts down on the calories and fat, and no one will even miss it.

2 teaspoons extra-virgin olive oil

1 medium yellow onion, chopped

1 red bell pepper, seeded and chopped (see Chef's Tips on chiles, page 316)

2 cloves garlic, chopped (see Chef's Tips on garlic, page 314)

½ pound extra-lean ground beef (93% lean) (omit for vegetarian version)

1 teaspoon chipotles in adobo sauce, seeded and chopped

1½ teaspoons ground cumin

½ teaspoon dried oregano

¼ teaspoon allspice

1 medium butternut squash, peeled and cut into 1-inch cubes (about 3 cups)

1 (28 oz.) can diced fire-roasted tomatoes

1 cup fat-free and low-sodium beef or chicken broth (or water for vegetarian version)

1 (15 oz.) can black beans, rinsed (an additional can for vegetarian version)

¼ cup chopped fresh cilantro

Salt and freshly cracked black pepper, to taste

Heat the oil in a large Dutch oven or wide-based pot over medium heat. Add the onion and bell pepper, and cook for 6 to 7 minutes until partially softened. Add the garlic, and cook another minute until fragrant. Stir in the ground beef and brown it, breaking it into pieces as it cooks. Season with salt and pepper.

Stir in the chipotles, adobo sauce, cumin, oregano, and allspice. Add the butternut squash, tomatoes, and broth (or water). Season with salt and pepper to taste. Bring the mixture to a boil, and then reduce to a simmer. Cover and cook for 20 minutes; then uncover and stir in the beans. Cook partially covered for another 15 to 20 minutes until the chili has thickened and the squash is cooked through. Stir in the cilantro.

Serve the chili alone or with brown rice. Top with the reduced-fat sour cream, if desired. Garnish with cilantro.

Real Texas Chili

James Garner *(Big Lake, Texas)*
Serves 6–8

2–3 strips bacon
3 pounds beef shoulder, chuck, or round steak, trimmed of fat and
ground or cut into ½-inch cubes
1–3 tablespoons dried chile pepper flakes (adjust to desired heat)
3 cups water
1 tablespoon dried oregano
1 tablespoon cumin seeds, crushed (see Chef's Tips on nuts and
seeds, page 318)
2 teaspoons salt
1–2 teaspoons cayenne pepper
2 cloves garlic, crushed (see Chef's Tips on garlic, page 314)
2 tablespoons corn flour (use masa harina if possible)
Fresh coriander leaves (cilantro) and sour cream, to garnish

In a heavy frying pan or skillet over medium heat, add the bacon, and
fry for a few minutes. Discard the bacon and leave the fat. Add the
beef, and fry in the bacon fat, stirring constantly until brown.

Add the dried chile pepper flakes, and cook for 1 to 2 minutes. Then
add water, and bring to a boil over high heat. Reduce the heat to a slow
simmer, cover, and cook for 30 minutes.

Add the oregano, cumin seeds, salt, cayenne pepper, and garlic. Cover,
again, and simmer for 45 minutes more. Uncover, and stir in the corn
flour or masa harina. Stir well until the corn flour is well-combined
with the rest of the ingredients. Cover, reduce the heat to very low,
and cook for 30 minutes more, stirring occasionally. If the mixture is
too thick, add small amounts of hot water, and stir. Serve with fresh
coriander leaves and sour cream.

▌ For those with real Texas stomachs, add diced jalapeños and/or ha-
▌ baneros to taste.

Posole

Santa Fe School of Cooking *(Santa Fe, New Mexico)*
Serves 8–10

> Posole, or spicy hominy stew, is traditionally served in New
> Mexico or Texas. Hominy, a dried and rehydrated white corn
> kernel, can be found in any international food aisle in your local
> grocery store. If you have never had hominy, posole is by far the
> best way to experience it.
> *Story by Chef Nicole*

2 cups posole, picked over for dirt or stones (may substitute rehydrated canned hominy)
¼ cup vegetable oil
2 cups chopped onion
2 tablespoons minced garlic (see Chef's Tips on garlic, page 314)
1 ounce New Mexico dried red chile pods (4 or 5 pods), stems and
seeds removed (see Chef's Tips on chiles, page 316)
5 cups chicken broth
½ cup coarsely chopped cilantro, divided
Salt, to taste

Put posole in a 6-quart pot and cover with cold water (until it reaches
3 inches over the posole). Bring to a boil, reduce the heat, and simmer
for 2 to 3 hours, adding water as needed until the posole has softened
and begun to burst. Drain the posole, rinse well, and set aside (if using
canned hominy, omit this step).

Heat the oil in a 6-quart pot, and sauté the onions until golden. Add
the garlic, and sauté for 1 minute. Add the dried chiles, broth, and
half of the cilantro. Bring to a boil. Reduce the heat and simmer for 30
minutes. Add hominy and salt, and continue cooking for 30 minutes.
Stir in the remaining cilantro. Taste and adjust the seasonings.

Avocado, Orange, and Strawberry Salad

Chef Michelle Moore *(South Pasadena, California)*

Serves 4

> Three of my favorite California fruits, avocados, oranges, and strawberries, are presented here in a simple, plated salad. Each is wonderful alone, but, when paired together, they create a colorful, delicious mixture of creamy, tart, and sweet.

Salad

2 firm, ripe avocados, peeled, halved, pitted, and cut into ½-inch slices (see Chef's Tips on avocado, page 313)
2 sweet oranges, peeled and sliced crosswise into ½-inch slices
1 pint fresh strawberries, half or sliced

Dressing

2 limes, 1 zested and both juiced (see Chef's Tips on citrus zest, page 311)
½ teaspoon salt
¼ teaspoon sugar
¼ teaspoon freshly cracked black pepper
Generous pinch cayenne pepper
¼ cup extra-virgin olive oil (see Chef's Tips on emulsification, page 320)

Salad

Decoratively layer the avocados, oranges, and strawberries on a serving platter.

Dressing

Whisk the lime juice and zest, salt, sugar, and peppers, and slowly drizzle in the olive oil to combine. Taste and adjust the seasonings as desired. Drizzle the dressing over the fruit, and serve immediately.

Confetti Corn, Red Pepper, and Bean Salad

Corrie Fukuda *(Inspired by Berkeley, California; resides in Riverside, California)*
Serves 6

> The main ingredients in this recipe are some of California's specialty crops. I have been obsessed with the idea of making fresh salads like this one. This recipe is made of kidney beans, pinto beans, red pepper, fresh corn, jalapeño, red onion, salt, pepper, olive oil, and store-bought Italian dressing. I honestly just use whatever is in the pantry or my refrigerator to create this refreshing, healthy, and delicious salad.

1 (19 oz.) can pinto beans, drained and rinsed
1 (19 oz.) can kidney beans, drained and rinsed
¼ red pepper, diced
2 cups fresh corn kernels (see Chef's Tips on corn, page 322)
2 tablespoons red onion, chopped
1–2 tablespoons extra-virgin olive oil
2–3 teaspoons diced jalapeño (see Chef's Tips on chiles, page 316)
Italian dressing, to taste
Salt and freshly cracked black pepper, to taste

Mix everything together in a big bowl. Refrigerate for at least an hour.

California Cobb Salad

Andrea Garro *(San Diego, California)*
Serves 4–6

Dressing
¼ cup red wine vinegar
1 ½ tablespoons fresh lemon juice
2 teaspoons Dijon mustard
1 teaspoon Worcestershire sauce
¼ teaspoon raw agave nectar
1–2 cloves garlic, minced
1 tablespoon finely chopped chives
½ cup grapeseed or canola oil (see Chef's Tips on emulsification, page 320)
¼ cup extra-virgin olive oil
Sea salt and freshly cracked black pepper, to taste

Salad
1 head organic romaine lettuce, shredded
1 head butter lettuce, shredded (or 2 heads romaine lettuce)
1 cup watercress or micro greens/sprouts
2 ounces bleu cheese, crumbled
2 hard-boiled eggs, peeled and sliced
8 strips turkey bacon, crumbled
8 ounces cherry tomatoes, sliced in half
1 avocado, peeled, pitted, and cut into cubes
2 boneless chicken breasts, grilled or cooked, and cut into small cubes

Dressing
Combine all the ingredients, except the oil, salt, and pepper, in a blender. While the blender is running, add the oil in a slow, steady stream to emulsify. Add salt and pepper to taste.

Salad

Add lettuce and watercress (or sprouts) to a large salad bowl. Toss with ¼ of the dressing. Arrange all the other ingredients in neat rows on top of the greens. Drizzle with the remaining dressing on top before serving.

Chorizo and New Potato Salad with Queso Seco

Andy Broder *(A Culinary Studio, Scottsdale, Arizona)*
Serves 6–8

> Chorizo is, by far, one of my favorite pork sausages. Classically burnt orange in color and spicy in flavor, this Southwestern specialty can be bought as crumbled, bulk sausage or cased links of sausage. My favorite Mexican queso seco (or "dry cheese") is cotija, which can be found in any Latin American food market.
> *Story by Chef Nicole*

8 ounces chorizo (crumbled or 1–2 links, casings removed)
½ teaspoon kosher salt
2 tablespoons olive oil
2 tablespoons water
1 pound new or yellow potatoes, cut into ½-inch dices (not peeled)
Juice of 1 lime
½ cup queso seco (or other crumbly Mexican cheese), crumbled

Heat a large skillet over medium heat. When hot, add chorizo. Cook thoroughly, stirring occasionally.

Transfer to a blender, and add kosher salt, olive oil, and water. Then puree.

Toss potatoes into the chorizo mixture, and place back in the skillet. Cover and cook over medium heat for 15 minutes, stirring every 5 minutes. When the potatoes start to become tender, remove the cover, and cook for 5 minutes longer.

When very tender, add lime juice, and toss to incorporate. Transfer to a cool bowl and chill (or allow to come to room temperature).

Just before serving, add cheese, and toss to incorporate.

Jicama Sticks with Spicy Cinnamon Dressing

Amie Valpone *(Inspired by San Diego, California; resides in New York, New York)*
Serves 2

It is not every day that you see a bit of jicama on your plate—or in the food store or farmers market, for that matter. Yet I have recently fallen in love with it. While I was out in San Diego, California, speaking at the BlogHer Conference this past summer, there was a fabulous spread of these cute, little white sticks (jicama). Let's just say that I devoured them. They were so refreshing and incredible. Now, I have had jicama before, but just as a mere topping on a salad, not eaten alone with hummus or salsa. Well, move over zucchini, because I have got a new love. Enter the pearly white jicama, so light and refreshing!

Cinnamon Dipping Sauce

5 leaves fresh mint, finely chopped
¼ cup ground flaxseed
1 extra-ripe avocado, peeled, pitted, and chopped (see Chef's Tips on avocado, page 313)
2 tablespoons almond butter
¼ cup rice milk
¼ teaspoon sea salt
1 teaspoon ground cinnamon

Jicama

1 tablespoon balsamic vinegar
Pinch cayenne pepper
1 large jicama, peeled and sliced into ½-inch sticks

Cinnamon Dipping Sauce

In a food processor, combine the mint, flaxseeds, avocado, almond butter, rice milk, sea salt, and cinnamon; pulse until smooth. Transfer the mixture to a serving bowl for dipping.

Jicama

In a large bowl, combine the balsamic vinegar and cayenne pepper; mix well. Add jicama; gently toss to combine until the jicama sticks are coated.

Arrange the balsamic-coated jicama sticks on a serving platter. Serve with the cinnamon dipping sauce.

Black Bean Salsa

Andrea Garro *(Vista, California)*
Serves 12

Here is a simple and delicious recipe that includes all the favorite local California flavors, such as corn, cilantro, avocados, limes, and jalapeños. I have been making it for years, and, whenever I bring this salsa to a potluck gathering, it is devoured. If you decide to make this (and I highly suggest that you do), be prepared to share the recipe—they *will* ask for it.

2 (15 oz.) cans black beans, rinsed and drained
1 (14 oz.) can whole kernel corn, drained
2 large organic tomatoes, chopped
2 large avocados (see Chef's Tips on avocado, page 313)
1 jalapeño, seeded and minced (see Chef's Tips on chiles, page 316)
¼ cup organic cilantro, chopped
3 cloves garlic, minced
½ large red onion, chopped
4 tablespoons fresh lime juice
¼ cup olive oil
¼ cup red wine vinegar
Sea salt and freshly cracked black pepper, to taste

Combine all the ingredients in a large bowl. Cover and chill for 1 hour or more.

Vegan Empanadas and Chimichurri Sauce

Andrea Garro *(San Diego, California)*
Serves 8–10

Empanadas are a traditional South American dish. They are often a staple at parties and family get-togethers because they are so versatile. You can make empanadas in any size or shape, and fill them with anything from sautéed greens to roasted corn and potatoes. Empanadas are a perfect little package of goodness. As a little girl, my mom would pack them in my lunch instead of the typical peanut butter and jelly. Thankfully, my mom has passed down her empanada recipes and techniques. Now, my children can enjoy them, as well.

I love Latin flare, flavors, and cuisine. My passion is to make traditional Latin favorites healthier, while maintaining the traditions that I have grown up with. Even the biggest skeptics and diehard traditionalists have loved these recipes, and I hope that you will, too. For an added touch, include a delectable chimichurri sauce on the side.

Vegan Empanada Dough
2 cups garbanzo flour (gluten-free) or spelt
3 tablespoons olive oil
¼ cup water plus additional water

Filling
Olive oil, as needed
1 yellow onion, diced
1 red pepper, chopped
3 cloves garlic, chopped
2 cups kale, finely chopped
1 cup spinach, chopped
1 portobello mushroom, chopped

5 tablespoons tomato paste

1½ cups cooked millet or quinoa

1 teaspoon paprika

2 teaspoons oregano

1 tablespoon cumin

Sea salt and freshly cracked black pepper, to taste

Chimichurri Sauce

¾ cup olive oil

¼ cup red wine vinegar

½ cup chopped parsley

3 cloves garlic, minced

1½ teaspoons dried oregano

1 teaspoon red pepper flakes, or to taste

Sea salt and freshly cracked black pepper, to taste

Vegan Empanada Dough

Add the flour to a bowl. Slowly add the olive oil, and mix; then add the water, and mix. Continue by kneading the dough and adding more water, 1 tablespoon at a time, until the dough comes together easily. Once you achieve the right texture, let it sit at room temperature while you make the filling.

Filling

Heat a large pan on medium heat. Then drizzle with olive oil. Add the onions and red peppers, and cook for 2 to 3 minutes until they begin to soften; then add the garlic. After about 30 seconds, add in the kale, and allow it to soften. Once the kale is reduced down, add in the spinach and mushroom. After about 2 to 3 minutes, add the tomato paste, and stir it in. Next, add the millet and the rest of the ingredients, and continue to stir until the filling is reduced and is well blended (approximately 3 minutes).

Spray a cookie sheet with a light coat of olive oil, and preheat the oven to 350°F.

Separate the dough into the desired size of the empanadas (I use golf-ball size). Then roll out the dough to about ¼-inch thickness. Take a spoonful of the filling, and add to half of the empanada dough. Then fold the other side of the dough over the filling side, and pinch over the edges to close. Place the empanadas on the cookie sheet and repeat. Once you have put together your empanadas, bake in oven for 12 to 15 minutes, depending on your oven. You want the dough to be just slightly firm to the touch. Allow them to cool. While they are cooling, make the chimichurri sauce.

Chimichurri Sauce

Add the olive oil, vinegar, and parsley to a bowl, and mix. Then add the garlic and remaining ingredients, and mix well. The chimichurri is then ready, but is even more delicious the next day, after the flavors have blended even more.

When serving, either drizzle the chimichurri sauce over the empanadas or serve on the side. Que delicioso!

Mammer's Sunshine Pickles

Flora Garner *(Denison, Texas)*
Makes 6–8 pickles or 1 (16-ounce) jar

6–8 Kirby cucumbers, with skin on, each 4–6 inches long
1 quart pure apple vinegar
2 quarts water
1 cup canning salt
3 grape leaves, washed and drained dry
1–2 cloves garlic, cut in half
1–2 hot peppers, cut in half (see Chef's Tips on chiles and roasting peppers, page 316)
1 teaspoon dill seed or fresh dill
1 teaspoon pickling spice

Boil the vinegar, water, and salt for about 2 or 3 minutes. Keep this mixture hot while you pack the jars. Place grape leaves, garlic, peppers, dill, and spices in the bottom of the jars. Pack the cucumbers on top, and pour the hot mixture over the cucumbers to cover. Seal according to the jar directions, and let cool. When cool, place upside-down outside in the sunshine. On the next day, turn right-side-up. Continue to alternate. Leave out for 8 sunny days (do not count the cloudy days). Do not use for 6 weeks.

Ceviche of the Big Island

Chef de Cuisine Johan Svensson *(BLT Steak, Honolulu, Hawaii)*
Serves 4

½ cup fresh lemon juice
½ cup fresh lime juice
1 clove garlic, sliced thin
½ red onion, sliced thin
1 jalapeño, core removed and sliced thin into rings (see Chef's Tips
on chiles, page 316)
2 Kamuela beefsteak tomatoes, core removed and sliced thin
½ cup olive oil
8 ounces sushi-grade tuna, sliced into 8 slices
8 ounces kanpachi (yellowtail fish), sliced into 8 slices
8 oysters
4 sprigs fresh cilantro
1 (2-inch thick) part fresh or canned heart of palm, sliced lengthwise
Good-quality olive oil, for garnish
Salt and white pepper, to taste

Mix the juices, garlic, onion, jalapeño, and tomatoes, and let sit for at
least 1 hour. Add olive oil, and season with salt and pepper.

Dip the fish and oysters in the mixture, letting them soak for 1 minute; then season and place on four plates. Fish out the vegetables from
the ceviche liquid and spread it over the fish. Garnish with the heart
of palm shavings and cilantro sprigs, drizzling some good olive oil on
top.

Fish Tacos

Chef Nicole *(Inspired by San Diego, California)*
Serves 4

> Traditional Mexican-inspired tacos are always served on freshly made soft corn tortillas with shredded cabbage and assorted toppings, such as pico de gallo, guacamole, fresh cilantro, chopped onions, fresh lime juice, and crema. The fish taco, now a staple among the predominant surfing culture along the coast of Southern California, combines this classic dish with fresh Pacific-caught fish. Recreations of this dish can now be found all over the United States, but there is nothing like this authentic recipe.

Batter

12 ounces beer (Tecate)

1 cup all-purpose flour

1 egg

1 teaspoon salt

1 teaspoon dried Mexican oregano

1 teaspoon paprika

½ teaspoon dry mustard

¼ teaspoon cayenne pepper

Fish

1 pound white fish fillets (cod, pollack, or snapper)

½ cup canola oil

White Sauce

1 cup crèma (Mexican mayonnaise; may substitute ½ cup each mayonnaise and yogurt)

1 tablespoon whole milk

½ teaspoon minced garlic

1 tablespoon chopped cilantro

Taco

8 small soft corn tortillas

2 cups shredded cabbage

Pico de Gallo

3–4 tomatoes, seeds removed and diced small

¼ cup red onion, diced small

1 clove's worth of garlic paste (see Chef's Tips on garlic, page 314)

1 jalapeño, seeds and ribs removed, and minced (see Chef's Tips on chiles, page 316)

¼ cup cilantro leaves, rough-chopped

Juice of 1 lime

½ teaspoon cumin

½ cup mango, diced small

Salt and freshly cracked black pepper, to taste

Guacamole

3 ripe avocadoes (see Chef's Tips on avocadoes, page 313)

½ cup red or yellow onion, minced

¼ cup cilantro leaves, rough-chopped

Juice of 1–2 limes

1 tomato, diced small (optional)

1 mango, peeled and diced (optional)

Salt and freshly cracked black pepper, to taste

Batter

Combine the first three ingredients. Add the remaining ingredients, and mix well. Allow to stand for 1 hour prior to use.

Fish

Check the fish for bones, and cut each fillet into 1-ounce pieces. In a frying pan, heat oil until hot, but not smoking. Dip four to five pieces of fish into the batter one at a time, and fry for about 1 minute on each side. Do not overcook. Drain on paper towels.

White Sauce

Place all the ingredients in a small bowl and whisk until well-combined.

Taco

Put a few tablespoons of cabbage in the middle of the tortilla. Add the fish, and garnish with the white sauce and your favorite traditional toppings.

Pico de Gallo

Combine all the ingredients, toss, and taste. Adjust the seasoning.

Guacamole

Combine all the ingredients, mix well, taste, and adjust the seasoning.

Pan-Seared Hawaiian Opakapaka and Macadamia Nut Gazpacho

Chef Aline Steiner *(A Table Hawaii, Honolulu, Hawaii)*
Serves 6

Fish

6 boneless pink snapper (opakapaka) fillets
2 tablespoons peanut oil (see Chef's Tips on blended oil, page 309)
Salt and freshly cracked black pepper, to taste

Sauce

½ cup soy sauce
¼ cup sake
3 tablespoons sesame oil
1 tablespoon fresh ginger, grated
3 cloves garlic, grated (see Chef's Tips on garlic, page 314)

Macadamia Nut Gazpacho

2½ cups unsalted macadamia nuts, divided
1½ cups water, more if needed
2 cloves garlic, peeled
2 tablespoons sherry vinegar
2 tablespoons olive oil
2 tablespoons walnut oil
2 star anise
Salt and freshly cracked black pepper, to taste

Fish

Place the fish skin-side-up on a cutting board, and score the fish using a sharp knife by making 3 to 4 shallow cuts skin-deep, exposing the flesh. Season with salt and pepper.

Place a sauté pan on medium heat, add peanut oil, and heat until almost smoking. Add the fish to the hot pan skin-side-down, and sear for approximately 3 to 5 minutes until skin is nice and crispy. Flip over and continue to sear for only 30 seconds on the other side. Remove the fish from the pan and place in oven-safe dish, skin-side-up. Set aside.

Sauce

Combine all the ingredients in a small saucepan and simmer over medium heat until reduced by two-thirds.

Macadamia Nut Gazpacho

Soak 2 cups of nuts in water for 30 minutes to 1 hour (do not drain). Place the nuts and water mixture in a blender with the remaining ingredients, and blend until smooth and creamy (not pasty). Add more water, if necessary, and salt and pepper to taste.

In a dry skillet, toast ½ cup of nuts until golden brown and fragrant (see Chef's Tips on nuts and seeds, page 318).

Place the fish in a preheated 450°F oven, and rest for 3 to 4 minutes. Plate fish skin-side-up, top each fillet with a spoonful of sauce, and garnish with toasted nuts.

Hatch Green Chile-Chicken Stew

Leila O'Connell (*Blue Plate Special Caterers, Albuquerque, New Mexico*)
Serves 4–6

> This chicken stew recipe features chiles, which are New Mexico's state vegetable.

1 large onion, diced
⅓ cup vegetable oil
4 cloves garlic, crushed (see Chef's Tips on garlic, page 314)
2 pounds chicken breast, cubed
2 teaspoons salt
1 teaspoon freshly cracked black pepper
2 pounds red skin potatoes (skin left on), diced
2 cups small diced tomatoes
4 cups chicken broth
2 cups hot fire-roasted diced Hatch green chiles (see Chef's Tips on roasted peppers and chiles, page 316) or frozen Bueno® diced green chiles
½ teaspoon cumin
¼ cup fresh chopped cilantro
4–6 flour tortillas

In a large pot, sauté onions in vegetable oil over medium-high heat. Add garlic, and sauté until golden brown. Then add chicken breast, salt, and pepper, and let it brown, again. Add potatoes, tomatoes, and chicken broth. Let it simmer, stirring often. Once the potatoes are soft, add chiles, cumin, and cilantro, and let it steam for 5 minutes so all the flavors integrate.

Taste for salt and spice from the green chiles; add more, if desired.

Serve it hot with flour tortillas. Bueno appetite!

Green Chile Stew with Potatoes

Chef Chris Maher *(Cooking Studio Taos, Taos, New Mexico)*
Serves 6

2 large Russet potatoes, peeled and cubed into ½-inch cubes
4 cups chopped onions
¾ cup minced garlic
½ cup olive oil
2 tablespoons cumin seeds, toasted (see Chef's Tips on nuts and seeds, page 318)
1 scant teaspoon ground cumin
1 teaspoon ground coriander
½ teaspoon cayenne pepper (optional, if chiles are mild)
1–2 pounds roasted green chiles, peeled, seeded, and chopped (see Chef's Tips on chiles, page 316)
8 cups liquid (combination of chicken stock and water) (see Index, page 343)
1½ tablespoons salt

Place potatoes in a bowl of cold water and set aside.

Sauté onions and garlic in olive oil until soft. Add cumin seed, cumin, coriander, and cayenne pepper, and continue to sauté for another 5 minutes.

Add chiles, and sauté thoroughly (about 3 minutes). Add liquid, mix thoroughly, bring to a boil, and immediately bring down to a simmer. Continue to simmer for 25 minutes.

Remove the potatoes from the water and add to the stew. Salt the stew and bring to a boil, again. As soon as it boils, quickly bring it down to a simmer, and continue simmering until the potatoes are soft (about 25 minutes). Serve with tortillas.

Gluten-Free Sweet Potato and Pork Stew

Chef Darnell Harness *(Simply Dine Catering, Henderson, Nevada)*
Serves 10

This pork dish is seasoned with Moroccan and South American spices, which are both popular in the Southwest. It is a perfect way to highlight Nevada's Southwestern cuisine fused with the original techniques of the Northwestern cowboys.

3 pounds pork shoulder, cut into cubes

1 teaspoon sea salt

1 teaspoon coarsely ground black pepper

3 tablespoons ground cumin

2 cups all-purpose flour

2 tablespoons canola oil

1 large Vidalia or any sweet onion, diced small

4 tablespoons garlic cloves

4 cups low-fat and reduced-sodium chicken broth

¼ teaspoon ground cumin

¼ teaspoon cinnamon

¼ teaspoon ground ginger

¼ teaspoon jalapeño powder (or cayenne pepper)

¼ teaspoon ground coriander seeds

⅛ teaspoon ground cardamom

½ teaspoon turmeric

2 pounds sweet potatoes, peeled and diced small

½ cup dark raisins

½ cup golden raisins

¼ cup cream sherry

Cube the pork shoulder, and season with salt, pepper, and cumin. Place the cubed pork shoulder in a large bowl with flour, toss, and shake off any excess flour. In a hot Dutch oven, with the oil, place the cubed pork in batches, and brown on both sides. Once all the pork has been browned, place the onions in the oven, and cook for 5 minutes until slightly browned.

Add garlic, and cook for only 1 minute longer; then add broth to the Dutch oven and bring to a boil. Reduce the heat to a simmer, and add the spices; whisk until mixed well. Add the browned pork, and cook for 1 hour or until the meat is very tender. Stir occasionally, and add the sweet potatoes and both raisins; cook for 20 more minutes. Add the cream of sherry, and cook for 5 more minutes.

Grilled Flank Steak with Mango Salsa

Sharon LaDuca *(Mesa, Arizona)*
Serves 4–6

> Mangos are readily available in Arizona all year long. They are always fresh, and people use them for many dishes, especially Southwestern salsas. Mangos are so popular in this region that our grocery stores even offer them peeled and sliced. This mango salsa recipe can also be served with chicken, pork, or fish.

Marinade

⅓ cup olive oil
2 cloves garlic, minced
2 tablespoons red wine vinegar
⅓ cup soy sauce
¼ cup honey
½ teaspoon freshly cracked black pepper

Mango Salsa

1 large mango, diced
1 red onion, diced
1 red bell pepper, diced
1 clove garlic, minced
¼ cup cilantro, minced
¼ cup fresh orange juice
2 tablespoons fresh lime juice
1 jalapeño pepper, minced (see Chef's Tips on chiles, page 316)
Salt, to taste

Steak

2 pounds flank steak
Kosher salt and freshly cracked pepper, to taste
Brown or wild rice and red beans (optional)

Marinade

Combine the marinade ingredients. Set aside.

Mango Salsa

Combine all the ingredients for the salsa, and chill for at least 2 hours before serving with the grilled steak. May be served over the steak or on the side.

Steak

Score the surface of the steak with ¼-inch-deep knife cuts an inch apart across the grain of the meat. Place the meat and marinade in a large freezer bag. Coat well. Seal the bag and chill overnight (or at least 2 hours).

Preheat the grill. Remove the steak from the marinade bag, and sprinkle on both sides with coarse salt and freshly ground pepper (the salt and pepper forms a savory crust on the steak).

Place the steak on the hot grill. Grill for 4 to 6 minutes on each side or to your liking (for this recipe, it is best if served medium-rare). Make thin slices against the grain at a slight diagonal so the slices are wide. Serve on a bed of brown or wild rice and red beans, along with the mango salsa.

Grilled Kulana Rib-Eye, Cured Shinsato Farm Pork Belly, and Green Zebra Tomato Chimichurri

Chef de Cuisine Johan Svensson (*BLT Steak, Honolulu, Hawaii*)
Serves 4

Chimichurri

1 sprig fresh curly parsley

1 sprig fresh cilantro

2 green zebra tomatoes, skinned and core removed (see Chef's Tips on tomato concasse, page 321)

1 teaspoon red pepper flakes

½ red onion, sliced

1 clove garlic, crushed (see Chef's Tips on garlic, page 314)

½-1 cup olive oil

Salt and freshly cracked black pepper, to taste

Meat

½ cup granulated sugar

½ cup kosher salt

1 sprig thyme

1 bay leaf

8 ounces Shinsato Farm pork belly

2 pounds Kulana rib-eye, cleaned and trimmed

8 ounces unsalted butter

8 ounces freshly cracked black pepper

4 bone marrows, roasted and marrow carefully removed

1 teaspoon aged balsamic vinegar

Salt, to taste

Chimichurri

In a high-speed blender, add all the ingredients. Blend until smooth, seasoning with salt and pepper.

Meat

Mix sugar and salt, add thyme and bay leaf, rub into the belly, and let it cure overnight. Wash off the salt mixture the day after.

Season the beef with butter, salt, and pepper. Grill and broil until medium-rare; then let it rest. Slice the pork belly into 4 slices, grill, and season with pepper.

Serve by placing some chimichurri on a plate, drizzling with balsamic vinegar, and topping with the pork belly and roasted bone marrow.

Michelada

Elvia Guerrero and Tianna Petersen *(San Antonio and Dallas, Texas)*
Serves 1

While dining with two colleagues, they introduced me to a michelada, a drink native to Texas, which I had never heard of before. I quickly jotted down the recipe on a cocktail napkin to recreate once I got home. It is a nice alternative to a margarita or a Bloody Mary.
Story by Mary Elizabeth

1 ounce fresh lime juice
1 (6 oz.) bottle beer
Dash Tabasco®, Worchester, or soy sauce
Kosher salt, as needed

Rub the rim of a 6-inch-high ball glass with a lime wedge, and then dip the glass in a flat plate full of salt until the entire rim is full of salt. Fill the glass with ice, and pour in the lime juice, followed by the beer and a dash of all or any of the sauces on top.

Chef's Tip

As an alternative, add half Clamato® juice and half beer with a splash of lime juice and hot sauce.

Chile Rellenos with Beef

Chef Chris Maher *(Cooking Studio Taos, Taos, New Mexico)*
Serves 6

5 poblano chiles (see Chef's Tips on roasted peppers, page 316)
½ cup onion, minced
1 heaping tablespoon fresh garlic, minced
1 tablespoon toasted cumin seed (see Chef's Tips on nuts and seeds, page 318)
1 Russet potato, boiled and cut into ¼-inch cubes
1 pound flank steak, grilled rare and cubed
1 cup asadero or soft Mexican cheese
Fresh cilantro, chopped, as needed
Olive oil, as needed
Salt and freshly cracked black pepper, to taste

Burn the chiles on a high, open flame until they are evenly blistered all over. Place into a metal bowl and cover tightly with plastic. Allow the chiles to steam themselves. Peel the skin, and set aside.

Sauté the onion and garlic in olive oil until soft. Toast the cumin seed, and then add to the onions along with the cubed potato and beef. Salt and pepper it gently. Add the cheese and cilantro, and mix thoroughly.

Make an incision on one side of each peeled pepper, and carefully open the pepper, removing the seeds. Take a handful of the filling, and stuff each pepper well, but do not overstuff.

Brush a baking sheet with olive oil, and place the peppers seam-side-up (as tightly closed as possible). Brush each pepper with olive oil, and place in a 425°F oven for 10 minutes or until the cheese is thoroughly melted.

Place a tablespoon of red chile on a plate, and float the pepper on top.

Ricardo's Stacked Red Chile Cheese Enchiladas

Beth Harper *(Keller, Texas)*
Serves 3

> My father-in-law Richard Harper was raised in El Paso, Texas. He is considered to be an expert in Tex-Mex cuisine. Richard has learned this dish from his parents, so it has been in their family for a few generations. For authenticity, we add eggs and enjoy his "stacked enchiladas" for breakfast.

1 large yellow or white onion, finely chopped
3 cups cheese, grated (Jack, yellow, gouda, sharp cheddar, manchego, or combination of all)
28 ounces red chile sauce (salsa de chile), medium or hot
10 ounces hot red sauce, or to taste
⅓ cup cooking oil or bacon grease
12 corn tortillas (4 per serving)
¾ cup iceberg lettuce, finely shredded
3 sunny-side-up or over-easy fried eggs

Preheat an oven to 350°F. Set the onions and cheese aside in separate, covered bowls.

Heat the red chile sauce in an 8-inch saucepan (do not boil). You can add a little water to "stretch" the sauce, if needed. Freeze any excess for later use.

Heat oil in an 8-inch skillet until it causes a sizzle when tested with the edge of a tortilla. Do not let the oil get too hot to avoid spatter. Place the skillet and saucepan adjacent to each other on the stove top. Have the cheese and onions, tongs, and plates nearby.

Assemble each stack using four tortillas. Place a tortilla in the hot oil, and then quickly turn it over (this softens it a bit and adds flavor). Remove the tortilla after 3 or 4 seconds, and transfer it with tongs to the red sauce in the saucepan. Submerge it, and then quickly, but gently remove it with the tongs, and transfer to the plate, laying it flat.

Spread 1 tablespoon of onions around the tortilla and sprinkle ¼ cup of cheese evenly.

Fry another tortilla as above and repeat the process, stacking one tortilla above the previous one, and repeat the onion/cheese process (to moderate the onion flavor, add onions to every other layer rather than each layer). Top the final layer with a heaping ¼ cup of cheese, and begin the process again for the second plate.

Pour the remaining sauce and cheese equally over each plate.

Before serving, heat each oven-proof plate of enchiladas at 350°F for about 15 minutes or until the sauce around the edge of the stack bubbles and the cheese melts.

Reheating can be done quickly in the microwave by covering the enchiladas with wax paper, and using 3 toothpicks to support the wax paper so it does not touch them.

Prior to serving, top each stack with ¼ cup of iceberg lettuce.

Chef's Tip

Refried beans are a perfect accompaniment to this dish. For authenticity, top with a sunny-side-up or over-easy fried egg.

When preparing enchiladas, make an extra serving or two, and place in aluminum pie tins, cover with foil, and place in the freezer. This makes a great breakfast dish or snack. To heat in a microwave oven, invert the pie tin over a plate, push on the bottom of the pie tin, and the frozen stack of enchiladas will fall onto the plate. Turn them over, add the wax paper, and heat.

Green Chile Enchiladas

Santa Fe School of Cooking *(Santa Fe, New Mexico)*
Serves 10

3 cups red or green chile sauce (see page 298), divided
16 corn tortillas, about 4 inches in diameter
4 cups chicken, cooked and shredded
1½ pounds Monterey Jack or cheddar cheese, grated
1½ cups diced onion or sliced scallions, with green tops
2 cups shredded iceberg or romaine lettuce
1½ cups diced tomato
1¼ cups sour cream, divided

Preheat the oven to 350°F. Oil a 9- by 12-inch baking dish or pan. Spread about 1 cup of the sauce over the bottom of the dish, and layer half of the tortillas evenly over the sauce. Top the tortillas with half of the chicken and one-third of the cheese, and sprinkle with half of the onion (for milder onion flavor, use scallions). Repeat for the second layer, and top with the last cup of sauce and the remaining cheese. Bake for 20 to 30 minutes until bubbly and lightly browned.

To serve, spoon portions onto dinner plates, garnish with shredded lettuce and diced tomato, and top with 2 tablespoons of sour cream. Serve with pinto beans and posole.

Carne Adovada

Santa Fe School of Cooking *(Santa Fe, New Mexico)*
Serves 8

Here is one of our favorite authentic New Mexican recipes using red chile (and for a recipe using green chile, see Green Chile Enchiladas on page 294). New Mexico is the only state with an official state question, "Red or green?," which refers to which type of chile that you would like served with your meal.

⅓ cup peanut or vegetable oil (see Chef's Tips on blended oil, page 309)
3½ pounds pork loin or butt, cut in ¾-inch cubes
2 cups diced onion
2 tablespoons minced garlic
4 cups chicken broth or water, divided
2 teaspoons ground coriander seed
2 teaspoons dried Mexican oregano
2 teaspoons chile caribe (crushed red pepper)
¾ cup Chimayo ground red chile, mild or medium
1 tablespoon red chile honey
2 tablespoons sherry or red wine vinegar
Salt, to taste

Preheat the oven to 350°F. Heat the oil in a large skillet, and brown the pork in batches. Set the pork aside. Add the onion to the skillet, and sauté until golden. Add the garlic, and sauté for 1 minute. Deglaze the skillet with 1 cup of the chicken broth, loosening the browned bits with a spoon.

Place the coriander, oregano, chile caribe, red chile, honey, vinegar, and salt in the work bowl of a food processor. Add the cooked onions, garlic, and broth from the skillet and 2 more cups of chicken broth. Process until the mixture is thoroughly combined.

Place the browned pork, chile marinade, and the remaining cup of chicken broth in an oven-proof pot or dish. Stir well to combine, and cook for 1 hour or until the pork is tender.

You can serve the Carne Adovada over chile rellenos or rice, wrapped in a flour tortilla as a burrito, or with beans and posole. This dish reheats wonderfully and tastes even better the next day.

Chef's Tip

The traditional method for making this dish is to mix the marinade ingredients together and pour this over the meat. Cover the mixture and refrigerate overnight. Pour the meat and the marinade into an ovenproof casserole dish or pot, and bake, covered, for 2 to 2½ hours or until tender. The method described above, although not so traditional, brings out the flavors of the onion, garlic, and pork, because the ingredients are caramelized or browned first. Whichever method you choose, the dish is full of flavor, and will be a favorite.

Calabacitas

Chef Chris Maher *(Cooking Studio Taos, Taos, New Mexico)*
Yields 2 pints

1 medium onion, cut in half and sliced thin
4 medium cloves garlic, chopped
2 cups zucchini, diced in ½-inch cubes
2 cups yellow squash, diced in ½-inch cubes
1 fresh poblano chile pepper, seeded and chopped (see Chef's Tips on chiles, page 316)
2 cups corn, cut off the cob (see Chef's Tips on corn, page 322)
1½ cups cooked black beans or 1 (15 oz.) can, preferably organic
3 tablespoons chicken or vegetable stock (see Index, page 343)
2 roma tomatoes, chopped (or cherry or pear tomatoes)
½ cup chopped cilantro
1 tablespoon fresh chopped oregano or 1 teaspoon dried
Olive oil, as needed
Salt and freshly cracked black pepper, to taste
Cayenne pepper, to taste

Sauté onions and garlic in olive oil until they begin to turn slightly translucent. Add zucchini and squash, and continue to sauté until you see touches of brown/carmelization on the vegetables.

Stir in the poblano chile pepper, corn, and black beans. Add the chicken stock, and cook until the vegetables are soft. Salt and pepper to taste. Before removing from the heat, add the tomatoes, remove from the heat, and stir in thoroughly. Add the chopped cilantro and a touch of oregano. Season with salt and pepper.

Green Chile Sauce

Santa Fe School of Cooking *(Santa Fe, New Mexico)*

Yields 2½ cups

¼ cup vegetable oil
1 cup chopped onion
2–3 teaspoons minced garlic, to taste (see Chef's Tips on garlic,
page 314)
1–2 tablespoons all-purpose flour
⅔ cup New Mexico green chile, mild-roasted, peeled, and chopped
(see Chef's Tips on chiles, page 316)
⅔ cup New Mexico green chile, hot-roasted, peeled, and chopped
1½ cups chicken stock (see Index, page 343)
Fresh ground coriander seed, to taste (optional; see Chef's Tips on
nuts and seeds, page 318)
Salt, to taste

Heat the oil in a medium saucepan, and sauté the onion until softened
(about 3 to 4 minutes). Add the garlic, and sauté for 2 minutes more.
Stir in the flour. Add the green chiles and coriander seed (optional),
and slowly stir in the chicken stock. Bring the mixture to a boil, reduce the heat, and simmer for about 15 minutes. Season with salt.

Red Chile Sauce

Santa Fe School of Cooking *(Santa Fe, New Mexico)*
Yields 3 cups

¼ cup vegetable oil
½ cup finely diced onion
2–3 teaspoons minced garlic
2 tablespoons all-purpose flour
½ cup pure-ground medium Chimayo red chile
2 ½ cups water
1 teaspoon dried Mexican oregano
½ teaspoon fresh-ground cumin seed
Salt, to taste

Heat the oil in a medium saucepan, and sauté the onion for 3 to 4 minutes until softened. Add the garlic, and sauté for 2 minutes more. Stir in the flour and chile, and slowly add the water, whisking to break up any lumps in the chile. Add the oregano and cumin, and bring to a boil. Reduce the heat, and simmer for about 20 minutes or until the mixture has thickened slightly. Season with salt.

Texas Barbecue Sauce

Yields 1 quart

1 pound bacon, whole strips
1 large onion, sliced
1 chile, diced large (see Chef's Tips on chiles, page 316)
3 cloves garlic, minced
½ cup whiskey
4 cups ketchup
½ cup honey
1 teaspoon liquid smoke
4 tablespoons whole chipotles with sauce
½ cup brown sugar
Crushed red pepper flakes, to taste
Kosher salt, to taste

Render bacon over a low flame in a deep sauce pot until almost crispy. Remove the bacon and reserve to cool. Place onions in the bottom of the sauce pot with the bacon fat. Sauté until soft and caramelized. Add chile and sweat with the caramelized onions. Add garlic, and deglaze the pan with whiskey. Simmer and reduce by half. Add ketchup, honey, liquid smoke, chipotle, brown sugar, red pepper flakes, and kosher salt, and stir. Chop the bacon and return to the pot. Puree and blend until a smooth consistency is reached. Simmer on a low flame and stir frequently until a thick consistency is reached.

Berry-Good Crisps

Chef Michelle Moore *(South Pasadena, California)*
Serves 8–12

> I love crisps; they are easy to make and very versatile. You just
> combine fruits of the season with a crumble-type pastry topping,
> and then bake until bubbly. Delicious!

Fruit

6 cups mixed berries (blueberries, blackberries, raspberries, and/or
strawberries)

⅓–½ cup brown sugar (amount depends on sweetness of fruit)

2 tablespoons cornstarch

½ teaspoon ground cinnamon

Topping

½ cup all-purpose flour

½ cup packed brown sugar

½ teaspoon salt

½ teaspoon ground cinnamon

5 tablespoons cold unsalted butter, cut into small pieces

¾ cup oatmeal (regular or quick-cooking)

⅓ cup sweetened and shredded coconut (see Chef's Tips on nuts and
seeds, page 318)

⅓ cup slivered or sliced almonds

Preheat an oven to 350°F. Butter a 9- by 12-inch baking pan (or coat
with cooking spray).

Fruit

If including strawberries, roughly chop to make pieces similar in size
to other berries. Then, in a large bowl, gently combine the berries with
the brown sugar, cornstarch, and cinnamon; place in a prepared pan.

Topping

Place the flour, brown sugar, salt, and cinnamon in a food processor fitted with the metal blade; pulse a few times or until combined. Add the chilled butter, and pulse until the mixture resembles coarse meal. Add the oatmeal, coconut, and almonds, and pulse a few more times. If you do not have a processor, gently mix the flour, sugar, and spices in a bowl. Using a pastry blender or your hands, work the butter into the dry mixture until it resembles coarse meal. Add oats and roughly chopped coconut and almonds.

Sprinkle the topping mixture evenly over the berry filling. Bake for approximately 30 minutes or until bubbly.

Serve warm or at room temperature. While delicious served as is, you can also dress it up with a dollop of crème fraîche, ice cream, or frozen vanilla yogurt.

Chef's Tip

As a variation, try mixing berries with other summer fruits, like peaches or plums. You can also substitute walnuts or pecans in place of almonds. Rather than making one large crisp, you can also bake this in ten individual 6-ounce cups. Place the cups on a baking sheet, and bake for approximately 12 minutes.

Clafouti with Plums or Pluots

Chef Michelle Moore *(South Pasadena, California)*

Serves 6–8

For a nice change, make this rustic French dessert with pluots, a fruit mainly grown in California that is a hybrid of a plum and an apricot. A clafouti is made by pouring a pancake-like batter over a layer of fresh fruit and baking it in the oven. It is traditionally served hot following baking, but I also serve it at room temperature or even cold. Creating the batter bottom underneath the fruit is a popular technique developed by Julia Child.

½ tablespoon unsalted butter
1 cup whole milk
¼ cup heavy cream
3 large eggs
½ cup plus 1 tablespoon sugar, divided
½ cup all-purpose flour
2 teaspoons pure vanilla extract
Pinch salt
1¼ pounds plums or pluots, sliced (about 3 cups)
Powdered sugar, for dusting

Preheat the oven to 375°F. Butter a 9-inch, deep-dish pie pan. Set aside.

Combine the milk, cream, eggs, ½ cup of sugar, flour, vanilla, and salt in a food processor or blender, processing until smooth. Pour a ¼-inch layer of batter in the buttered dish, and bake for a few minutes until a film of batter sets in the pan. Remove from the oven.

Spread the fruit evenly over the batter. Sprinkle with the remaining tablespoon of sugar, and pour the remaining batter evenly over the top. Bake until puffed and golden brown (a knife inserted in the center should come out clean; about 40-50 minutes). Remove from the oven and allow to cool briefly on a rack.

Using a small strainer, dust the top with powdered sugar. Serve immediately, or at room temperature or chilled. If served hot, serve with a little cream.

Chef's Tip

Try using different fruits such as peaches, nectarines, cherries, berries, or a combination. In place of the powdered sugar, you can sprinkle white sugar over the top prior to baking.

Bread Pudding

Leila O'Connell *(Blue Plate Special, Albuquerque, New Mexico)*
Serves 6–8

> This is a very popular dessert in New Mexico. It is especially
> enjoyed around the winter holidays.

1½ pounds sourdough or 24 ounces white bread, cut into cubes
4 eggs
2 cups milk
1½ cups half-and-half
1 cup sugar
1 teaspoon pure vanilla extract
1 cup brown sugar
½ cup unsalted butter
½ cup chopped pecans (see Chef's Tips on nuts and seeds, page 318)
½ cup dried cranberries
½ teaspoon nutmeg
½ teaspoon cinnamon
½ teaspoon allspice
½ teaspoon salt
⅓ cup spiced rum

Place bread in a well buttered and greased 8- by 12-inch baking pan.
In a blender, mix eggs, milk, half-and-half, sugar, and vanilla, pour
over the bread, and let it soak for 10 minutes. In a saucepan, add
brown sugar, butter, pecans, cranberries, spices, salt, and rum. Bring
to a boil and pour over the bread mixture.

Bake it in a 350°F oven for 30 minutes or until golden brown and the
center is cooked.

Capirotada

Santa Fe School of Cooking *(Santa Fe, New Mexico)*
Serves 10–12

Capirotada is a traditional Mexican bread pudding made for Lent. This recipe is the most brilliant balance of savory and sweet ingredients, such as caramel and cheddar, wine-soaked raisins, and vanilla ice cream.

10 ounces day-old French bread, torn into bite-sized pieces
½ cup raisins or other dried fruit
½ cup madeira or other sweet wine
2 cups sugar
3½ cups water
5 tablespoons unsalted butter
1 teaspoon canela (cinnamon)
1½ teaspoon Mexican vanilla
2 ounces (½ cup) pecans or toasted pignoli/pine nuts (see Chef's Tips on nuts and seeds, page 318)
1 cup shredded Monterey Jack or Longhorn cheddar cheese
Whipped cream or vanilla ice cream

Preheat the oven to 350°F. Butter a 9- by 12-inch baking dish or pan. Place the bread in the prepared dish, and toast in the oven for 20 minutes or until lightly browned. Soak the raisins in madeira for 20 minutes and drain, reserving the madeira.

Place the sugar in a heavy saucepan or large skillet over medium-high heat. When the sugar starts to melt and turn golden around the edges, mash it gently with a large spoon (stirring will create more lumps, and the sugar will take longer to caramelize, so the mashing motion is more effective). Cook the sugar until it turns a deep caramel color. Immediately add the water, being very careful, as the hot syrup will bubble and splatter. The caramel will partially solidify but will re-liquefy as it reheats. Reduce the heat, and add the butter, canela, and vanilla to the caramel syrup, stirring until the butter has melted.

Top the toasted bread with nuts and raisins, pouring the reserved madeira over the mixture. Pour the syrup over the bread, and allow it to sit for 5 minutes. Sprinkle the top with grated cheese and additional canela to taste. Bake for about 25 minutes until lightly browned and bubbly. Serve warm with a dollop of whipped cream or vanilla ice cream.

Individual Mexican Chocolate Cheesecakes

Andy Broder *(A Culinary Studio, Scottsdale, Arizona)*
Makes 20–24

2 sheets puff pastry dough (available in the freezer case of most grocery stores)
3 tablets Mexican chocolate (3 ⅛ ounces / 90 grams per tablet)
4 ounces dark chocolate, roughly chopped
½ cup heavy cream
16 ounces cream cheese, softened
1 (10½ oz.) can sweetened condensed milk
3 eggs, beaten
All-purpose flour, as needed

Preheat an oven to 400°F. Spray two muffin pans with baking spray. Cut each piece of pastry into twelve equal-sized squares. With a little flour on the work surface, roll each piece of dough into a 5-inch square. Line each space in the muffin tin with a square of dough. Heat both chocolates on the defrost setting in the microwave just until melted. Stir in the heavy cream until well incorporated.

Place the remaining ingredients into a food processor fitted with the blade attachment. Process until the mixture is smooth and uniform (about 2 minutes). Add the chocolate, and beat until thoroughly incorporated.

Pour the filling into the prepared crusts, and bake in the 400°F oven for 15 to 18 minutes. When the crusts are golden, the cheesecakes are done. Cool for 15 minutes and remove from the tins.

Chef's Tip

For videos of the tips in these sections, visit www.youtube.com and type in "Chef Nicole Roarke".

Mise en Place

Mise en place [MEEZ-ahn-plahs] is a French term that literally means "set or put in place." *Mise en place* refers to a chef's setup of essential ingredients and tools that are necessary to begin the actual cooking process. Before beginning any recipe, it is important to:

1. Have all the ingredients and equipment readily accessible.
2. Read the entire recipe and make sure that you understand all of the instructions and steps that you need to follow. If your *mise en place* is set out and organized right in front of you, it allows for a steady flow of production. Essentially, organization leads to less error. For most professional and at-home chefs, a *mise en place* consists of:
   - *Kosher salt:* Keep readily accessible in a small finger pot.
   - *Freshly cracked black pepper:* Keep in a refillable pepper mill with whole black peppercorns.
   - *Blended oil* (see below).
3. **Flour/cornstarch:** Not only is flour or cornstarch essential for baking, they oftentimes act as a thickening agent.
4. **Sugar/honey:** Just as a pinch of salt is added to almost all baking recipes to bring out the sweetness and balance the flavor, I add a pinch of sugar or a tablespoon of honey to my savory soups and sauces. I believe that this creates a well-rounded depth of flavor.

Blended Oil

The term "blended oil" refers to two or more oils combined together and bottled as one oil blend. Professional chefs and cooks may purchase this bottled oil blend from industry suppliers featuring various ratios of oils, but we will show you how to make your very own blend at home.

A blended oil typically includes a higher percentage of a mild tasting, light-bodied, and inexpensive oil that has a high smoke point. In other words, the oil can reach the high temperatures needed for deep and shallow frying, sautéing, and stir-frying. The most common of these oils include, but are not limited to, canola, corn, vegetable, soybean, peanut, grapeseed, or zero-trans-fat frying oil.

A blended oil also includes a lower percentage of a flavorful, costly, richly colored, and dense-bodied oil. Some favorite oils are virgin olive, extra-virgin olive, sesame, and truffle oil. Most possess a low smoke point, meaning that these oils begin smoking, then burning, and often catching fire when heated to high temperatures. Alone, these oils are best used to drizzle over a finished dish, to add toward the end of the cooking process, or when preparing a pesto, vinaigrette, or any other cold sauce.

An example of a blended oil is one with 90% soybean oil and 10% olive oil. To prepare your own blended oil, mix two or more of your favorite oils in a mixing bowl, and store at room temperature for 3 months. (If using garlic oil, store in the refrigerator for up to 3 days. Do not keep homemade and untreated garlic oils for any longer than 3 days.)

Be sure to use a higher ratio of the high-smoke-point oil to the low-smoke-point oil if you plan on cooking with the blended oil. If the blended oil will be used for vinaigrette or marinade, any combination of oil is permitted.

Reduction

The desired consistency of a reduction should be a little thicker than syrup and thinner than honey. Not only will the liquid that you are reducing thicken as it reduces in volume, but its flavor concentrates will also produce a rather sweet finish.

The success of this single-ingredient recipe is solely based on technique and some helpful "tricks of the trade." Below is an example of a balsamic vinegar reduction:

Choose a shallow pan to maximize the surface area of the vinegar, which enables the volume to reduce faster and more evenly without having to stir it.

Bring the vinegar to a boil over medium-high heat, and then immediately lower to a simmer. Allow the vinegar to reduce by half of its original volume. Check its consistency by dipping a spoon into the reduction. It should coat the back of the spoon when removed. If the reduction slides off the spoon, it is still too thin; allow it to continue to reduce to approximately two-thirds of its original volume.

If it has over-reduced, it will be thick and sticky like molasses and will taste bitter. As it cools, it will harden like tar. Unfortunately, there is no way of reversing over-reduction, and the mixture will have to be discarded. This mistake is quite tough to remove from your pan, but a great trick is to fill the pan with water and bring to a boil (this will loosen any over-reduced vinegar from the pan, which can then be simply poured out, and should be easy to wash out). This trick is also great for any burnt or caked-on food that is tough to remove.

Citrus Zest

The "zest" of any citrus fruit (such as lemon, lime, grapefruit, and orange) is only the outermost colorful edge of the citrus. It is important to understand exactly where the zest is because just underneath the surface of the zest is what is known as the pith of the rind, which is extremely bitter. The zest is considered the most flavorful part, and can be used to infuse citrus flavor into a wide range of recipes. Using the zest as opposed to the juice allows you to extract the flavor without sacrificing the consistency of your recipe, which would otherwise "break" or curdle if the juice were added to the recipe's other ingredients, such as cream or milk.

A great "trick" is to run the side of the citrus along a microplane, because the small, sharp teeth will gently scrape off the zest without cutting deeply into the bitter skin. The microplane should remain stationary (over a bowl or measuring cup), and only the citrus should be scraping up and down the sharp surface of the plane. When scraping the citrus against the microplane, roll or rotate it in your hand so no one area of the citrus is over-zested. If the recipe calls for large strips of zest, use a vegetable peeler to remove the large strips.

If the strip of zest contains white, bitter pith, place the strip zest-side-down on the edge of a cutting board, and hold the knife parallel to the zest. Press the blade against the zest and, with large strokes, shave off as much of the white as possible.

If you are succeeding at this "trick," you will notice that the area where the zest was removed will appear to be smooth and have a lighter shade of the citrus' color. For instance, if you are zesting a lemon after running and rolling it over the plane, you will remove the bright yellow outer edge, but a lighter tint of yellow should remain. If you are over-zesting, you will see the white pith of the rind exposed.

Compound Butter

Classic compound butters are made with chopped herbs, minced shallots, roasted garlic, citrus zest, roasted peppers, sliced olives, sun-dried tomatoes, toasted nuts, cheese (such as gorgonzola or Parmesan), honey, maple syrup, caramelized onions, and/or freshly cracked black peppercorns. It is a simple way to customize the flavor and texture of an otherwise unsalted butter. This can be served with just about anything, including freshly baked bread, roasted vegetables, and pan-seared meat.

To make your own compound butter, remove the whole butter out of the refrigerator and cut it into pieces (if you are making 1 stick, then cut into 8 tablespoons; for a whole pound, cut all 4 sticks into 32 tablespoons). This will spread out the surface area of the butter so it will soften faster. Set aside and allow the butter to come to room temperature (do not melt the butter). While the butter is softening to a spreadable consistency, prepare your other ingredients (any and all combinations of ingredients should always be fully cooked and cooled before combining with the room-temperature butter).

Place the fully softened butter into a standing mixer, and whip the butter with the paddle attachment until a smooth consistency is reached. Then add your ingredients and mix until fully combined. If you do not have a standing mixer, you can place the fully softened butter into a mixing bowl, and stir with a wooden spoon or rubber spatula until smooth. Fold in the remaining ingredients until combined.

Compound butter can be served in a small bowl at room temperature. To store the compound butter, tightly roll it into a log with waxed paper and/or plastic wrap, and then twist the ends closed. Store in the freezer.

When needed, simply cut a medallion straight from the frozen log, and then remove the waxed paper and/or plastic wrap. Serve immediately; the butter will begin to melt over hot food.

How to Prepare Avocadoes

Removing the buttery, rich, green flesh of an avocado may seem daunting if you have never done it before, but this method makes it rather easy. Stand the avocado upright on a cutting board. Using a large chef's knife, cut downward through the top until your knife reaches the large pit in the center (do not remove your knife and allow the avocado to fall to its side). While holding the knife in place, spin the avocado around so the knife continues to cut the entire way around the pit. Remove your knife.

With one hand on each side, twist the avocado in half. In one half of the avocado, you will see the large center pit. Lay this half skin-side-down on your cutting board with the pit facing upward. Carefully whack your knife into the middle of the pit. The blade should remain in the pit while you twist the knife (this should loosen the pit so that when you pull your knife out, the pit should be attached to the blade of the knife). Carefully remove the pit from the blade and discard.

You can take a large, metal spoon and simply scoop the flesh out of each half. Or, you can "score" the flesh with the tip of your knife by making several vertical cuts and then several horizontal cuts through the flesh of the avocado (this will make a cross-hatch cut, like a tic-tac-toe board). To remove the scored flesh, either scoop out with a spoon or, if the avocado is very ripe, you can simply squeeze the skin, and the flesh will come out.

If you are making a guacamole or looking for a smooth consistency of avocado, you can sprinkle with a coarse ground salt (such as kosher salt), and mash with a fork.

Avocados are extremely prone to browning when exposed to air. To avoid this natural oxidation, add a citric acid such as lime or lemon juice to the cut avocado or guacamole.

When storing, press a layer of plastic wrap directly against the cut avocado or guacamole, and then add an additional piece of plastic wrapped tightly around the storage container or bowl (this is an extra prevention measure taken to preserve the bright green flesh and avoid oxidation).

Garlic

How to Peel Garlic

Most professional chefs do not care to rely on gadgets and gizmos that are used for one specific task, like garlic peelers. Instead, I will share with you a few tricks of the trade that I have learned.

For minced or chopped garlic: Lay the garlic clove on a cutting board, take the flat surface of a chef's knife, and lay it on top of the garlic. Smash your fist against the flat-side of the blade. Now, remove the peels. This releases a lot of the flavorful oils from the garlic and helps to break it down so mincing it into smaller pieces is easy.

For whole peeled garlic cloves: Loosen the garlic cloves from the head and place individual cloves into a small, metal mixing bowl. Cover the mixing bowl with a second similar-sized metal mixing bowl to create a dome. Shake the two bowls vigorously enough to hear the garlic cloves bouncing around inside. Do this for 60 seconds. Once you remove the cover, you will find that the garlic peels have come off with little to no effort.

How to Prepare Garlic

There are so many ways to incorporate the flavor of garlic into your recipe. Raw garlic can sometimes be a bit strong (especially if you bite into a large piece), and the unexpected crunch of raw garlic overpowers any additional flavors. The following preparations are some of my favorite ways to incorporate garlic's strong aroma and flavor.

Roasted garlic: This technique uses a combination cooking method so the garlic roasts within the circulating dry heat of the oven while it steams in the foil pouch. The roasting lends to garlic's unmistakable golden color, and the steaming makes the cloves soft and spreadable.

Keeping the entire head of garlic intact, make one large cut, removing ⅛-inch or ¼-inch off the top (opposite end of the root). Without cutting off too much of the garlic, expose each individual clove within the head.

Place the head, cut-side facing upward, onto a small piece of foil. Pour a teaspoon of your favorite oil over the head of garlic. Add a pinch of kosher salt, freshly cracked pepper, or a few leaves of your favorite herbs, such as rosemary, basil, or oregano.

Bring the edges of the foil up around the garlic, creating a pouch. Place the pouch of foil onto a sheet pan. Place the sheet pan on the middle rack of a 350°F oven for approximately 35 to 45 minutes. Check that the garlic is golden brown and soft by inserting a skewer/toothpick into a clove; there should be absolutely no resistance. If so, remove from the oven and open the pouch to cool. Once cool, squeeze the root-side of the head to remove the individual cloves.

Poached garlic: Once you learn this technique, you may find yourself poaching all the garlic that comes your way so you will always have soft, sweet poached garlic on hand at all times.

You can purchase whole-peeled garlic cloves so the bulk of your work is already done for you, although it does cost more than purchasing whole heads of garlic, removing all the cloves, and tediously peeling each one.

Place all the whole-peeled garlic cloves into a saucepan or pot. Cover the garlic with oil (such as vegetable, canola, corn, grapeseed, or extra-virgin olive oil).

Place the sauce pot over medium-low heat and bring the oil to a poaching temperature of 165°F to 180°F. If you do not have a long-stemmed thermometer, simply heat the oil until you see small bubbles forming on the top, outer edge of the oil where it touches the pot. If the oil is too hot, it will essentially deep-fry the garlic, which will make the outside the correct color, although the center of the garlic will still be raw and crunchy. Do not stir the garlic.

Continue poaching the garlic until it is soft. Remove the pot from the heat and cool to room temperature before use. You may choose to strain it, and use both the poached garlic and the garlic-infused oil.

Garlic paste: This method of preparing garlic is ideal for recipes that require the garlic to be raw, such as Caesar salad dressing, pico de gallo, or tomato bruschetta.

Begin by removing all the cloves from the head of garlic. Place the garlic on a cutting board, use the flat-side of a knife blade to smash each clove of garlic, and remove the peels. Discard all of the peels and wipe the cutting board clean.

Place the smashed cloves in the center of the cutting board. Begin to chop them roughly until the pieces are small enough to start mincing. Continue mincing the garlic until it is as finely chopped as you can get it.

Sprinkle the finely minced garlic with a pinch of coarse ground salt (such as kosher salt). The salt will draw the moisture out of the garlic and help break down the solid compound into a smooth, paste-like consistency.

Use the flat side of the blade, again, but, this time, crush and bruise the salted minced garlic between the flat blade and the cutting board. Do this until a smooth, fragrant garlic paste remains.

This garlic paste can now be whisked into a vinaigrette, pesto, herb oil, or just about anything in which you want raw garlic flavor without an offensive raw garlic bite.

Chiles

There are essentially two types of peppers—sweet bell peppers and spicy chiles. Chiles (such as jalapeño, red and green habañero, and poblano) contain a compound known as capsaicin, which is strongest on the white ribs found inside the chile, and is responsible for making it spicy.

When handling chiles, you should take caution to wear disposable gloves. Otherwise, the oil will permeate your hands, and can be easily transferred to anything else you touch, such as your face, eyes, mouth, and other foods. After removing the gloves, be sure to wash and sanitize your hands and any equipment that you have used (such as knives and cutting boards).

How to Remove Ribs and Seeds

In order to enjoy a milder version of chiles, you can remove the fiery inside and consume only the colorful flesh. Here is an easy way to remove the ribs and seeds of your chiles:

Lay the chile flat on your cutting board, and cut it in half from the stem to the tip. Then cut each half, again, from the stem to the tip so you have four quarter cuts.

Lay the chile skin-side-down on the edge of the cutting board. Hold your knife parallel to the cutting board, and slice from the tapered end of the chile through the stem, removing the seeds and rib with one cut. Repeat this technique with the remaining three-quarters. You should now be left with the colorful flesh to cut into julienne strips or small dices, depending on what your recipes calls for.

If using char-grilled or fire-roasted chiles, leave them whole to roast, and, after removing the skin, follow the procedure above to remove the ribs.

Roasting Peppers and Chiles

Below are two suggested ways to roast peppers/chiles.

Oven-roasting for a milder version: Lightly coat the outside of the peppers with a bit of blended oil. Place the glossy peppers on a shallow sheet pan, and place in a preheated, 450°F oven for approximately 30 minutes, or under a broiler until the outer skin is blistered and/or shriveled, and the inner flesh is soft and has released juice. Occasionally turn the peppers so they blister evenly.

Char-roasting or fire-roasting: Do not coat the peppers with oil, as this would burn over a direct flame. Place the peppers directly on the stove-top burner and turn on high heat (for gas stove tops or grills). Ideally, the flame will get close enough to touch the skin and ultimately scorch it. Periodically rotate the peppers once each side is fully blackened and charred. Repeat this technique until the entire pepper is charred black. Immediately place each charred pepper into a metal mixing bowl, and quickly cover with tightly fitting plastic wrap to trap the steam that will build between the layer of charred skin and sweet, juicy roasted flesh. The top of the plastic wrap will bubble outward as it fills with steam, and the inside will be covered in condensation. Once cooled, the plastic wrap should appear deflated. Uncover the bowl and check to see if you can now handle the roasted peppers. Wipe off the charred skin with a dry or slightly damp towel, but never wash off the charred skin with water, as this will remove a lot of the natural smoky, rustic flavor that has been created. Once all the skin is removed, the flesh will be soft enough to be hand-torn or sliced open to remove and discard the stem, ribs, and seeds. Cut or puree as desired.

Nuts and Seeds

Anytime you come across nuts or seeds (such as almonds, hazelnuts, coconut, pumpkin seeds, or sesame seeds), regardless if the recipe is for a savory dish or a sweet dessert, I always recommend toasting them. Nuts and seeds contain an exuberant amount of natural oil, which, when heated, will be extracted and produce a golden color and strong aroma.

This task, however, does require caution, as nuts are one of the most commonly burnt items in professional kitchens.

I would not advise adding additional oil or butter to the pan, as the natural oil that is released when heated is all that will be necessary to gently toast the nuts. Below are two methods for toasting:

· Spread the nuts or seeds in a single layer on a sheet tray, and place in a preheated 375°F oven for 2 to 10 minutes depending on their size.
· Spread the nuts or seeds in a single layer in a sauté pan. Toast on the stove top while constantly stirring or flipping them (if the nuts stay in one place in the pan over direct heat, they will scorch or burn rather than toasting evenly).

Never crush or chop the nuts before you toast them. Only do so after they have toasted and cooled. When chopped ahead of time, the inconsistent shapes and sizes will cause them to toast unevenly, and the smaller fragments will burn while the larger ones do not get enough color. This will make your entire mixture taste bitter.

You should also never toast two or more different varieties of nuts or seeds in the same pan at the same time. Each is a different size, and will require different cooking times. As such, always toast different nuts and seeds in separate pans.

Nuts and seeds are often quite costly, especially in a professional environment. Because of this, I always instruct my cooks to toast them in separate small batches. This way, if you do, in fact, burn them, you will not lose the entire stock, and the monetary damage will not be as severe.

The cooking time varies depending upon the size and shape of the nuts and seeds, as well as the heat source and temperature. Because there are several variables, it is difficult to say exactly how long they will take to toast, but what is an absolute surety is they do not take much time, at all. I frequently check them in 2-minute increments until well-toasted. You will often smell the scent in the air when they are ready. Halfway through the cooking process, I will often rotate the pan to avoid unevenly cooking due to "hot spots" in your oven. I also use a heat-resistant or flat metal spatula to flip the nuts or seeds often to ensure even color.

Standard Breading Procedure

This procedure is meant for food that will be baked, pan/shallow-fried, or deep-fried. First, prepare the "dry" flour mixture (typically, the main ingredient is all-purpose flour, although you may use a whole-wheat, rye, or rice flour). I always add cornstarch to this dry mixture. The ratio that I follow is 2:1, meaning 2 parts flour to 1 part cornstarch. This trick lends to the crispy and crunchy texture characteristic of fried food. Season the flour mixture. Use your imagination; in addition to using kosher salt and freshly cracked black pepper, paprika is fantastic for adding a bit of color, and spices such as curry, cinnamon, and cayenne will add a great depth of flavor. Place the flour mixture into a large, shallow pan. The pan should be large enough to lay the dredging item flat.

Secondly, prepare the "wet" egg mixture. Always beat the eggs well in a separate bowl, and then add to a large, shallow pan. I always add 1 or 2 tablespoons of water, milk, or buttermilk to the egg mixture. This lends to a creamy texture to the eggs, which act as an adhesive between the dry ingredients.

Lastly, prepare the "dry" breadcrumb mixture. Typically, this is Italian-style breadcrumbs, although I love the Japanese-style "panko" breadcrumbs (found in the international foods' aisle of most grocery stores). Panko is characteristically light, and adds a lot of texture to fried foods. You can also season this mixture with kosher salt, freshly cracked black pepper, and minced fresh herbs. Other flavor additives include Parmesan cheese, sesame seeds, and toasted coconut. Avoid adding fresh garlic or onion when deep frying, as this will often burn and add a bitter flavor.

To assemble, place the flour mixture, egg mixture, and breadcrumb mixture side by side, in that order. When dredging in the flour mixture, be sure to completely coat the entire surface area of the food item, and pat it off to remove excess flour that would otherwise burn in the oil. Next, fully submerge the food item into the egg mixture. Finally, place it into the breadcrumb mixture until fully coated. Another great trick is to lay fully coated food onto a flat pan, being careful not to overcrowd it, and place the pan uncovered in the refrigerator for 30 minutes before frying. This helps to adhere the breading onto the food item.

Seasoning

Coating food with dry seasoning may seem like a simple task, but, by following the procedure below, you can be sure to do it as evenly and adequately as possible every time. First, combine the dry seasoning (such as kosher salt, freshly cracked black pepper, and dry spices) in a small bowl and mix well. Set aside. Lay the food flat on a cutting board or sheet pan. Pinch a generous amount of the dry seasoning and hold your hand approximately 12 inches above the food. Sprinkle the dry seasoning onto the food while simultaneously moving your hand side to side (this should mimic falling snow).

Emulsification

The emulsification process combines two or more ingredients that do not typically mix in order to create one stable sauce or dressing. Examples of emulsified food include hollandaise sauce, mayonnaise, and vinaigrettes.

Vinaigrettes are made with a ratio of 3:1, meaning 3 parts oil to 1 part vinegar. Vinegar and oil do not mix by nature, but, by following this procedure, it is possible to emulsify these ingredients together.

In a large mixing bowl, place 1 part vinegar and any other flavorful ingredients (such as garlic paste, roasted garlic, onions, shallots, herbs, spices, fruit, or citrus), and set aside at room temperature for 20 minutes. This allows the flavor to infuse the vinegar.

Next, whisk in a binder. This ingredient acts as the glue that aides in keeping the oil and vinegar together. Binders include mustard, honey, and egg yolks (some recipes will call for one or all three).

Measure three parts oil in a volume measuring cup or a cup that has a spout for easy pouring. While vigorously whisking the vinegar mixture, slowly pour the oil in a steady stream. Be sure to add the oil slowly and continuously until all of the oil has been added, and do not stop whisking during this entire process. The mixture should get thicker as more oil is added. If emulsified properly, this mixture will remain stable for 3 days in the refrigerator.

Simple Syrup

This mixture is easy to make, and lasts for 5 days in the refrigerator. It is always prepared with equal parts of granulated sugar and water. It is often used to sweeten beverages such as iced tea, lemonade, and alcoholic cocktails, as well as desserts like sorbet or berry coulis.

Add one part water to a small saucepan and place over a medium-high flame. Immediately stir in one part granulated sugar and bring the mixture to a low simmer. Allow this mixture to reduce by half of its original volume, creating a syrupy consistency. Remove from the pan and pour into a heat-resistant container to cool.

Tomato Concasse

Many chefs and cooks use canned, peeled, and diced or crushed tomatoes, which are perfectly acceptable when preparing tomato-based recipes. A higher quality product can be achieved, however, when you make your own, known as a tomato concasse.

Use a small paring knife or vegetable peeler, and remove the stem. Score the tomato using a paring knife by making two shallow cuts in the shape of an "X" on the bottom of the tomato (opposite end from the stem).

Blanch the tomatoes by fully submerging the prepared tomatoes in salted, boiling water (212°F) for 1 to 2 minutes. Once the skins loosen, remove from the water with a spider or slotted spoon. Shock the tomatoes by fully submerging them in iced water (32°F), also known as an ice bath. Once cool, the skins should peel off easily (use a paring knife if you have any difficulty). Cut the tomatoes in half lengthwise, and either squeeze out the seeds or continue to cut the tomatoes in half, again.

Place the 4 quarters flesh-side-down on the edge of a cutting board. With your knife held parallel to the board, make one cut from the tapered end of the tomato straight through the stem-side. This should remove all the seeds and ribs. Dice the peeled and seeded tomatoes.

Some recipes require you to only blanch and shock fruits and vegetables without any further preparation, whereas other recipes direct you to continue peeling and discarding the skin, and keep the item whole for further use (see Sausage-Spinach Calzones with Marinara Sauce, page 45).

How to Thicken a Sauce or Soup

To prepare a slurry, dissolve ½ cup of cornstarch into ¼ to ½ cup of cold liquid or water until a heavy cream consistency is reached. Bring your recipe (for example, sauce or soup) to a boil, and whisk in the slurry. Return to a simmer (5 to 7 minutes). If you add cornstarch directly to your recipe, it will clump and not alter the thickness, which is why it is necessary to mix the cornstarch with cold water or any other cold, flavorful liquid (such as wine, stock, or juice) ahead adding it to your recipe.

Citrus Bath

When cutting up apples to serve on a cheese platter or for dipping into a fondue, you can prevent the apples from oxidizing by making a "citrus bath," which is essentially an anti-browning solution. Squeeze lemon juice into cold water, and cover your whole or sliced apples with the mixture. Leave them in this solution until ready to use.

Preparing Fresh Corn

If using fresh corn kernels in your recipe: After you have shucked the corn, stand the cob upright on a cutting board. Cut kernels off the cob by slicing downward and rotating the cob until all the kernels are removed. Put the corn kernels in a large bowl, and add water until it reaches 1 inch above the kernels. Let it sit for 5 minutes to allow the impurities and silk to rise to the top. Using a wire-mesh strainer or a slotted spoon, skim the silk. Drain and repeat the process 3 times until the water begins to run clear.

If using corn on the cob in your recipe: After shucking the corn, remove as much of the silk as possible by hand. Another easy trick for removing the silk is to use a soft-bristle toothbrush and comb out the fine silk. Rinse thoroughly and cook as directed.

If using cooked corn in your recipe: Boil water in a large pot, turn the heat off, and place 1 cup of milk and 1 tablespoon each of sugar and salt into the water. Return to a boil. Place the shucked and cleaned ears into the water. Turn the water off, and keep the corn in the water for 10 minutes until tender. You can now keep the corn in the water so it will stay warm until ready to serve.

Basic Recipe for Vegetable Stock

Makes 2 quarts

1. Fill a stock or large sauce pot with vegetable trimmings from your stock bin. For example, use 1 yellow onion, 2 carrots, 1 bunch of celery, and fresh herbs such as bay leaf, thyme, parsley stems, rosemary, and peppercorns.
2. Add cold water (just covering the vegetables), bring to a boil, and immediately reduce to a simmer. Simmer for 1 hour.
3. Remove from the heat and let cool for 30 minutes.
4. Strain contents through a colander, and then a second time through a fine-mesh strainer called a *chinois*.
5. If you prefer a darker stock, add 2 tablespoons of tomato paste and any tomato trimmings that you have.

Most chefs agree not to salt the stock. Use the stock as a basic foundation for a soup or sauce that can be further flavored or salted later. This way, you can control the amount of salt that goes into the finished product.

Basic Recipe for White Chicken Stock

Makes 2 quarts

1. Fill a large stock pot with raw or cooked chicken, including gizzards, bones, trimmings, and neck—do not use internal organs (e.g., liver or kidneys). Also include vegetable trimmings (for example, 1 yellow onion, 2 carrots, 1 bunch of celery, and fresh herbs such as bay leaf, thyme, parsley stems, rosemary, and peppercorns).
2. Add cold water to just cover the chicken parts and vegetables.
3. Allow to simmer for at least 1 hour, but no more than 2 hours.
4. Remove from the heat. Allow it to cool for 30 minutes.
5. Strain contents through a colander, and then a second time through a fine-mesh strainer called a *chinois*. If the stock is for immediate use, skim off any excess fat from the top of the stock with a large spoon or ladle, and discard. If the stock is to be used at a later date, cool in the refrigerator; the fat will rise to the top and solidify, which can easily be removed with a large spoon before use.

Basic Recipe for Brown Chicken Stock

If you prefer a dark stock, coat the chicken bone with vegetable oil, and roast in an oven for approximately 20 to 30 minutes at 350°F until a brown color is achieved. Then proceed as above, but include an 8-ounce can of tomato paste and any tomato trimmings that you have on hand.

Now, it is up to you to season with salt to taste. Otherwise, use as a flavor foundation.

Baking Tips

Have you ever tasted something that you absolutely loved, but when you got the recipe and attempted to reproduce it, you could not come up with the same results? Baking is a precise science. You cannot deviate from the directions; when they say "do not over-beat," they mean it. If you follow the directions exactly, the end result will be consistent every time.

Read your recipe from start to finish. Every baker can tell you a story of leaving out a key ingredient when they were distracted or multitasking, as many of us do. Or, after beginning their recipe, they got to the end and read that it must chill for three hours, and their guests were arriving to eat in one hour. See Chef's Tips on *mise en place* (page 309) for tips on how to avoid this from happening to you.

Preheat your oven. If you are unsure whether or not your oven is accurate, purchase a small oven thermometer so you can double-check that the temperature that you set on the outside of your oven is the same as the internal temperature required for the recipe. If not, you will need to calibrate your oven (refer to your oven's manufacture's handbook for details on how to do this).

Prepare or grease your pan for baking. Only grease your pan when the recipe calls for you to do so. Cut out a piece of parchment paper to exactly cover the bottom of the baking pan (this piece should not overlap onto the side at all unless directed to do so in your recipe). Generously spray the bottom and sides of your baking pan with baking spray (available in the supermarket) or pan-coating spray. Then place the pre-cut piece of parchment paper on the bottom and once again generously spray the paper and the sides of the pan.

Weigh your ingredients. The most accurate form of measurement is weight. Always use a kitchen scale to weigh your dry ingredients. First, put the empty measuring container on the scale to determine the weight of the container. If using a digital scale, hit the "tare" button once so the screen displays zero weight. If using a manual scale, turn the dial back to zero. Next, place your ingredient in the container. The scale will now only register the weight of the ingredient.

In lieu of weighing your dry ingredients, you can also scoop them into a measuring cup. To remove the heaping excess, place the cup on a flat surface, and tap the top of the cup with the back of a knife so the contents settle. To level the contents, use the back of your knife to push or sweep the excess ingredients off the top of the container.

Liquid measurement. Use a measuring cup with a spout or a volume measuring cup to measure your liquid ingredients.

Eggs must be brought to room temperature. If the recipe calls for this ingredient, immediately place your eggs in a container on your counter top so they will reach the appropriate temperature when needed.

Butter. Always use unsalted butter (sometimes referred to as sweet cream butter), unless the recipe specifies otherwise. If the recipe calls for the butter to be cold, leave it in the refrigerator until needed. When using softened or room-temperature butter, do not melt or microwave the butter. Instead, cut it into tablespoons or cubes to expand the surface area of the butter, enabling it to come to room temperature faster. The desired consistency should be spreadable. If a recipe calls for melted butter, cut the butter into tablespoons or cubes, and put in a saucepan over low heat until all the butter has liquefied. Do not simmer.

Fresh whipped cream. To make fresh whipped cream, first place the bowl and beaters in your freezer, and keep the heavy cream in your refrigerator while assembling your ingredients. Beat the cold cream until peaks are formed or it appears to double in volume. Do not add any additional ingredients before air has been whipped into the cream; otherwise, they will weigh down the cream, and the end result will be deflated and dense rather than light and fluffy whipped cream. After beating the cream, add any other ingredients, such as vanilla and sugar, while the mixer is running. As soon as the ingredients are fully incorporated, stop mixing, cover with plastic wrap, and keep in a cold bowl in the refrigerator.

Buy good-quality chocolate, vanilla, and cinnamon. Whenever purchasing these ingredients, I spare no expense on quality. Using bargain or store brands will inevitably compromise your end result. Any time that I find these high-priced items on sale, I buy in bulk to keep my pantry full at all times. My favorites are Ghirardelli® or Val-rhona chocolate, Madagascar and/or Tahitian vanilla bean, and pure vanilla extract. Vietnamese cinnamon is also wonderful for making your recipe more flavorful, and will make your desserts pop.

Melting Chocolate. Choose a pot large enough to have a heat-proof bowl sit snugly on top of it so that little to no steam can escape. Fill the pot with water and bring to a rapid boil. Turn heat off. Place bowl on top of pot and place chopped chocolate in the bowl. Wait 10 minutes and then stir until a smooth consistency is obtained.

Resources

Labensky, Hause, Martel, *On Cooking*. New Jersey: Prentice Hall, 2011.
The Art Institute, *American Regional Cuisine*, New Jersey: Wiley, 2007.
The Culinary Institute of America, *The Professional Chef*, New Jersey: Wiley, 2006.
State Symbols USA, *www.statesymbolsusa.org/Lists/American-FoodSymbols.html*

A heartfelt thanks goes out to our contributing chefs, cooks, CHCs (Certified Health Coaches), cooking classes, and caterers for sharing their recipes and stories with us:

Adwar, Reshma, *www.cookmehealthy.com*
Brandes, Annette, *www.annettebrandes.com*
Chef Andrea Beaman, *www.andreabeaman.com/health*
Chef Eric Wilson, *www.chefericwilson.com*
Chef Michelle Moore, *www.NaturalStyleHealth.com*
Chef Nicole Roarke, *www.NRcatering.com*
Chef and Dr. Sonali Ruder, *www.thefoodiephysician.com*
Damboragian, Jackie, *www.simplifiedwellnesswithjackie.com*
Foster, Melanie, *www.mjcooks.com*
Franzen, Nicole, *http://nicolefranzen.blogspot.com*
Fukuda, Corrie, *http://corriefood.blogspot.com*
Garro, Andrea, *www.goodcleanhealth.com*
Giannone, Heather Pierce, *http://heatherpierceinc.com*
Hamilton, Angie, *www.leionthewater.com*
Henderson, Marguerite, *www.margueritehenderson.com*
Kessner, Eve Lynn, *www.lovelifeandlollipops.com*
Kohler, Jessica, *www.kohlercreated.com/blog*
Ratulowski, Andrea, *www.foodembrace.com*
Rice, Lori, *www.fakefoodfree.com*
Robertson-Smith, Amber, *http://blissholistic.com*
Segal, Emily, www.TriumphWellness.com
Smoragiewicz, Julie, *www.dakotathyme.com*
Wilson, Eric, *www.chefericwilson.com*
Valpone, Amie, *www.TheHealthyApple.com*
Younger, Kath, *www.katheats.com*

Index

D

Damboragian, Jackie, 57
Derr, Laraine, 224
Dessert
    Apple Pie, 243
    Baked Pears, 241
    Baked Stuffed Apples with Walnuts and Raisins, 65
    Banana-Bourbon Scones with Walnuts, 77
    Banana Hazelnut Upside-Down Cake, 246
    Bananas Foster, 123
    Bavarian Blueberry Tart, 201
    Berry-Good Crisps, 301
    Best Apple Crisp, The, 66
    Blueberry Cobbler Doughnuts, 7
    Bosc Pear Sauce, 242
    Bumbleberry Pie, 198
    Carolina Sour Cream Pound Cake, 121
    Clafouti with Plums or Pluots, 303
    Crêpes with Blueberry Marmalade, 5
    Frying Pan Fudge Cake, 205
    Georgia Peach Pound Cake, 122
    Gluten-Free Apple Strudel, 67
    Gluten-Free Red Velvet Cake, 132
    Gooey Butter Cupcakes, 203
    Grammie Jayn's Blueberry Coffee Cake, 141
    Grandma's Rhubarb Kuchen, 194
    Honey Maple Roasted Pears, 64
    Indian Pudding, 63
    Individual Mexican Chocolate Cheesecakes, 308
    Kentucky Derby Pie, 128
    Kim's Key Lime Pie, 130
    King Cake, 134
    Moon Pie, 129
    New York Cheesecake, 71
    Peppermint Semifreddo, 248
    Persimmon Pudding, 193
    Pralines, 119
    Rainbow Cake, 70
    Rhubarb-Strawberry Crumble, 68
    Risotto Napoleon with Dried Door County Cherries, 190
    Sautéed Strawberries in Wine-Pepper Sauce with Vanilla Ice Cream, 245
    Shaker Lemon Pie, 200

M

N

O

P

Request for Future Submissions

We have thoroughly enjoyed collecting these stories. As we received each story and recipe, we would anxiously read through and decide if it could be included in our book. We knew that it would be included if it evoked in us the emotions and memories that come to mind when we remembered our own traditions. We reached out to family, friends, neighbors, and colleagues, and now we are reaching out to you, our readers. We would love to have you share your stories with us.

To do so, please e-mail your story to us at countrycomfortcookbooks@gmail.com or "like" us on Facebook at "Country Comfort Cookbook." Please be sure to include your name, e-mail address, city, and state.

There is no word count or previous writing experience necessary, and we only require one rule—that you write from your heart.

Thank you,
Mary Elizabeth and Chef Nicole

About the Authors

Mary Elizabeth Roarke has a Bachelors of Science degree in nursing, and has worked in the field for over 30 years. In 2008, she earned a certificate in Pastry and Baking Arts. Currently she works in pharmaceutical clinical research and prepares all the baked goods for NR Catering on Long Island, where she lives with her husband.

Mary Elizabeth's published work can be found in *Potluck Wisdom for the Pharmaceutical Professional* and *Country Comfort: Harvest, Country Comfort: Holidays, Country Comfort: Slow-Cooker Favorites, Country Comfort: Summer Favorites,* and *Country Comfort: Casserole Cooking.*

Her philosophy is that sharing recipes creates lasting memories!

Chef Nicole Roarke is an honors graduate of the French Culinary Institute in New York. While earning her Bachelor's degree in Psychology at the State University of New York at Stony Brook, Nicole began her career in restaurants in 1997. She honed her cooking skills in many restaurants including the Bon Appetite favorite The Linkery, Loews Coronado Bay Resort in San Diego, CA, the Aviles at the Hilton Historic Bay Front in St. Augustine, FL, Trattoria Aroma in Buffalo, NY, and Jean Georges' Spice Market in New York, NY. Nicole participated in such events as the 2005 Chaine de la Rotisseur and the 2006 Taste of St. Augustine. Nicole worked as the exclusive caterer of the Frank Lloyd Wright Davidson House in Buffalo and as an Executive Chef in Long Beach, NY where she resides today. Along with her mother, Nicole established NR Catering in 2010, specializing in off-premise catering. Nicole began teaching private cooking classes in Lynbrook, NY and presently instructs at a NY accredited Culinary School in Syosset, NY.

Nicole's published work can be found in the Chef Tip's and Menu Planner sections of *Country Comfort: Harvest, Country Comfort: Holidays, Country Comfort: Slow-Cooker Favorites,* and *Country Comfort: Summer Favorites.*

Her philosophy is: cook with your senses and your food will come alive!

Also in the *Country Comfort* series...

Country Comfort: Casserole Cooking
ISBN: 978-1-57826-404-9

Country Comfort: Harvest
ISBN: 978-1-57826-359-2

Country Comfort: Holidays
ISBN: 978-1-57826-380-6

Country Comfort: Slow-Cooker Favorites
ISBN: 978-1-57826-374-5

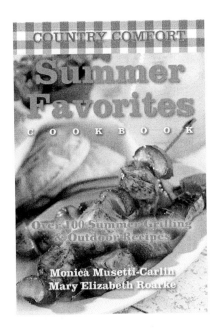

Country Comfort: Summer Favorites
ISBN: 978-1-57826-384-4